WOMEN

WHO

CHANGE

THE

WORLD

Women
Who Change
The World

STORIES FROM THE FIGHT
FOR SOCIAL JUSTICE

EDITED BY LYNN LEWIS

CITY LIGHTS BOOKS—OPEN MEDIA SERIES
SAN FRANCISCO

"I love this book. I love that every chapter is the voice of an incredible woman at the forefront of social justice, sharing her story directly with me and in her own words. And I love that each woman gave me new ideas about everything from organizing and family life to how I think about grief. This is a necessary and radical book for our collective futures."

　　—DAISY HERNÁNDEZ, co-editor of *Colonize This! Young Women of Color on Today's Feminism*

"*Women Who Change the World* is oral history at its finest. The stories will draw you in; the profound insights about self-care, collective action, trauma, and power will stay with you."

　　—AMY STARECHESKI, author of *Ours to Lose: When Squatters Became Homeowners in New York City*

"Lynn Lewis's longtime organizing experience, political insight, and loving heart shine brightly through this collection of oral histories. She introduces nine changemakers from across the United States whose lives reflect the intersection of personal experiences with the legacies of history. Each woman describes her transformative journey to becoming an activist and community builder. These inspiring accounts offer urgently needed ideas, strategies, and actions that women pursue to create a more just society."

　　—IRIS MORALES, author of *Revisiting Herstories: The Young Lords Party*

"A bevy of brilliance and tactics to be learned and used by new and emerging generations of activists, *Women Who Change the World* is at once a gift of witness and a Social Justice master class for a world in need."

　　—THEODORE KERR, co-author of *We Are Having This Conversation Now: The Times of AIDS Cultural Production*

"Lynn Lewis's book is a gift of cool clear water to a world parched of movement histories. If, as Dorothy Allison wrote, telling a story all the way through is an act of love, this collection is a great big hug for all those thirsting for inspiration. The women here are heroes, but as their oral histories reveal, heroes are all around us, made of regular and radical stuff. The voices here will stay with you: personal, political, persuasive."

—**LAURA FLANDERS**, host of the *Laura Flanders Show*

"This rich oral history collection of nine women social justice activists is a must-read for our challenging times. The narratives of these working-class leaders speak to the passions, struggles, deep knowledge, and love that shape their practices of resistance and organizing for a just world."

—**TARRY HUM**, author of *Making a Global Immigrant Neighborhood: Brooklyn's Sunset Park*

"Lynn Lewis has gifted us with a treasure of powerful narratives by nine brilliant, fierce, and caring women dedicated to social justice— some that I know, some I now know better, and some I want to know. Their individual and collective journeys leave me with radical hope that each of us can and will do what is necessary to keep changing the world."

—**LYNN ROBERTS**, co-editor of *Radical Reproductive Justice: Foundation, Theory, Practice, Critique*

"Women indeed ARE changing the world! This truth comes through loud and clear, gently and subtly, humbly and proudly in the oral histories that make up *Women Who Change the World*, edited by Lynn Lewis. You have got to read the narratives of the nine powerful, fierce women organizers included in this oral history! They tell stories of true social justice heroines whose lives and actions are transforming society from the bottom up."

—**REV. DR. LIZ THEOHARIS**, pastor, organizer, author, Director of the Kairos Center for Religions, Rights, and Social Justice and Co-Chair of the Poor People's Campaign: A National Call for Moral Revival

"Lynn Lewis knows that listening and asking questions can spark a revolution. These stories contain all the clues we need to build a better world."
—**JAMES TRACY**, co-author of *No Fascist USA! The John Brown Anti-Klan Committee and Lessons for Today's Movements*

"This powerful collection of oral histories provides firsthand accounts of how social change is won through movement organizing. The women at the heart of this book share inspiring life stories behind the barricades, picket lines, and protests. It is a narrative of global resistance."
—**BENJAMIN DANGL**, author of *The Five Hundred Year Rebellion: Indigenous Movements and the Decolonization of History in Bolivia*

"In *Women Who Change the World*, Lynn Lewis has worked in the grand oral history tradition of Studs Terkel and the Lomax Brothers, but with an explicitly feminist and intersectional lens. An outstanding collection harvested with great care, the women in this book remind us we are not alone in our struggles against empire—that we have contemporary sisters and ancestral mothers waiting to share plans for liberation. If 'we must love and support each other,' as the great Assata Shakur is quoted in the introduction, a great way to start doing so is by listening to the stories Lewis presents in this powerful book and taking them as a call to action."
—**STEVEN W. THRASHER**, author of *The Viral Underclass* and former editor at the NPR StoryCorps project

This book is dedicated to my mother, Violet
to Carol, my birth mother
to Frances, my movement mother
to my daughter Rocio
and to all of my movement sisters.

Open Media Series Editor: Greg Ruggiero

Cover and text design by Patrick Barber

ISBN: 9780872868748

Library of Congress Cataloging-in-Publication Data

Names: Lewis, Lynn (Historian), editor.
Title: Women who change the world : stories from the fight for social justice / edited by
Lynn Lewis.
Description: San Francisco, CA : City Lights Books, [2023]
Identifiers: LCCN 2023006705 | ISBN 9780872868748 (trade paperback)
Subjects: LCSH: Leadership in women—United States. | Feminism—United States. |
United States—Biography.
Classification: LCC HQ1421 .W664 2023 | DDC 305.420973—dc23/eng/20230213
LC record available at https://lccn.loc.gov/2023006705

City Lights Books are published at the City Lights Bookstore
261 Columbus Avenue, San Francisco, CA 94133

citylights.com

TABLE OF CONTENTS

Introduction

THIS COLLECTION OF ORAL HISTORY INTERVIEWS documents the journeys of nine women who have played critical roles in contemporary organizing struggles in the United States. In that process, they have each participated in making history. They are brilliant thinkers who put theory into action, even though they probably would not describe themselves that way. As they generously share some of the personal and political choices that moved them to dedicate their lives to constructing justice, you may see yourself in their journey. I hope you will find joy and inspiration in their example, as I do.

The nine women presented in this collection span a range of identities and life experiences. They have taken different paths into organizing and social justice work. In their own words you will learn how some have taken a leap of faith by accepting an invitation to a meeting or a protest, seeking to connect with others to solve a problem in their own or their families' lives, or attempting to address an issue in their community. Others were born into movement, deeply conscious of their lineage. All have stayed involved because they want to make sure that the harm caused to them and to others would not be repeated. Each of them is doing the work of building a more just future that benefits us all.

Their work has shifted narratives and created new frameworks for thinking about critical issues, but they may not be well known beyond the sectors where they have worked. For some, that is a reflection of their approach to organizing. These women stand on the shoulders of historic figures we have learned about, and millions of others whose names we will never know. It isn't the famous few who make the revolution; it is the many who are harmed by oppression and choose to respond by mounting collective action to build political power through community organizing. It is in this spirit that *Women Who Change the World* was conceptualized. I am deeply grateful to each of the women for taking the time to reflect, to share, and to teach.

Why Focus on Community Organizing?

Community organizing is the foundation that all movements for social change rest upon. To quote Frances Goldin, a brilliant housing organizer and literary agent representing radical leftist authors, "Without the troops, we have nothing."[1] Without listening to folks harmed by systems of oppression and welcoming them into a collective process to identify solutions, how would organizers know what the problems are, what solutions to fight for, and what alternatives to build? Some of the women interviewed no longer work primarily as community organizers. They have tapped into and developed their skills as educators, media makers, and cultural workers, or are holding down other roles within organizations because they determined their contribution to social transformation would be more meaningful that way. All of them remain connected and accountable to their communities.

Community organizing at its most powerful compels us to listen, learn, and support the collective analysis and action of the many, not the few. Because of them, the rest of us have more choices. Because of them, the rest of us have more rights. Because of them, the rest of us live with less danger, and because of them, we are more free. The truth is that we may not always win, but we *never* will if we don't organize. "In the process of struggling in community, we learn how to glimpse new possibilities that otherwise never would have become apparent to us," writes Angela Y. Davis, "and in the process we expand and enlarge our very notions of freedom."[2]

The mission of social justice organizing is to build power *with* those who don't have it, in order to transform the conditions of all our lives. That starts with building relationships, so that we can begin to analyze and strategize together. Through organizing, power is redistributed horizontally to the many, away from the hierarchies of the few. As Ella Baker continues to teach, "What is needed, is the development of people who are interested not in being leaders as much as in developing leadership in others."[3] This requires nurturing a political space that creates the conditions where folks can envision a different social construct and build the skills needed to fight for it. The social and institutional formations nurtured, and in some cases founded, by the women presented here are examples of such political spaces.

While organizing requires us to recruit people to meetings and mobilize people to protest, moving bodies isn't the end goal. The purpose of organizing is to support individual and collective leadership in order to shift consciousness, and to build power so that we may transform the conditions of our lives. Movements for social change require theory, infrastructure, and members with many skill sets and talents. In activities from street outreach and meeting facilitation to relationship building, research, critical analysis, direct action, strategic planning, and teaching others these skills, an organizer brings a combination of strength and humility, agility, vision, hope, patience, capacity for emotional labor, deep listening, and love. An organizer is a learner, teacher, artist, planner, friend, media maker, and witness. Through their stories, we learn how each of the nine women in this collection discovered those skills within themselves and how they were sharpened through collective struggle.

Oral History: Basic Definitions

Oral history is a dynamically evolving and even contested field. For example, there are critiques of false dichotomies that differentiate oral traditions and oral history.[4] The definition of archive is another example, with critical questions around who the intended audience is when an oral history project is conceptualized and undertaken.[5]

While there is no one correct way to conduct oral history, there are some core values. Open-ended questioning that centers and honors the reminiscences of a narrator is primary. Posing open-ended questions, an oral historian creates space for the narrator to share their memories and interpretation of events, thereby complicating and contextualizing the past and filling gaps in the historical record. Oral histories generate qualitative and quantitative data that illuminate the past and allow us to analyze current conditions in our efforts to organize for a more just future.

Increasingly, the voices of oral history practitioners of color have moved the field to acknowledge the role that privilege plays in the dialogic relationship between an interviewer and a narrator. The boundaries of what is oral history practice are continuously being interrogated, reclaimed, and expanded, including considerations around narrator identification, recording, archiving, and sharing what we create from an oral history interview.

Interviews are recorded with an audio and/or video recorder, and after the interview, may be transcribed or remain in audio or video form. The interview is shared with the narrator for purposes of editing and approval prior to publication. Once approved by the narrator, an oral history interview may be digitally archived or printed, in full or excerpted. Questions around copyright ownership, interviewing locations and techniques, and concepts such as participation and collaboration are among basic considerations in the design of an oral history project.[6]

Oral history interviews often take place within the context of a broader oral history project. Choosing which narrators to invite to participate is often determined by the project's goals. An oral history project may document a family, a neighborhood,[7] a community, an organization, a social movement,[8] or an experience collectively shared, such as the Great Migration.[9] The New York City Trans Oral History Project is a community archive devoted to the collection, preservation, and sharing of trans histories, organized in collaboration with the New York Public Library. With the goal of documenting transgender resistance and resilience in New York City, it is an example of ways that community members are participating as oral historians and documenting their own communities.

Each dialogic encounter is shaped by the relationship between the oral historian and the narrator, their understanding of the purpose of the interview and the larger project, how the interview will be publicly shared, and who benefits from the project. The dialogic encounter at the core of oral history, therefore, occurs within a much bigger context, and powerful relationships often emerge from the collaboration.

Oral History as an Act of Resistance

Prior to the written word and to this day, the transmission of knowledge through traditional stories, songs, poems, and directives determines our understanding of the world. "Telling" history happens in many ways and for many reasons. Oral transmission of knowledge through songs was just one example of a survival strategy used by enslaved Africans in the United States. The sharing of history and the calling to action through songs and chants are resistance strategies used by many social action groups, such as the International Workers of the World with its *Little Red Song Book*.

The knowledge that people before us have struggled to end oppression, create spaces of liberation, and build movement infrastructure inspires us to follow in their footsteps. Stories and examples of resistance may appear as visual symbols, such as Harriet Tubman's face on T-shirts of United Workers in Baltimore. They may be chanted after many an organizing meeting, as Assata Shakur's words often are:

> It is our duty to fight for our freedom.
> It is our duty to win.
> We must love each other and support each other.
> We have nothing to lose but our chains.[10]

These words and stories bond us to past struggles and help us to situate ourselves within the arc of history. Knowledge requires an awareness of events as well as an understanding of what those events mean. Such understanding shapes our identity, assigns us a social location, and tells us what to believe is possible for ourselves and our communities. Gentrification does not have the same meaning for those who were displaced from substandard housing as it does for those who moved into those renovated brownstones afterwards, or the property owners who accrued wealth from real estate sales and higher rents. The stories describing the process and results of gentrification differ depending upon how you are affected—whether you benefit or are harmed. Narratives associated with colonization contain a catalogue of events that hold one meaning for colonizers and another for the colonized—and their descendants. Inherited memories become the stories and myths that uphold power structures, just as inherited memories of resistance and struggles for social justice can transform our understanding of ourselves and our communities.

Oral history is a method of recording events and their meaning. It is a tool by which we may contextualize historical narratives with added nuance, detail, and analysis. For oppressed peoples in particular, oral history is a way to offset erasure and ensure that a more complete history—including the history of resistance—is told, recorded, documented, and shared. Howard Zinn, in *A Power Governments Cannot Suppress*, writes, "To omit these acts of resistance is to support the official view that power only rests with those who have the guns and possess the wealth."[11] One obstacle to liberation is that histories of grassroots resistance are often little known, and their lessons obscured by time. But, Zinn adds, "if history is to be creative, to anticipate a possible future without denying the past, it should, I believe, emphasize new possibilities by disclosing those hidden episodes of the past when, even if in brief flashes, people showed their ability to resist, to join together and occasionally to win."[12]

The oral histories presented in this collection bridge struggles, communities, generations, and geographies. In order for us to believe we can change the conditions of our lives and of our communities, it is critical that we see ourselves in a landscape of change—and that we understand how social change happens and who makes that change possible.

Representation Matters

Systems of oppression function to control women's bodies and labor, but we cannot ignore the hierarchies of privilege *among* women if we are truly committed to women's liberation. The histories shared by the women in this collection illustrate the ways that disparate issues are connected, and their harm compounded, vividly evoking the meaning of intersectionality.[13]

Women who are members of multiple marginalized communities experience the exponential harm that results from each of these sources of injustice. As women engaged in justice work, it is important to listen, to acknowledge not only the ways we are oppressed but any privilege we have, and to actively support the dismantling of systems from which we benefit, not only those that oppress us. Our privilege implicates us, because our privilege can't exist without the real and tangible oppression of others. This collection of oral histories offers a window into the experiences of both oppression and resistance embodied by the lives of the nine women interviewed, and is not intended to erase difference in the name of commonality, solidarity, or unity.

When addressing the Occupy movement at an outdoor gathering in New York City in 2011, Angela Davis asked, "How can we be together in a unity that is complex and emancipatory?"[14] Conscious of these questions, the nine oral histories offered here are examples of women who have faced many forms of oppression and adversity and chosen to commit to social transformation. I am hopeful that readers will find resonance and lessons within these pages.

Notes on the Oral History Process for This Book

There were choices to be made in shaping this book. I prioritized racial, generational, and geographic diversity among a range of working-class women, with an orientation towards paradigm shifting—transformational organizing that propels us beyond short-term focus on winnable campaigns. I prioritized the inclusion of women who are gender non-conforming and women who are mothers and caregivers of loved ones, and sought to explore how they balanced their responsibilities while organizing.

I started with a short list of women whose work I deeply respect. I reached out to each person, sending a one-page description of the process and the goals of the book. There were women who were unable to or who chose not to participate. Mutual friends introduced me to women in their networks to expand the pool of narrators. Once each agreed to an interview, I asked them to recommend materials for me to read or listen to in order to prepare myself. Most of the interviews were conducted over Zoom and lasted over two hours. Open-ended questions can stimulate tides of memory, and because memory isn't always chronological, responses sometimes took us to a new subject or time in the narrator's life. There were follow-up questions that I didn't ask, for the sake of deferring to the narrator's flow.

I transcribed the interviews with a commitment to preserving each narrator's voice and the meaning they assigned to the events in their lives. I deleted my questions so that the chapters would flow as a first-person narrative. I also deleted many of the "you know, um, like, sort of" speech elements and other ways we often speak that don't gracefully translate to the page. I then shared the transcript with each narrator, who further revised the text as they saw fit. Endnotes are used sparingly to cite sources, to explain a reference, or to direct readers to additional resources. Italics are used to denote where the narrator emphasized a word or phrase.

Nine Women

The women interviewed here have organized around a host of issues throughout the course of their lives, because they and their communities have been harmed by multiple systems of oppression. The analysis embedded in their stories shows the impact and connection of these systems; the diversity of their approaches to organizing and movement building offers insight and hope. The power of their descriptions of the harm effected by racism, poverty, gentrification, displacement, housing insecurity, homelessness, hunger, domestic violence, rape, reproductive injustice, police brutality, migration, climate change, labor exploitation and economic exploitation, attacks on welfare, silencing, government surveillance, lack of health care, colonization, and countless other forms of discrimination and harm lies in their resilience, commitment, and creative strategies to dismantle those systems.

The women you will meet in the pages ahead have founded and co-founded organizations, coalitions, and movements that range from reformist to revolutionary. Sharpened by years of toiling in the fields of grassroots organizing, their analyses suggest that reform and revolution are not necessarily mutually exclusive. Several narrators' political work subjected them to COINTELPRO and related tactics during the 1970s and 1980s, including political assassinations of comrades and invasive surveillance that continues to this day. While the women interviewed for this book have founded or are deeply engaged in movement work within nonprofit structures, their work has not been limited to such formations. However, all the women featured here explicitly align themselves within a range of anti-racist, anti-fascist movement politics and radical progressive values.

Not all racial, sexual, or class identities are represented within this collection. There is a lot missing, given that all nine are women live within the artificial and colonial borders of the United States. The collection does not include undocumented women, youth organizers, trans women, Muslim women, or differently abled women, nor the full range of ethnicities and languages spoken by Latinx, Indigenous, Afro-descendant, or Asian women. These omissions are not intended to be exclusionary or dismissive, or to minimize in any way the experiences of those women and the critical organizing work happening in their networks and communities. A compendium of oral histories of nine women can only hope to provide a humble gesture toward the full spectrum of those networks and the fights they are waging.

This collection contains long-form oral history interviews with nine narrators, with each chapter devoted to one narrator. We learn from them their formative early experiences, what moved them to attend their first meeting or protest, their reflections on their experiences, and why they remain involved in social justice work. The choice of long-form interviews, however, meant that I would interview fewer than a dozen women for the book. Spanning their early childhood to the present in one chapter also means that not everything is included. What each narrator chooses to share, and not to share, also conveys meaning. There will inevitably be questions about aspects of a narrator's life and work, and I encourage you to seek out the powerful body of work that each has created, as well as pieces created about them.

Women Who Change the World is an invitation to look around and acknowledge the women in your lives who are making change. Take the time to listen to their stories, and if you and they are up for it, record and transcribe their reflections. Find out who they are and what moved them to take up the responsibilities and risks of being a changemaker. Listen to their reflections and find the lessons within. Books such as *Comrade Sisters: Women of the Black Panther Party*, by Ericka Huggins and Stephen Shames, and *Through the Eyes of Rebel Women: The Young Lords: 1969-1976*, by Iris Morales, share first-person accounts and analysis by women organizing in their communities, and there are others out there. Take the time to explore feminist archives such as the one at Smith College, or organizational/movement archives such as the Digital SNCC Gateway, The

Freedom Archives, those available through NYU's Tamiment Library, or the Brooklyn-based, volunteer-run Interference Archives.

This collection of personal and political movement histories is shared in the hope of inspiring and informing all who reject the systems of oppression that confront us on a daily basis. It is critical to reflect on our place in the struggle for social justice. Learning about the choices that others have made can help us to understand our own choices, possibilities, power, and privilege. If you are engaged in movements for social justice, thank you for being one of many making history. If you aren't part of some type of social justice organization, please find and join one. We need you.

ONE

Vanessa Nosie

⁘

In order to change this system,
we have to heal.
In order to heal,
we have to acknowledge the First People.
For so long
we were the dust underneath the rug.
Now we've got to pull that rug back
and show we exist.
Our voices need to be heard.
This is the reason I fight,
so that my daughters
can be Apache.

Vanessa Nosie is a Chiricahua Apache, enrolled into the San Carlos Apache tribe. The US government created the San Carlos Reservation, where she lives, as a concentration camp for several Apache tribes, who were forcibly relocated as prisoners of war and were expected to die due to the harsh conditions there. Vanessa links her work to that history of colonization and genocide, and to their continuing legacies today. She is an organizer and spokesperson for Apache Stronghold, "a nonprofit community organization of individuals who come together in unity to battle continued colonization, defend Holy sites and freedom of religion, and are dedicated to building a better community through neighborhood programs and civic engagement." She also works as an archaeology aide with the San Carlos Apache Tribe Historic Preservation Office and Archaeology Department.

Vanessa's work is inseparable from being Apache. In her oral history, she reflects on her spiritual and political journey, informed by her family and community. She also considers her role as the recorder, the one who has the knowledge and experience to pass on the fight when it's time—just as her father, grandmother, and ancestors have passed those skills on to her. She directly connects the themes of motherhood and lineage to the history of colonization and racism in the United States, and the need to understand that history in order to heal and identify solutions. Her organizing work is a struggle for the very survival of the Apache people and Mother Earth. She reflects on the immediate need for unity among all people to confront the forces of greed and power that threaten us all.

Vanessa currently resides on the San Carlos Reservation.

I WAS BORN NOVEMBER 10, 1979, IN PHOENIX, ARIZONA. I AM a Chiricahua Apache enrolled into the San Carlos Apache tribe. The San Carlos Reservation is very unique. San Carlos is the concentration camp where the United States placed all the Apache people. The reservation is a prison. It's a concentration camp. They placed us there because there is no way to survive on this land. It's extremely hot. There was no shelter for shade. There's no water. There's no food. It was once known by the US Cavalry as Hell's 40 Acres. That's where they placed us at first, thinking we weren't going to survive.

Seven different Apache tribes were taken away from our ancestral homeland and placed on the San Carlos reservation. You have Muscalero, Chiricahua, Tonto Apache, Jicarilla, you have Camp Verde Yavapai Apache, the Western Apache, the White Mount Apache. Apaches also had our own Trail of Tears. They rounded up five hundred Muscalero Apaches with the Navajo people, but they were able to go back to Muscalero, where they are from. White Mountain Apache is back in White River, Arizona. Yavapai went back up to Camp Verde, Arizona. Some of them have been able to go back to their different lands. But San Carlos is still very, very diverse. Within those seven Apache tribes, there's several bands that stem from them. I am a Chiricahua Apache, and I reside on the San Carlos Apache Tribe Reservation.

I was raised by my father and my grandmother. His name is Wendsler Nosie Sr.[15] and her name was Elvera. They were always adamant about us knowing the truth. My grandmother, as far back as I can remember, has been my mother. It was my grandmother who took the lead in my life, and my father. That's just where my heart was at, and that's where I wanted to be.

Prisoners of War

At a very young age, I knew that I was a prisoner of war. I knew that I still belonged to the United States government, and how we didn't come from San Carlos. My grandmother would take us to go pick acorn at *Chi'chil Bildagoteel*, or Oak Flat in English,[16] and tell us that this is where her family came from. We would go to *Dził Nchaa Si'an*,[17] known as Mount Graham in English, and we would talk about how that's where my grandfather's people came from.

13

On the political side, understanding the fight, and what's happened to our people, those conversations started around the age of seven. That's when I started to have really intimate talks with my dad and my grandmother about who we are, the genocide that happened to our people, and the ongoing fight for our survival. My dad would take my siblings and myself running. This is when he would talk to us about *Nagosan*, Mother Earth. He would talk to me about Mother Earth, how *Usen*[18] created everything, and how everything is alive, from the smallest pebble to the biggest tree. He would talk to me about the wind that was blowing when we're running—that the wind hears us and takes our prayers. It was just the way that we were raised.

We Weren't Supposed to Exist

When I was pregnant with my first one, I remember my grandmother sat me down and gave me all the protocols and instructions about what I could and couldn't do as an Apache woman being pregnant. There were protocols about things I couldn't watch, couldn't see, couldn't do. I couldn't cut my hair, because if I cut my hair, that's a life and I could cut my baby's life short. I mean, there were so many guidelines that I had to follow. She said, "You need to talk to your stomach, your baby can hear, even though it's not physically in your arms. *You have to teach it now, about respect and the things that are in life. Because when you have the baby and it takes its first breath, that is the moment you prepare them for the ceremonies. That is the moment that you prepare them to fight.* That moment when the doctor says, 'It's a girl' is the moment you start to prepare her for her ceremony." We have the coming-of-age ceremony for the girls to become a woman.[19] So, I did that when I was pregnant. I get emotional talking about my grandmother since she is no longer physically here with us.

I was being prepared for the things that were going to happen in my life the moment I took my first breath. On the spiritual side, going through the ceremonies is what got me where I am today. It started when I was born, when I took that first breath. My family was preparing me to become a woman. They were preparing me for all the things that were going to happen, from that moment. My daughter Naelyn always says it best. "For all Indigenous people, the day that we started fighting was the day that we took our first breath. *We were people that weren't supposed to exist.* We were fighting and going against a system that was trying to extinct us." I really believe that. As much as I can remember, this is what we were taught.

It Is Not Only Historic Trauma, Because It's Still Happening

I live about twenty, thirty minutes from the town of Globe, Arizona. Our reservation is surrounded by these little border towns. They're predominantly white towns. My grandmother was very strong, but at the same time, I could see the historic trauma. Her parents were gathered and put on the reservation. She was born when the concentration camp first started. She was raised in this concentration camp, having to be quiet, not speak our language, not practice our ceremonies and our prayers. She witnessed all the tragic events. Adding to this devastation is that this historic trauma *is still happening* to us today. It was trying to kill our spirit then, and is trying to kill our spirit now.

As my grandmother got older, she would tell us stories about those times. Up until the 1970s, Globe had signs in restaurants and stores that would say "No Dogs, No Indians Allowed." She would tell us the way things were and how she was treated; as if she was a "dirty, savage Indian woman." She talked a lot about the racism that happened to her, along with my father. He also would share similar stories of racism that he dealt with living near the town of Globe, and attending Globe High School.

Stripped from Our Families

During the boarding school era, my grandmother's first two older kids were rounded up and sent off to boarding school. It wasn't until the late 1970s that they quit forcing Indian children to go to boarding schools. My grandmother told us stories of seeing a van driving around and if they saw kids, they would just throw them in the vans! Families would hide their children if they saw the vans. It wasn't even safe for children to play outside. Families knew that their children could be taken. My late uncle was the third oldest. When they quit taking our children to boarding schools, my grandmother was happy because she wasn't going to lose one of her children. I heard all of these stories growing up, of children being stripped from our families.

My grandmother used to tell us that when she would go to *Chi'chil Bildagoteel*, they would hide and have to run and try to get their acorn and their medicine, and then they would have to try to sneak back onto the reservation. She was afraid of the cavalry and the people from the border towns, because they would punish people if they were caught. The stories of my grandmother and father dealing with racism have been very hard to hear. My father went to the high school in Globe. Dealing with the system and fighting back, he organized a walkout of Indigenous students, grew his hair, created a radio station, and many more events, as ways for the Indigenous students to be recognized, and to stop the oppression. Even though I come from a strong family where my grandmother was willing to step out of the box, there were moments when I saw her *hide*. If we were going into town and she was asked if she wanted to go eat, she would say, "I'm not going inside, just bring me food back." Or "I'll sit in the car and wait." The same with my dad. My dad is an extraordinary person, but there were moments when I saw the generational trauma in him. It is not something that you can turn off easily. It's an internal battle to unlearn the lies and the fear that were placed on you.

The Story of When My Dad Had Enough

My father was very young when he already had enough of it. He knew that it shouldn't have to be this way. He was really angry at the white people, at the system. My grandmother said, "Son, you have every right to be angry. You have every right to be mad. You go over there, and you could hurt them. You could kill them. But do you want to live that life? Do you want to be that person?" Those are those same teachings for me.

It hurt me to see what my dad was going through. The frustration, the letdowns, the fatigue. Being sad that nothing was changing for us Indigenous people, just fighting, and fighting. Seeing the way my grandmother was, made me angry, too. When I look at my kids, I think of those same talks with my grandmother and my dad. They used to say, "Remember, Creator made all things. He even made those people, and they are here for a reason. But something comes and changes them. They go bad. So you just pray for them. You even pray for those people that are hurting you. You pray for them." I remember those same teachings. I have so many intimate talks with my kids. When they were very little and we had racist things happen to us, I would be mad and ask them, "Do you understand what just happened to you? Do you understand that they kicked us out because we are Native American? Do you understand? How do you feel?" So I had that anger, too. Those moments took me back to the stories that were shared with me and the events I experienced as a child, teenager, and young adult. I wanted my children to understand the situation, what was happening to them, and that this racism must end.

Early Acts of Resistance

We were in Safeway, in Globe. I was around age eight or nine. My father and I were going down the aisle and these white people came around the corner. They were coming down the aisle and my father said to me, "Ness, scoot over. Move, get out of the way for them." And I said, "No! Why? Why do we always have to move out of the way? They can go around us." Then he looked at me and he was kind of upset because I was defying him, too, as a parent. I was like, "I'm not moving." So we stood there. He froze and he didn't know what to think, and they went around us. I didn't want to look at him because I didn't know if I was going to get in trouble. He just touched my shoulder and didn't say anything to me, and we kept going on with our grocery shopping. I think in that moment *I was just done.* I could envision my grandmother and all the people who dealt with the hardship of having fear placed inside them for being Apache.

As a child, I started to experience racism too, in school. It's sad, because not only is it a very white-dominant town, there's also a lot of Mexicans there, but they're very Americanized. You see them, they're trying to fit in with white society. So, when it comes to the Indian kids, we're "dirty Indians." They made sure that there was no place for us in their world. Telling us to go back to where we came from, which meant the reservation.

I went to Catholic school. I was chosen to speak at a church when I was eleven. I talked about how they used religion against our people. Not too long after that, I quit standing up for the Pledge of Allegiance. I think I was around twelve. The nun was telling me to stand up and I said, "No." I just sat there. I wasn't disrespectful. I wasn't making noise or saying anything bad. I just sat there. My grandmother used to tell me to "just pray." So I remember praying and the nun came, and she got mad at me, and she hit me with the ruler. I did it again the next day. Then she finally asked me, "Why aren't you standing up?" And I said, "You see all those stars that are on that flag? They represent a state, right? That's what you teach us, they represent a state." And she just looked at me. I said, "Well, in order for those states to exist, they had to kill my people." She didn't say anything. I said, "So I'm not going to salute a flag that wanted us dead." Then they left me alone. A lot of that was the rolling effect of learning how to speak up. After I refused to move out of the way in Safeway, my father knew that I was understanding what he and my grandmother were teaching us, understanding our talks.

My dad was in tribal political government for over thirty years. He was one of our tribal council members, and I was able to learn the political side of the United States government and our tribal government. I started to listen a lot more and was very interested in what was going on. I was my dad's tail. He was the type of parent that didn't leave us at home. If he had meetings or events, his kids went too. I know he was probably hoping that we were paying attention to what was being discussed. He was giving his children an opportunity to know what was going on in the government and be involved with the community.

I was born into this. I was fortunate to come from a family that was going to step out of the box. It became the norm for us. Even to this day, I tell my kids, "I feel bad because we're not a normal family." At the dinner table, it is not just asking how your day went. We talk about spirituality, the ways of our people, and the government. We discuss what is going on with our people, the history of who we are, and why we are still here. It is really heavy at times, especially because that history is ongoing. These conversations we have as a family are what has rooted us in the fight for our people, our religion, and Mother Earth.

My father is the founder of Apache Stronghold. He has sacrificed his life and made this his life's work. *This is his life, his heart, and his spirit.* I am blessed to have a father like him, because he shares his knowledge with me and my children. We all have a role in this fight and this way of life. It's going to take all of us to create change. Each day, I am using the same teachings my ancestors gave my great-grandmother, my grandmother, and my father, who has passed it on to me. I have had many special moments with my father. He tells me I am ready. He sees it in my heart. He hears it in my voice, because he can feel my spirit when I speak. I believe him when he tells me I am ready. It is *my* life, *my* heart, *my* spirit also. As his daughter, I know I have big shoes to fill. He is healthy and alive, and the fire is still burning in him. When you look at us as a family and you see this dynamic, it is the teaching of the balance between man and woman. In the Apache Way, there is a balance. We have Man Mountain, Woman Mountain, Man Rain, and Woman Rain. Everything is man and woman. These teachings have helped us to understand our role, and we all balance each other out.

As I was growing up, my father instilled all these tools in me. He showed me his heart and how passionate he is about his people and saving Mother Earth. My grandmother is the root of why he is the way he is. My grandmother is not in the spotlight as much, but you hear her story. She was in the back, praying and protecting her son.

I started my journey learning all of the tools that are passed down to me to fight for people—not just the Apache people, but all people. Indigenous people have been fighting this for over five hundred years, but now we are in a world where everyone is involved, no matter what race you belong to or what religion you believe in. When we are talking about protecting Mother Earth and protecting the water and protecting our religion, that includes everybody now.

It's My Job To Protect and To Show My Children the Way of Life

I got married at the age of eighteen and became a mother at nineteen. When I became a mother, my role switched. I now become the root, just like my grandmother. When they told me, "It's a girl," my job *changed*. Now, I had to protect and show my children the way of life, to prepare them to take on the fight for our existence. When I became a mother, I took a step back from being right next to my father. I have four daughters. Three are young adults, and the fourth is a one-year-old. Instilling in my children the same teachings that were given to me, I am creating spiritual warriors.

My three older daughters have been able to carry on the fight for our existence, but my one-year-old has a different, and harder, fight in front of her. The fight right now for Indigenous people is even worse. The United States is a corporate government. Their views and the way the system works is like a corporation. Everything is being stripped from our Indigenous people. You see my generation, you see my kids' generation, you see my dad's generation. We knew that we were going to have to pick up the fight. We didn't know where it was going to go and where it was going to lead us. *Chí'chil Biłdagoteel* is a perfect example. I was able to raise my older kids like my dad and my grandmother raised me. I was able to have ceremonies. I was able to finally go back to *Chí'chil Biłdagoteel* to pick our acorn, pick our berries, get our medicine, all the tools that we need. I am able to teach that to my children because *Chí'chil Biłdagoteel* still exists.

Now, I look at my youngest daughter. She has two fights. Is she going to pick up the fight? Are we even going to be allowed to continue to fight? Will she have to fight for her existence as an Apache? If *Chí'chil Biłdagoteel* is destroyed, she will no longer know what it is to be Apache. I won't be able to pass on the tools that were passed from my ancestors to my grandmother, to my parents, to me. They will be gone forever. My youngest daughter won't be able to physically learn the songs and the prayer before you pick your acorn, before you pick the berries, before you pick the medicine. Because they will be destroyed. She will only hear the stories. It's different when it's hands-on, compared to trying to paint a picture for her of how it used to be.

That is why you see me in and out. My role did change, and I was very proud to be able to take a step back because, for whatever reason, Creator blessed me to have children. That was the biggest win for me, because we were not supposed to exist. Having a child, let alone four children, is to know that we exist. The fight is for our existence. I have children who are twenty-three, twenty-one, and seventeen. Their names are all in Apache. Naelyn means girl. She was my first girl. Then I have Nizhoni, which means beautiful. I have Baase, which means the sacred hoop. And I have Shá'yú. Her name means "in the sunshine." My three older children were able to pick up the fight. That is what you see my eldest Naelyn doing. She is able to fight. But my one-year-old? She will have a whole different fight.

This Generation Is Different

I don't see the same fear in my daughter's eyes as I have in some of the older generations. When it comes to all Indigenous people . . . the white terminology for it is historic trauma. Our ancestors were forced onto a reservation or killed at gunpoint. Their families saw them having to be prisoners. That is what a lot of people don't understand. *We are prisoners.* If you look at our court case, that the Apache Stronghold filed against the United States, government attorneys cite case law and use the same language that they use in cases about federal prisons and federal prisoners. According to the way the Constitution is written, Indigenous people belong to the United States government. I have two numbers from the United States government that can be used to identify me. One is my Social Security number and the other is a tribal enrollment number, which any federally recognized tribe has. We were given tribal enrollment numbers when the Cavalry came. The United States gave every Apache a number so they could keep track of us. I and my kids have an enrollment number. As a result, the United States government knows the population of the tribe, where we're at, and what we're doing. Just like a person that goes to prison, they have their Social Security and then they have their federal prison number, and *that will never go away.* We are no different when it comes to the system. Putting us on a reservation, we are viewed as prisoners. Historic trauma and generational trauma are very real. Being shot at, killed, starved, all these things have been passed down and they are still happening because the system was designed and put in place to kill us or control us. But we are still here.

These things continue to this day. My third daughter felt bad because her friends were being picked on by these white kids. They didn't want to tell the school, because they didn't think anyone would do anything. That's the trauma! We are told to be quiet, that we'll get hurt or killed if we speak out. That teaching has been passed down, "Shhhh, don't say nothing, just leave it. They'll go away." Not having a voice, that is very much still alive today. We witness it. We see it.

My daughters have my heart. My daughter Naelyn is very vocal, she is not afraid to speak. It is different with this new generation. They give us hope and they make us proud because they're going to fight for us and those yet to be born. When I hear Naelyn talk, or when I see my girls pray or have ceremony, they give me hope because we are a people that are still here. We are not forgotten and we're not going anywhere. Naelyn says things so eloquently. I wish I could talk the way she does, because I want to give that hope to people. I too, still feel that hurt and that anger.

Apache Stronghold

My dad was the founder and has been the leader of Apache Stronghold. The two major fights that Apache Stronghold is involved in are *Dził Nchaa Si'an*, or Mount Graham, which is in Safford, Arizona, in the Coronado National Forest, and *Chi'chil Bildagoteel*, or Oak Flat, which sits five miles east of Superior, in the Tonto National Forest. Those are the prominent fights that we have been really involved in.

Dził Nchaa Si'an

We've been fighting against the University of Arizona and the Vatican for *Dził Nchaa Si'an* for over thirty years. My dad started that fight when I was seven years old, and I'll be forty-three soon. *Dził Nchaa Si'an* is one of our holy mountains, and they wanted to put telescopes on top of it. The Vatican wanted to find a physical being of God. They wanted to actually touch the gates to heaven, and they wanted to use it to find alien life. They wanted to build thirty-some telescopes when the fight initiated, and the University of Arizona got involved because they were building the telescope lenses. *It was just huge.*

One of the Cardinals was sent from the Vatican. He actually drove up to *Dził Nchaa Si'an* and told them to give him fifteen minutes. He stood outside and then walked back and said, "It's not holy, it's not sacred." So it's just been this constant battle. A Coalition to Save Mount Graham/*Dził Nchaa Si'an* was formed, and we took the

US government to court and went all to way to the federal Ninth Circuit. The university had already started building the telescopes, but when the final judgment came down, they weren't allowed to build any more, they could just keep what they had. What's crazy is that the name they gave the last telescope they built is *Lucifer*.

My father has traveled all over the country to have companies disinvest from this project. This year is our thirty-first annual Sacred Run to Dził Nchaa Sí'an.[20] We are called the Mountain of the Spirit Runners. We also hold an annual march and run to *Chi'chil Bildagoteeł*. We've had so many people from all over the world participate and become involved with us in this fight. There were only a handful of us running that first year. It was mainly my family—my cousins, aunts, uncles, and siblings. I was eleven during our very first run, and now it's my second year actually organizing it. It has been amazing to watch the number of runners that come every year as it has grown so much. What's beautiful about the run is that it's sacred. When we are running, we are running the same path our ancestors once roamed. Our feet, hitting the ground, are the heartbeat connecting us to Mother Earth. The purpose of the run is to show them that we still exist and to highlight the desecration of the holy mountain and our way of life.

I have to go meet with the Forest Service every year. We've learned that as long as there's no documentation, we don't exist. Each time they relocate staff, we have to deal with a new administration. There was a moment when a great relationship was created, and it seemed like we were finally knocking down these barriers. Eventually that ended, and that forest staffer was relocated. Then, all of a sudden, all our documents disappeared. So now we are back to square one, having conversations about why the mountain is holy, and explaining why we pray on our holy mountain and why we don't want to sign any permits.

So we have a meeting every year to go over the logistics of the run. We are going to have the run regardless of what they say. I'm going to continue to stand for my people and our way of life. If I have to go back every year and explain everything over and over, I will. This is the life I've chosen, and the run is too important to lose. It has opened so many doors for us to conduct ceremony and to be Apache, just like my ancestors were before being killed or imprisoned.

The Fight for Chí'chil Biłdagoteel

Chí'chil Biłdagoteel sits on the Tonto National Forest. The fight for *Chí'chil Biłdagoteel* started in the late 1990s with a road widening. It was deceitful because they were hiding the real truth of their intention to mine our holy land. In the early 2000s we got word of lobbying happening in D.C. for a proposed copper mine called Resolution Copper. It wasn't until 2012 that Representative Gosar (R-AZ) was going to put a bill on the floor for the "land exchange."[21] At that time, they had no support, because they all knew it was a terrible bill. They knew the devastation it was going to have on the environment. Even the Forest Service, at the beginning, was telling Congress not to do this because it was going to be such an environmental disaster. And of course the government doesn't ever want to talk about Native people because then the truth would have to come out about what really happened to us. And no one wants to touch religion.

It wasn't until 2014 when Senator McCain slipped the "land exchange" bill into the National Defense Authorization Act for FY15. The NDAA was a *must-sign bill*.[22] McCain slipped it in as a midnight rider at the eleventh hour, which gave the green light for the mine to go forward.

What makes it even worse is that in the small print of that bill, it states that the National Environmental Protection Act, NEPA, didn't apply. Resolution Copper was exempt from all federal laws, including NEPA. The normal route of NEPA is to first create an environmental impact statement to determine if a project is good or not. But because Resolution Copper's proposed mine at *Chí'chil Biłdagoteel* is exempt from all federal laws, regardless of what the outcome of the final environmental impact statement is, the land swap is still going to happen.

My father sat on the tribal council when they were informed about what McCain had done. They created resolutions to fight against the land exchange. Once that bill was signed, the occupation by Apache Stronghold started. We were there for longer than a year, maybe two. Groups of people from San Carlos banded together to fight it. Everybody was getting educated about the bill and what was happening to us spiritually in our religion and our way of life. That is how Apache Stronghold came to exist. Apache Stronghold is a

24

spiritual movement. Everything we've ever done is through our spirituality, our religion, our way of life. That is how we move forward in every decision that we make.

Fighting the Oldest Evils in the World

We believe that we are fighting the oldest evils in this world—greed and power. Our creation stories talk about what non-Natives call Lucifer. He was on the other side of the world, and he came to this side, but he couldn't penetrate. He couldn't destroy us, because at that time, all tribes were one. We weren't all one tribe, *but we were in sync.* My dad says we were "one drum, one circle, one prayer." Lucifer couldn't penetrate his evil into the Indigenous people because we were still very entwined and in sync with, and rooted in, the blessed gifts the Creator had given to us. It wasn't until assimilation came when things started to divide us. In prophecies Lucifer told us that he would be back and that we would know it was him.

This is how we look at these corporations and this government system that continue to want to destroy us. We keep it spiritual because we are fighting evil. We're fighting Lucifer, who came over but couldn't break us then. We are fighting. But now, because of the way the system is and how we are divided and conquered through colonization, what assimilation has done to put us to where we're at today, ripping everything from us. That's why Apache Stronghold keeps it spiritual.

My Roles within Apache Stronghold

I'm a spokesperson. I'm an organizer. But my most important role is being Apache. This is who I am. I don't call myself an activist or an advocate. I manage my dad's schedule, my schedule, and Naelyn's schedule. I cook, I take care of our elders. I play so many roles that it's hard to put it all in job titles, because we're also taught that we don't do this work with titles, or job descriptions. I don't know how to do that, because it's so real for us.

Being Apache is to fight for our way of life, to fight for our religion, our spirituality, our identity, and to fight for Mother Earth because she is our mother. She gives life to us in *Chi'chil Bildagoteel*, she gives us all the tools to be born there, to survive there, and even to die there. It's the circle of life. Mother Earth has provided all that for us. It's our job to protect what's left so that we can exist. It's been a very heavy, but a very honored and humbling experience. I am a mother, and I want my girls to be able to have a voice and to be able to be Apache and to be able to pray at their holy places. It's really a difficult and emotional fight because we're doing it spiritually. *We just need to matter.* That's the hard part to swallow. It seems like our people don't matter.

I am learning. My father's life's work and passion became mine. My heart is my people. My heart is all people. My heart is for those yet to be born. My heart is protecting our way of life so that we all can survive. In Apache Stronghold, I fight to be able to carry on for the next one, so that all the work that my dad and those that passed before him contributed to the fight for our people, and doesn't just end.

I always tell myself, "I'm the recorder." I tell Naelyn, and I tell all four of my girls—because I talk to my baby, too. But even for my nieces and my nephews, or those not even within our family, if there's someone that's supposed to take it on, *I'm that recorder.* I have it. I have the experience and the knowledge of what each person has went through, so that when it's their time, I can pass on the torch. I can pass on the fight. It's sad because we want to win! But now, hopefully, there will be fight to pass on, because of the way the system is.

The Apache Wars Haven't Ended

On Friday, the judgment on our appeal came out from the Ninth Circuit Court.[23] We lost the injunction against the mine. It was two against one. Even though we didn't win the appeal, the fight is not over, we're going to take this all the way to the Supreme Court.[24] This is where we will see actual change happen. The United States government will acknowledge us and admit that we have a religion, or the world will finally know the truth and the deceit of how America was founded. The system was established to destroy us.

The Apache wars haven't ended! We're still fighting. It's just a different fight now. We're not just fighting for us. We're fighting for everyone! No matter who you are, no matter what color you are, no matter what religion you believe in, no matter if you don't believe in a religion. We're still fighting for everyone, because we can't exist without the natural resources. We can't exist without the water. If our religion is at stake, so is theirs.

My Journey Home to Chí'chil Biłdagoteel

It began when my father decided to move back to Oak Flat. On November 28, 2019, my father ran from Old San Carlos to Oak Flat, for three days. Seeing the burden, the heaviness on his face throughout his journey, lift when he reached his home—that is when I could see that he was happy and free. You could feel his spirit. My dad is residing at *Chí'chil Biłdagoteel* now.

My father had been organizing our annual march and run to *Chí'chil Biłdagoteel*, and I told him that I didn't want it to just end. I thought that we needed to keep it going, because people like myself need it. It's a part of healing. For all of our spiritual runs and walks, we say, "It's a personal journey to a sacred unity, because it's not us calling on the people, it's the mountain that makes you come. We inform the public that we're having the sacred march-run, but what brings you is the spirit of our holy mountains.

It is healing even for non-Indigenous people. We have so many good friends and allies that have joined us. My dad had a really good friend who asked him how he could help. "Wendsler, what can I do to help? My people are the ones that put you on this reservation. I feel bad. What do we do?" And my dad said, "Walk with me. You could walk me out." His friend said, "Okay." Because it is healing for everybody.

Organizing Our Sacred Run

This was the second year that I organized the Oak Flat march-run. I had a vision that there were runners coming in from all four directions. I told my father about my dream, and he said, "I think that needs to happen. It's going to take all of us." We started organizing and meeting people, and I had seen certain people in my dream. I explained my dream and the response was amazing. They knew the importance of unifying and to be in prayer to save Oak Flat and our religion. Organizing from the four directions, we had people from Tohono O'odham and the

Pascua Yaqui of south Arizona, Navajo Nation from the north, Apache Stronghold from the east, Onk Akimel O'odham, Piipaash, and the Yavapais coming from the west. I would visit my father and we would meet with other organizers to prepare for the sacred march-run. I realized how focused I was on the other three directions, helping them go through ceremony, getting them ready and establishing the foundation for their run. They, too, were preparing their own personal journey.

On one of our visits, I was around the fire pit speaking with my father and one of the organizers from the north. I said, "Dad, I got to tell you something, but I don't know how you're going to take it." He's real protective of us, especially his girls. I said, "I want to start the run from Old San Carlos, where they first placed us as prisoners of war." That's where they actually had the concentration camp, where the Cavalry had their station and everything. He looked at me and goes, "Are you ready?" And I said, "Yes." He said, "Are you sure? Because your life's going to change forever." And I said, "I want to come home. Don't worry, I'll be okay. I want to be free."

Feeling the Chains on My Ankles and Wrists

I ended up staying an extra night at *Chi'chil Biłdagoteel* because I didn't want to return to the reservation. That night, my fiancé Morgun and I were going down the hill and I started crying. I told Morgun, "I was raised knowing that I'm a prisoner of war. That I belong to the United States government. I've known that my whole life." You have that idea. You have the knowledge and awareness of the truth. *But I never really felt it.* I said, "I feel it. I literally can feel the chains on my ankles and on my wrists. They feel so heavy. *They feel tight.* I can really feel it like it's on me!" Then he looked at me and asked, "Are you okay?" I said, "I feel it! I understand now. I don't like it. I want the chains off."

In 2020, I decided to do my own journey, to start making it slowly back home, to reside at *Chi'chil Biłdagoteel*. I had just had a baby and I had a torn meniscus and was in a lot of pain, but this wasn't going to stop me. I remember my father explaining the process that would take place, a ceremony that I would have to go through. He told me that my world was going to change. "You're a mom, you just had a baby. You have Morgun. Things are going to be different. Are you ready?" I said, "I have to set the example for my children. I have to do it. I know Morgun and I are strong enough. He'll support me." He looked at me and gave me a hug. That moment changed me forever.

We got to Old San Carlos, and he said, "Okay, I'll ask you one more time. Are you ready?" I said, "Yes." He said, "You're walking away from this colonization, this colonial world we live in, and you're going to go home someday, but this is the beginning." He prayed for me and then he said, "Okay. You're ready." My run home began.

Leading up to that, I was telling my dad that night that I felt like when you're in an abusive relationship and you're the victim. "My abuser is physically, emotionally, and verbally abusive. I'm watching the clock waiting for him to go to sleep, and then I'm going to leave!" That's how I felt. I really felt like that—all that anxiety, being scared, nervous, anxious, happy. I said, "I feel so many emotions." That's why he talked to me that next morning to make sure I was ready. I said, "Dad, he's asleep. It's my time to escape." So, I left, and I did my first leg in 2021. I'm hoping to do the second part of the leg, making my journey home. All these events and experiences are leading up for me to carry on the fight. That spiritual and personal journey—standing up for our religious rights—is setting the example for my children.

Messengers for Creator

My dad has taught us that we're all messengers for Creator. We are that funnel. Whatever decisions that need to be made are going to come spiritually. Whether it's in a dream or a vision or a message, even from talking to somebody. There have been times that my siblings, children, or even a friend outside of our family comes to me or my father and tells us that they have a message. There's a feeling that comes over you. You know in your spirit that Creator's talking to you. My dad and I don't make a move unless it's a message from Creator. All of our decisions are based on our spirituality. I can't say it enough, our reason to fight the way we do is because it was prophesied at the very beginning that he would be back, and he would be in different forms. We are in a spiritual war. We can't fight this evil without spirituality, because you need it to win, to save Mother Earth, the water, the people, and those yet to be born.

One Drum, One Circle, One Prayer

When we started Apache Stronghold, we had ceremony done and these elderly women asked my dad, "What do you want? What do you want to happen?" My father said, "I want religious people." They looked at him and they said, "That's what you want? You don't want anything else? Do you only want Apache people?" He said, "No, I need religious people to stand with us, no matter what color they are, or what religion they believe in. We need religious people because we're fighting the oldest evil." So that's what they did. They shot these arrows and that's what we have received. Numerous people of all faiths standing with us. Our religion is on trial, and that means the continued genocide of our way of life. To fight this is to stand united with all faiths.

When we file our case in the US Supreme Court, we are going to have to be unified. *One drum, one circle, one prayer.* We're going to have to be in sync. Standing Rock, Mauna Kea, Line Three, Keystone Pipeline, in all of these you have Indigenous people fighting against the greed of money and power to protect the water, to protect our natural resources, to protect our spirituality. You and I cannot survive without it. It is time for the world to wake up.

Breaking Down the Walls of Divide and Conquer

From the Sierra Club to the Center for Biodiversity and the Poor People's Campaign, all of our supporters and allies who have joined the fight have been a blessed gift. We are breaking down the walls of divide and conquer. It's going to take every one of us. All the support we can get to help fight to protect *Chí'chil Biłdagoteel*. This is a fight for everyone because *Chí'chil Biłdagoteel* sets the precedent of what's going to happen for all people. If a foreign mining company can come in and be exempt from all federal laws—a genocide on the religion and on Mother Earth, water—how are we going to survive? We are all witnessing a premeditated murder. Mother Earth is alive, but it has become the norm to hurt her.

Remember, *I'm a ward* to the United States government. In the Constitution, in order to speak to Congress, in order to knock on the door and visit your senators, as an Indigenous person enrolled into a federally recognized tribe, I don't have that privilege. They do not have to listen to me, even though I am a voter. Why? Because I do not hold a political seat in my tribal government. The way the Constitution is written, it's government to government between federally recognized tribes and the US government. Any other nationality can speak to their congressional leaders as a constituent, but there is an exception when it comes to Indigenous people.

That's why it's going to take all of us. While we're at the forefront protecting Mother Earth and the water, we need you to help get our voices elevated. We need letters written. We need those calls to senators, to congresspeople. We need you because it's on federal land. Anybody can help us fight to protect *Chi'chil Bildagoteel*, no matter what state you live in. You can tell your congressmen and senators to support the Save Oak Flat Act.[25]

Our next step is to go to the Supreme Court. It is time now more than ever to unify. We have been blessed with religious organizations and institutes joining us on the lawsuit. The people are slowly waking up, but there are other organizations and religious groups that can join us. We all have a role. We have said it before, this system does not have the best interests of the people at heart. We have to conquer this system that was meant to divide the people. It will take us working together to actually make change.

I've been co-leading Apache Stronghold's participation in the Poor People's Campaign with my father. It has been a blessing to work with the Poor People's Campaign as an ally. Having the opportunity to speak on a national level has been a blessing, but also an awakening. There are five hundred and seventy-four federally recognized tribes, but there is very little awareness among non-Indigenous people that we even exist.

We Were the First Chapter

Understanding the first chapter of what happened to Indigenous people helps you find solutions to what you're fighting for. We were forced by military to live in exile. We were put on this reservation, this concentration camp, with no way to survive. We have the poorest health care that exists. That's one of the reasons why alcoholism is such an issue and we're so stereotyped with it. When they placed us on reservations, they took us away from our religion, our traditional ways. We were hit with these diseases—with smallpox and all these other sicknesses that our people were dying from, that our medicine people didn't understand. We didn't know what it was, and they didn't know how to cure it.

It was a way for the US government to come in and say, "Here, we got a doctor. Our doctor's better than your doctor." But they were giving us whiskey! Instead of treating us medically, they were giving us alcohol. Our people did not understand what was happening. We had never consumed alcohol before. When they did, and no longer felt the pain of their illness, they thought the white man's medicine was working, but they were killing us.

There are so many issues that we as Indigenous people are facing, from alcohol to diabetes, et cetera. People don't understand the history. The US government had their campaigns. First it was "A good Indian is a dead Indian." Then they realized that they couldn't kill us all. So the campaign went to "Kill the Indian, but save the man." They wanted to strip us away from who we were and make us civilized and assimilate us. We were a healthy people that lived off the land. When they forced us on the San Carlos reservation, another form of punishment and control was taking away our rights to hunt and harvest food. They started making us stand in line for food rations. It was another way of controlling who we are.

Apache Tribal Historic Preservation

I work as an archaeology aide with the San Carlos Apache Tribe Historic Preservation Office and Archaeology Department. I work with the director, Vernelda Grant, the tribal historic preservation officer and archaeologist. My director has been a role model for me. She has taught me so much and has allowed me to grow. She's a strong Apache woman who was educated in this white world, but she has never lost her connection to our way of life.

We are called "the war department." Too many people only know the history of Indigenous people during the time of war. We're not taught "pre-reservation." You don't hear a lot of the history prior to colonialism. In my job I'm able to be with the land and gain knowledge of how our people were before invaders came. So it's really given me even more of an understanding of the teachings my grandmother instilled in me of how we were pre-reservation.

One of my duties is to go out and survey the land. When someone applies for land to build a home or create a project, I'm able to protect my ancestors and not disturb them. When I was pregnant with my youngest one, and after she was born, I would take her to survey the land with me, and I still do. We pray and I say, "I'm not here to bother you. If there's something here, show me. I'm here to protect you. But if there's nothing here, then I want to create a home for a family so that they can have children and have a place to live and set a foundation."

As Much as We Need You, You Need Us

I am passionate about sharing our story because in order for us to make a better world, we have to know what really happened to the Apache/Indigenous people. The one thing that I stated at the Poor People's campaign, and it is really true, is that "as much as we need you, you need us." We were all given a gift. The way that I was raised—and what our people would tell us—is that there are all these different people. There's white people, Black people, Asian people, and Indigenous people—which includes Mexican people. It is said that white people were given the gift of fire. Black people were given the gift of water. Asian people were given the gift of air. Indigenous people were given the gift of earth. We all have the power in these elements. It's a gift. But there are people that are going to misuse it. There are good and bad people. All these elements need protection. So we need one another. This will help secure a future for those yet to be born.

My Hope for My Daughters

I hope that my daughters don't have to fight for their survival. I hope for a world where they have equal rights as do those who are not Indigenous. I hope for a world for them to be free to be Apache. I hope that they can go to *Chi'chil Bildagoteel* and *Dził Nchaa Si'*. I think about my youngest one. Her future is so unpredictable because she's so little. I want her to know who she is without being ridiculed. I'm worried about our spirituality—that our holy places and identity will be taken from her and from our future generations. I want them to be able to pray in Apache at their holy places and not be worried about being shot at or arrested. These are just some of the things that have happened to us! I just want them to have this beautiful life, but the reality of that is that we don't know if things will change, and if they do, if I'll see it in my lifetime, or if my children will see it in their lifetime, but I hope someday our future generations will have a win.

It's just the simplest things. You hope that they can drink clean water. You hope they can breathe! The basics of survival. As First Nations people, we've been through it. If we can tell the very first chapter of how America was founded, and if people would actually listen to us, instead of jumping to chapter two, three, and four, and forward, then we would have solutions. It's going to take all of us. In order to change this system, we have to heal. In order to heal we have to acknowledge the First People. For so long we were the dust underneath the rug. Now we've got to pull that rug back and show we exist. Our voices need to be heard. This is the reason I fight, so that my daughters can be Apache.

TWO

Roz Pelles

⁎

People might come into a housing struggle
just because they want to get a certain thing fixed.
They may end up understanding that it's not just
about me getting my sink fixed.
It's more about *there's a reason* that the sink isn't getting fixed.
There's a reason bigger than that sink.
That's where people get access to other people's experiences,
other people's knowledge,
and they can continue to be engaged.
Organizing is a place where people get engaged,
get educated, get moved to act,
and in many cases, become engaged for a lifetime.
That's an amazing thing to be a part of.

Roz Pelles is an award-winning organizer, strategist, movement builder, and attorney. Joining the civil justice movement as a young teenager, she became active in the Congress for Racial Equality in Winston-Salem, North Carolina, in the early 1960s. Roz has organized around connecting issues of civil rights, workers' rights, police brutality, and anti-racism to broader issues of social justice and liberation. Embracing an anti-capitalist and anti-racist framework during a period of white supremacist resurgence across the US, she joined the Workers Viewpoint Party, which became the Communist Workers Party. Roz is a founder and former executive director of Repairers of the Breach and a former director of the North Carolina NAACP, and has held leadership positions with national labor unions and the AFL-CIO. She was the executive director of the National Rainbow Coalition and special assistant to Reverend Jesse L. Jackson Sr. Roz is currently the Strategic Advisor to the Poor Peoples Campaign: A National Call for Moral Revival.

While sharing her personal and political trajectory, Roz describes the need for a multi-racial, multi-issue movement developed from the bottom up, and reflects on her organizing philosophy of leading from behind. She also describes what it means to balance parenting and family life within the context of organizing while menaced by government repression and political assassination. She details her experiences of the fracturing of the left in the wake of the Greensboro Massacre and offers lessons for organizing today.

Roz currently resides in Maryland.

I WAS BORN IN WINSTON-SALEM, NORTH CAROLINA, IN 1948. I'm a Black Southern woman who only moved to the Upper South in 1986. I spent most of my early life in North Carolina. I am the daughter of a tobacco factory worker who was proud, wrote songs, and spoke French, and a registered nurse who taught at a Black nursing school. My parents were Ruby Monroe Woodward and Robert Ernest Woodward Jr. My mom was born in South Carolina. My father grew up in Brooklyn. He came to the South to be with family for the summers and at other times, as did many kids growing up in the North with extended family in the South. It was during one of those transition moments that they met. My mother is still alive. She's ninety-seven and fiercely independent. I've got one younger sister who still lives in Winston-Salem.

We have traced my family roots on my mother's side back eight generations to an African village in Anomabu, Ghana. We were able to trace my father's paternal ancestry four generations back to a plantation near Spartanburg, South Carolina.

I grew up in a home where there was a lot of talk at the dinner table about what was happening in the world around us. It was during these meals that I developed my sense of who I was and acquired the values that would guide me throughout my life. For example, my father taught me at a very early age that if you see something wrong, it's your responsibility to do something about it. This is a daunting thing to hear if you are a four- or five-year-old. But if you live into that, it really can be a guide. It guides how I work today. This is basically who I am.

Segregation

Growing up, the signs of inequality and segregation were present: separate water fountains, hospitals, churches, and schools. In Winston-Salem, segregation almost allowed dignity. That's an odd concept, but there was a highly developed Black middle class in Winston-Salem. This made possible certain structures, such as Black-owned businesses—a public bus company, pharmacy, and movie theater—and Black organizations and institutions that in some ways protected some of us from the harshness and humiliation of segregation. But my personal experiences could not override what I was seeing on TV and hearing in discussions at my dining room table. I was seeing young people across the South resisting all forms of segregation. I remember seeing a *Life* magazine issue dedicated to the civil rights movement and then translating what I was seeing outside of Winston-Salem to what I was seeing and feeling inside my city. Ours was different, *and it was still wrong.*

The Congress for Racial Equality

I first learned that I could be part of the change—making something wrong, right—when the civil rights movement came to my town. It came not only to my town, but to my church. St. Stephen's Episcopal Church became the headquarters for the Congress of Racial Equality (CORE) and for the civil rights movement. I was thirteen years old. That was the beginning of my involvement in the civil rights movement.

We were trained, and we were on the picket line, and it was a scary thing if you've never done it. But there was a spirit that just made it all right. There was the singing, there was the camaraderie, and there was the confidence that *we could win.* I don't think we were thinking about what we were protesting as a system, it was thought about more as a pattern and a practice. There were laws that needed to be changed, and there was the confidence that we could do it and that it was happening beyond my little town. It was happening all over the South and in other places. Pretty soon it got to be so common to the point where I was not afraid, except when the police showed up differently than they had the time before. But there was never an attempt to attack the protesters where we were. When I was on the picket line, there was no attempt to actually hurt people. There was confrontation, but not in a way that I ever felt like, "I've just got to get out of here," even as a kid. That confidence grew over the years, of trying to understand and growing up knowing that you have to do what's right. It became a normal thing for me. A lot of people did it sporadically. I was a regular. I went to the March on Washington and just got grounded in a movement for change.

The target of the movement in Winston-Salem had earlier been the typical one, Woolworth's, but the focus in Winston-Salem quickly became K&W Cafeteria. K&W Cafeteria was significant. It not only had a practice of segregation; its owner was a known member of the White Citizens' Council. Our single focus was trying to make a breakthrough at this one place.

The irony is my parents were not engaged directly. They were not on picket lines. They trusted me to our priest at church, his wife, and that community. They knew them and they came to mass meetings, but they were *not* on picket lines. My father showed up in parking lots when there were picket lines, especially if there was some concern about how the day would go. He and my Uncle Mike would be in the parking lot, and I would look out and see them. His reasoning was that he did not believe he could be nonviolent if somebody hit him. He felt that he would have had to respond, so he would just sit there watching. I often wondered what he would do if there was a problem, especially since we were supposed to be nonviolent. Who knows? But that never happened.

I was one of the younger people in CORE. My house became a place where the college kids came, mainly because of my father. It was an intimate kind of relationship to the struggle because it was not just about showing up and getting trained, it was about being totally integrated into the process. It involved my interacting with students, Black and white, who came to my dining room table. I listened to and participated in their conversations with my father, and my mother even made birthday cakes for the kids from Wake Forest. It was a unique perspective, and it situated me to think about the need to change the world. That stuck with me. How I saw change then, and what I see is the problem now, are of course different. But that's where I was situated at the time, and it put me in a position to do the things that I've done.

There were a lot of things that I didn't understand back then that my later politics helped me understand. In the South, often the main occupations were the basics—undertaker, teacher, nurse. One of my friends' father was a funeral director, and he also had a gospel radio show on Saturday. I was in and out of their house all the time. When the sit-ins started, he referred to us as hooligans. He was one of the first Black aldermen. Later in my life, I got to understand how some people identify with the oppressor, even though they're in an oppressed class themselves.

That was my life, on picket lines and in marches, and I'm very grateful for that experience. I was in the ninth grade, entering high school, but I was not exceptional in that way. It was not unusual for children to be engaged in the civil rights movement, because young people were thrust into these struggles *by circumstance*. I could choose to be involved or not, but some people were so in the crosshairs that they didn't have a choice. There were kids as young and younger than me who were engaged. There were the Birmingham Children's Marches, for example. There were people younger than me who actually got thrown into jail, bitten by dogs, or got fire hoses turned on them. This was not unusual. I had folks who were in school who were with me. I had the ability and the support to take part in this and not cause my parents negative consequences for my actions. In some places and circumstances, a child's involvement cost their parents things, cost their parents their livelihood, and caused family conflict. That was not my case. I don't think I was particularly exceptional. I just stayed in the struggle.

Staying in the Movement

My understanding of the world and situations I was in created the conditions for me to stay in the social justice movement. I went from understanding that segregation was wrong, to understanding voting rights were important, to seeing the larger ills. Registering to vote was a critical part of it. I was even part of the team that had the honor of registering my grandfather to vote for the first time. I was not a senior on the team, I was just tagging along because it was my grandfather.

I read a lot. I took in a lot. When I was at North Carolina A&T State University, there was a Black student union on that historically Black college campus. It sounds unusual, but it was a group of progressive students who were trying to understand the world. There were students from A&T and Bennett College. There I was introduced to readings that explained the world I lived in and the importance of being active in the movement. We watched Malcolm X evolve, then King got killed and there was an analysis of that. We were also looking at the liberation struggles from around the world. All of those things influenced me. There were all these things throughout my life that came together and deepened my understanding of the problems that exist in this country and in the world, and which also helped me figure out opportunities to address them.

Situating Myself in Struggle

Through reading and talking to people and trying to understand why things existed in the way that they did, I finally got an understanding of how *systemic* these things were. I also understood that there was a system in this country that perpetuated these things, often in the service of profit and power. As that understanding grew, I had to figure out where to do my work. I started to understand that it wasn't just a question of being able to go to a restaurant or to have equal access to things. It was also a question of being able to have a good job. My father worked in a cigarette factory for most of his life. He hated that job. On Fridays he would be happy and on Sundays he would be dreading work, because it was oppressive and my father was a creative, thinking man.

I knew that something needed to be done about how people worked and lived. People were profiting off these various things. There was a whole system that I came to understand as capitalism. Capitalism was the problem. A minority of people ran everything, and the majority of people worked for them. There needed to be a system where people had a voice in how they were treated and how they lived. That guided my thinking. It was not an aha moment, it was over the course of time. I was also seeing that maybe people could move away from being oppressed if there was struggle, if there was a movement. I was looking around and I saw the liberation struggles in Africa. I made a big connection with Africa during my early days, and was what people would call a nationalist. There was a tremendous identity with Africa. Then I started to look around and moved beyond just an identity of Black is beautiful. While that is true, there was another way to identify, which was with the revolutionary nature of the work that people were doing in other countries, how they were winning, and how people were able to start to build the lives that they deserved.

Community Organizing Training

While I was at North Carolina A&T there was a huge community organizing movement led by Howard Fuller, who was Owusu Sadaukai at the time, conducted through the Foundation for Community Development in Durham, North Carolina. In much later years, he became a national proponent of charter schools. People have trouble seeing that link, but he is probably one of the best organizers I've ever seen. This whole community organizing movement was coming into being and included, a few months later, the Malcolm X University.

A program was developed to take progressive college students, train them to be community organizers, and put them across the state of North Carolina, living in the communities where they organized. We had ten intensive days and nights of study. There might have been fifty of us that were trained. It was a combination of Alinsky-type organizing that was connected to a political framework that explains why people are poor. That people *are made to be poor*. It's not something that has to be. That's where I worked that summer, and it changed my life. That training changed the way I saw things, and the way that I understood how I could be engaged in making change. That was the first time I'd ever been a community organizer. I must have been nineteenish. I could see change. I could see what it meant to talk to people and listen really hard, and work with them to bring about the things they wanted to see in their community, and how, ultimately, *I was them.*

It's that training that got me on the road to organizing. That's what got me on the road to seeing that not only was there was something wrong, but that I could actually do something about it, that I could actually be a part of the change in a real way, not just picketing, but actually delving into root causes and then figuring out with others how to make that change. It's a powerful thing to understand that you can actually be a part of the change, that you can actually make change, and that you can actually help bring others to a similar realization just by talking to people, by listening to people, by being with people. That was the beginning of my real involvement and commitment to doing the work and understanding what I was to do, and I'm thankful for that time.

The Meaning of Collective Struggle

Community organizing removes the idea that one person can make history based on charisma. It removes that idea that changing the laws is what fundamentally makes change. It reveals that people can be in control of the change that they seek and that change best happens when people come together and identify problems and then identify ways to collectively solve them. In the absence of that, it's not likely that you can have long-term change. Even when the laws change, sometimes the laws are not enforced or barely enforced, or they just sit on the books. That's not the end-all and be-all for change in people's lives. People have *to fight*, even when the laws change, even when there's a call from charismatic leaders. People are best able to protect their rights by coming together, understanding what their rights are, agreeing to make sure they have those rights, and then taking the necessary steps to achieve those goals and those rights. It's through that coming together, through community organizing, that this kind of change can happen. Those are the series of steps that have to happen for change to come and to last. Through that process people learn that change is possible. People might come into a housing struggle just because they want to get a certain thing fixed. They may end up understanding that it's not just about me getting my sink fixed. It's more about *there's a reason* that the sink isn't getting fixed. *There's a reason bigger than that sink.* That's where people get access to other people's experiences, other people's knowledge, and they can continue to be engaged. Organizing is a place where people get engaged, get educated, get moved to act, and in many cases, become engaged for a lifetime. That's an amazing thing to be a part of.

Balancing Family and Movement Work

I married my childhood sweetheart when I was nineteen. We had our first kid when I was twenty. He was also a community organizer. It's not easy. We later separated and divorced. For a number of those years, I was a single parent. I really tried to continue to do whatever work I could do.

The whole question of balance, I didn't know how to do it just right. I think that my generation of activists may in some ways have impacted the way people think about how you do movements now.

Back then there was little to no talk about self-care. I was able to do it because I was committed to doing it. I found a partner with the same commitment to family and to building a movement. I had found a community that embraced me and others who needed the support to do it. That made it easier. The other piece of balancing family life and movement work is knowing that you don't have to stop your life to change the world. There has to be a way for people to make change without giving up the family, and without giving up a "normal life." One way that I learned how to do this was from watching people who did not have a choice. I watched tenants' rights advocates and folks who were in the street who had been doing that work for a long time, and who raised families. They didn't have the luxury to not do it. They wanted a family and they wanted change, and they did it all, and in much worse conditions than I ever had. There was something about learning from people who were doing that very thing that seemed hard to me. I looked at them and understood how people were committed to both. That boosted my commitment. The other thing was, I didn't ever separate my family life from my movement life.

When I was going to demonstrations, my kids were going to demonstrations. My youngest got lost in a Central America rally in Washington! My kids have been totally integrated into the movement. I have at times felt like, "Oh, my God, what have I done to them?" We've talked about it over the years. This is sometimes a discussion at Thanksgiving or during some other gathering when there's all this storytelling about how they grew up and what they were seeing. They seem to have no regrets. I think that's what folks who are committed to change can actually expect to happen when they build families. *And we're doing this because of families!* So, to deny the prospect of having healthy families, or think that there has to be a choice, would be incredibly discouraging, but it's not necessarily true. It does takes planning and thinking things through. It's a matter of trying to make sure that family is not out here and movement work someplace else, that they are together. I've done that my whole life. It never dawned on me to separate them.

Even when I was a single parent working in a factory on the third shift, I always tried to make sure that they understood what I was doing. It was critical that I just didn't "disappear" for meetings, but that they understood fully that they had books that they could read and things that they could do and that they understood what I was doing. They also had friends whose parents were doing similar work. It was a conscious choice on my part to not separate it out. I think it's totally possible. I have three adult sons who have taken the values, thinking, and curiosity about the world from our household into their own work. They are not organizers like me. They are very different, but one of the things that I can count on is that they will always be on the right side of history. Always! I've got one son who is a filmmaker. He teaches film at a school in the state of Washington. Another one is a psychologist in North Dakota, for God's sakes, and another one is working in New Jersey as an assistant commissioner for Labor. They've all been proud of how they grew up. They've used it to their advantage, and it shows in their work, and that makes me so proud. That really solidifies my belief that you don't have to do one or the other. You *can* continue to build family and you can continue to build a better world.

As an organizer leading a normal life, you find some balance where you can, and realize that every struggle is not *the* struggle. We're not always under a state of siege. That helps to moderate how we respond to the things around us. I am so saddened every time I hear a young organizer questioning whether they should have a family, based on the perceived contradiction between family and commitment to social justice. I'm very sad by that. People can have other reasons, but that particularly saddens me because I know that it's possible to do it. It's not easy, but it's possible. Often family was a respite. It was a place to come home to. There was safety, there was understanding. There was appreciation. There was a chance to have real discussions, as a family. I've so much appreciated my choice to organize and have a family.

Identifying Capitalism as the Problem

The movement work that I've been involved with goes from trying to desegregate public accommodations to being a Black revolutionary nationalist, to discovering how countering capitalism can connect everything. Seeing that the struggles for civil rights, workers' rights, and the environment were connected. This led me to take all that I had learned and thought about in the movements as I knew them, to an understanding that it was capitalism that was the problem.

During the time that I worked in the factory, I was a part of a group called the Workers Viewpoint Organization, which was a Marxist organization. Many folks in my generation had been in various silos in movements and were not satisfied with the progress being made. Many started to look deeper at the problems people were facing and came to understand that the cause was capitalism. Understanding that capitalism was the problem meant you had to lift up work in the communities and the workplace. I went to work in a textile mill in Greensboro, North Carolina, because organizing workers was important. I learned a lot. I learned to listen to people, and I learned so much from the women there—how to have family and work hard.

I also learned that you cannot talk politics with people if you don't do your work. I would just be chatting away, and somebody would say, "You know, this is all fine, but right now, you need to make production right here. You need to do your job!" I went to work in a plant to organize workers because at that point the thinking was to go to the places that were most critical in upholding capitalism, which are workplaces, the point of production. So I, like many young people who came out of struggles on campuses and in other movements, went to newly formed organizations that were popping up all over the country, and we became members of these groups. This was in the mid-1970s.

In 1977, I remarried and moved. I lived in Greensboro, and he lived in Durham. He was also working with Workers Viewpoint. I'd known him before that, which is another nice and different story. But his work was good and so we moved to Durham. I worked for that first year, and then in December 1978, we had a baby who was sick and in the hospital for four months, so I did very little work.

Organizing Tenants and Families to End Police Brutality
During this period I worked for a year and a half on a high-stakes police brutality campaign. I totally loved that organizing, and I did the work. I was in the Workers Viewpoint organization at the time,

and also with the African Liberation Support Committee. I read in the local paper that a person had been beat up by the cops. It just didn't seem right. I talked with some of my friends and found out the address of the person that this had happened to, and I just showed up at their door. From there I learned that the person who got beat up was the son of the woman—Mrs. Farrell, bless her heart—who was a community leader of a tenants' organization. When she went to get him out of jail, the police roughed her up! So the question was, *what do we do about this?*

Together we organized other tenants. She was already a leader in the housing community. We did that for over a year. Every chance I've had to organize, I've always learned something. That was a wonderful experience. There were a lot of attempts to split her off from me. I remember somebody asking her, "Why do you want to associate with those communists?" Mrs. Farrell said, "I don't care what you call her. I know she's doing God's work." That was the quote. It was great! It was absolutely wonderful work. Then Greensboro happened on November 3, 1979.

White Supremacy and the Greensboro Massacre

I am a survivor of the Greensboro Massacre in that I was there that day and part of the group that was under attack.[26] My husband, Don Pelles, was wounded there. The whole back of his body was sprayed with birdshot. We were not living in Greensboro at the time. We were organizing and living in Durham. I'd been doing police brutality work and he was working in a factory there.

An understanding of Greensboro is an understanding of white supremacy in its more violent forms. There are lessons to be learned from the Greensboro massacre. I thought a lot about Greensboro during the violence in Charlottesville.[27]

The massacre in Greensboro happened because there was a coming together of white supremacist and government forces. This is not hyperbole. There were indications that the Bureau of Alcohol, Firearms and Tobacco (ATF) was involved, actually helped people convert weapons into more powerful ones to be used on November 3, and was with them in the caravan as they made their way to Greensboro. The attack came as a result, I think, of the strength of the good work we were doing in cities across the country. We were a new organization among a series of organizations. We were working in plants and in the mines and in various places.

Greensboro had a history of activism, and some of the same people who were engaged in that history were part of what was then the Workers Viewpoint Organization. Just weeks before the attack, Workers Viewpoint became the Communist Workers Party (CWP). It was right then that the name shifted. It was a model that included Asians, African Americans, and white women and men in leadership. It probably was one of the more multiracial groups on the left at that point.

The attack in Greensboro on November 3 was an attempt to stop the work, to stop the exposure of how capitalism works. I'm trying not to be grandiose about this because I don't want to give the impression that this was *the organization* on the left. I'm not trying to give the impression that this came from the highest ranks of the US government. But I am acknowledging that there is proof that at least the ATF and Durham police were involved in what happened. The question is, why would they even be involved in this? Why would they join ranks with the supremacists and drive halfway to the attack? Why would the police make a decision not to be at a demonstration? It is the first time I've ever been in a demonstration and there were no police. Why? The police actually were called off. There was only us when the Klan drove in.[28] I believe it was an orchestrated attempt. We, the Communist Workers Party, probably didn't do everything right, but a system that allows people to drive into a Black community and shoot people down in the street, there's nothing, there's no rhetoric that makes that okay. There's no one statement, there's *no nothing* that gives anybody the right to do that, and that's what they did.

The Klan drove into a poor Black community that was not even the announced starting point for the march that we planned. It was where people were going to set up and drive to the publicized starting point. They drove in as a caravan. It was fall, but it was a warmish day. We were singing and there were children around. At first, some of us thought that they were going to just drive through, and that it was harassment. That they were just trying to scare people.

Then the caravan stopped at the end of the block. The person in the lead truck shot a gun in the air. People in the last car got out and opened the trunk of their car. It was a very surreal moment because they just opened the trunk, pulled out guns, and started to shoot! There were children! How do you get the children out? How do you do all of this? The people that they murdered were our leaders. My husband got sprayed with birdshot, but the four people who were leaders were killed with big ammunition.

My friend Sandy Smith was the only woman killed. She was also the only Black person killed. She had been a leader in the factory and a spokesperson for many kinds of things for a very long time. There was a woman with her who survived, Claire Butler.[29] Claire stuck her head out from around the corner of a building where they found shelter during the attack to see what was happening. Claire reported that she said to Sandy, "This guy was pointing a gun right at me and he didn't shoot me. I don't know what's happening." So Sandy decides to look, and they shot her right between the eyes. One didn't get shot for looking, and one does.

It was a very difficult time, but it did not stop the work. We buried our dead and we continued to work. It was a bad time for us and had a chilling effect on the movement. For Marxists and leftists who were doing similar work, it created a moment where people didn't know what was going to *happen to them.* It also created a moment where many of those people decided that there had to be a separation between us and them. It was a very difficult moment for a long time. But we did our work, raised our families, and continued to do those things that we were supposed to do.

A White Supremacist Backlash

The reason that we were so violently attacked is that our organizing was anti-racist and anti-Klan. The Klan in the South was having a rebirth. Folks in the plants were talking about the Klan and leafleting neighborhoods. We had a campaign all over the South that was anti-Klan. We were marching and educating about the rise of the Klan. What often gets lost in the retelling of that day is that there was to be a march to a church to have a conference. That gets lost.

We were doing anti-Klan work, but there are those who have criticized some of the rhetoric. If I look back, it probably was excessive, but it's one of those things where it's *not* excessive if everything goes right. It's excessive if something goes wrong. People in communities all over the state were putting up our leaflets and posters in grocery stores and barbershops and all of that. The slogan of the demonstration—which was an anti-Klan demonstration taking place during a time when people were saying "Death to the Shah, death to this, death to that"—was "Death to the Klan." But those words were not unusual. That was the slogan for movements around the country. I don't want to minimize that it was an anti-Klan, anti-racist demonstration. No, I don't want that at all, but our work was not anti-Klan work, solely.

Our work was deeply embedded in communities and deeply embedded in workplaces. In North Carolina, we became leaders and took over trade unions in Cone Mills plants. I don't think that these issues can be separated. So, while it was an anti-Klan demonstration, there was also this educational element of how racism divided the working class, how the Klan was used to divide workers, so they didn't organize to get better wages at the textile mill.

Death to the Klan

At that time, the "Death to the Klan" slogan became a wedge on the left. In retrospect, I could see how it created a situation where people didn't know what was going to happen to them. People did not want to defend us and did not want to associate with us. Several months after the murders, there was a big demonstration in Greensboro. It was on February 1, and they did not want us to be a part of the coalition, *and it was about us*.

We were finally invited to be in that demonstration but with very strict admonitions about what we could and couldn't do, what we couldn't say, *what we couldn't be*. I attribute it to Anne Braden's work[30] that it was possible for us to attend and participate. Because of her long history, Anne understood that this was not the time for separation, but for coming together. So there was a big problem within the left. It hurt our ability to win, because we were not only trying to continue our organizing. Everybody in the organization had lost their jobs. People lost their jobs all over the country! We were trying to organize, and at the same time we had a legal battle. All of it was made more difficult because we didn't have the support of the left. We were able to gain support as time went on, but the left at that time was afraid. I understand that. But at the time, these were people who were my good friends. Some people even said we brought it on ourselves by the "Death to the Klan" language. That was hard to swallow.

We did have some victories. We had several trials that were not successful, but once we filed a civil suit, we were able to get documents that implicated the government and that connected a lot of the dots that we had not understood before. The CWP filed a civil suit against the Ku Klux Klan, the Nazi Party, and city of Greensboro. Several years later we won a wrongful death suit. That validated our claim of white supremacist and government collaboration. There were some people who came to this struggle because they knew that was fundamentally wrong. People like Reverend Jesse Jackson and folks who didn't care about the labels. They just knew that this was wrong.

Lessons Learned and Decisions to Be Made

We survived and learned a lot of lessons about oppression, language, about the necessity to fight in the streets and the courts. We learned a lot of lessons about what do you do after that attack. Do you go underground, or do you stay above and fight and continue the work? That was a question. We did the right thing, I believe. We did not go underground. *We would not be forced underground.* We took care of ourselves and took care of each other, but we had to continue to live and fight for what we believed in. There's a lot written about it, and it has truly impacted my life. It was a critical time in my political work where I had to decide *what to do and where I stood.* It was a time when I had to decide if I was still an activist. I had to ask myself if I still cared about this country. Did I still care about the kind of place that my kids were going to have to raise their kids in? The answer was yes.

Was I afraid? I was very much afraid. I was a spokesperson for the CWP in Durham, which meant that I received more attention than I sometimes would have liked. But questions remained. Which side am I on? Am I going to be an observer or am I going to be a doer? Am I going to remember that admonition that my father gave me, which was, "If you see something wrong, you should do something"? So this is the work that I chose to do.

My youngest child was nearly a year old on the day of the massacre. He was staying with a friend that day. That was in November, and he had been in the hospital the year before for four months. So, how do you *still* raise a family? I had older boys who were ten and six years old. They knew all the people. They were their uncles and their aunts! We had to figure out how to do the explaining, how to keep them from being scared, how to do all of that. We did it, and we did it the best way we could. That's what activists who want to do family and want to do work have to do. You do it the best you can, and you live with it. I did the best I could with what I had, and *that's a thing*. The massacre does not define me. It informs me. My experience there and with the Communist Workers Party is really part of the body of knowledge that I have accrued that made me able to do everything else. So, it's not the massacre, it's the work, the study, and the understanding of the world during that period that makes me able to fully be who I am and to be present even at this age.

After Greensboro, I worked at Duke Hospital, where I also learned so much. I was adding experience and knowledge to this trunk, along with some very good relationships that I carried with me. We were rooted in our community before November 3 and after November 3. I was the president of my PTA, which was astonishing. It was a conscious decision to keep living in a way that I could be proud of who I am and what I was contributing. *We* did that. We did it as a family. It made sense then, and it makes sense now.

Organizing at Duke University

In 1980, in the midst of the anti-Communist, *anti-everything* heat against the CWP, I got a job at Duke University Hospital, which was a prime place to do organizing. Folks at Duke were particularly aware of the massacre because several of the people who were killed had relationships to Duke Hospital or Duke University. They had either been students, professors, or doctors there, or something. There had also been a lot of stuff written about it in their student paper, and all over.

I was trained to be a phlebotomist and worked all over the hospital. The thinking was, how do you organize in this space? It's not just a job, it's a place to organize. I went to work there with the idea of building a workers' organization, a grievance committee. Duke had been the target of organizing by the American Federation of State, County, and Municipal Employees (AFSCME), but AFSCME could not make a breakthrough in the hospital. They made a breakthrough at the University and in some small areas of the hospital. During past unsuccessful organizing efforts, Duke had given concessions to entice people to vote against the union, including a grievance procedure, the right to be represented by other workers in grievance meetings, the right to arbitration paid for by Duke for certain offenses. These concessions were policy but were going unused. My work along with others was to use these "gifts."

We basically set up a union in exile, with newsletters and shop stewards. It was probably some of the best work I've ever done, until now. It was powerful work. We trained a lot of people and we beat Duke's lawyers on many fronts. That's what made me think I could probably do law school. That's what I did at Duke for about five years until we moved away. It was remarkable work. I was also on the editorial board of the student newspaper for a while. Duke hated us and respected us. It was *worthy work*. People referred to Duke at that time, and maybe they still do today, as the plantation, because of the way Duke employees were treated and how people were treated when they went to the hospital.

A couple of years ago, the medical school asked me to organize a panel of folks, including a couple of doctors who worked at Duke and were members of the Communist Workers Party. There was a whole discussion about Duke and its relationship to the community and its patients. There was no denial of that history.

Needing to Breathe

I went to law school and thought of it as a reprieve. Even all those years later, it was still hard to be in North Carolina. There are some people who have stayed in North Carolina for all these years,

Nelson and Joyce Johnson, and many others. But it was still very hard. There was still a whole left liberal community that was always questioning, "But what is she really saying?" That wasn't so much among community members, but there was that dynamic among some of the left. So, in some ways I was just glad to *breathe a little bit*, because there was almost no breathing in North Carolina.

I didn't finish college until 1986. I realized that there probably wasn't going to be a revolution, and so I had to get a job and a degree. My husband had a PhD, he had been a professor before at the University of North Carolina in the 1970s. He had started to do that work again, and I had the opportunity to keep working at Duke while finishing up my degree. I didn't have that much to go, and I went from there directly to law school. We moved the kids with the idea that my husband, Don, could choose where we went next. Everybody wanted to stay in Silver Spring, Maryland, for God's sake. I expected that we'd move back to North Carolina, but everybody was happy in Maryland. The schools were good, so different, the kids were prospering, Don found good jobs, and so we stayed. It was a good decision.

Howard University School of Law is a school with mostly young people. There's not a night school. There were probably less than a dozen of us that were older. I graduated when I was thirty-nine and just integrated myself with the students and got into study groups. I thought that I would use my law degree in the traditional way, but I ended up doing different types work. It's always served me well, because there's this kind of blessing that goes with having a law degree, some sort of thinking that if you could do that, you're pretty smart. I finished law school and then started to do other work here in the Washington, D.C., area. I had no idea what I was going to be doing, but I ended up having some amazing opportunities that I hadn't expected. I had a series of jobs, including as a legislative analyst for a session and a staff director for the National Education Association staff union, and I worked for the National Treasury Employees Union.

The Rev. Jesse Jackson and the National Rainbow Coalition

I ended up as executive director at the National Rainbow Coalition, with the Reverend Jesse Jackson. I really loved that job. It was great.

It wasn't organizing on the ground per se, but I learned a lot. It was a place where my opinions were asked. I think it's a side of Reverend Jesse Jackson that most people don't know. He is brilliant, and I still call him a friend, to this day.

This was the rainbow. This was before it became Rainbow PUSH. It grew out of the political campaigns of the 1980s. At that point it was a mass organization, and at the same time, Reverend Jackson was the national civil and human rights leader. What I think people don't realize about him is how much he was called to struggle and showed up to struggle. We used to say that he had walked more picket lines than any labor president, and that was true. The main thing is that he's really smart, analytical, and strategic. He sought the advice of folks who were situated around him. I appreciated that. I wasn't always right, but I was asked. A lot of it was trying to figure out where he would head, politically. It was during a time when there were great questions for him and our place in the movement. I have a lot of deep respect and love for Reverend Jesse Jackson.

I've been so lucky to be in these situations where I don't have to explain about Greensboro. I can't run away from who I am, because I was so public. Some people can just disappear into their past. I don't want to, and I couldn't if I wanted to. I worked next for the AFL-CIO and retired from there in 2013. I was with the AFL—I cannot believe it—for eighteen years and had different jobs there. I think what initially held me there was that I had a job as the head of a labor version of the United Way. We set up a fund that workers could contribute to through their paycheck, and the money would go to community organizations in their cities that supported labor. I did that for a couple of years. We were trying something new, and we raised a lot of money, and we were able to give a lot of money after 9/11, as solidarity, not charity. I later ended up being the Director of Civil, Human and Women's Rights there. During my tenure in that position, we were able to get a diversity resolution passed by the AFL-CIO executive council. The resolution mandated that affiliated national unions' delegates represent the diversity of their memberships and also included studies and recommendations for changes within the AFL-CIO and its affiliates. I did that for a number of years and then I retired.

I met Reverend Barber once or twice. We knew mutual people and I'd been at a meeting or two with them. I didn't really know him that well, but I knew people around him. I'd talked to him before, and we had talked a little bit about the Moral Mondays movement, but no big conversation.

I do an annual beach trip with my old comrades and our families. There are three or four generations that have come to this gathering for over forty years. In 2013, Don and I were on our way home. I get this call from Reverend Barber, and he says to me, "This is Reverend Barber, and this is a Macedonian call." I didn't say anything, and he realizes that I don't have *a clue* about what a Macedonian call is. Because I didn't! So, he says "Oh, let me tell you what I mean." So, Paul is on the road to Macedonia and God says, "Do something else." It is a call that you're not supposed to be able to refuse, and you're supposed to change your plans to do what you're called to do. Reverend Barber invited me to come to work with him. He was then the president of the NAACP, and they were at a critical point in the Moral Mondays work. There was no expectation that Moral Mondays would last a year and a half and experience 1,040 arrests. There was no plan for that. They knew that this was going to last longer than they had initially thought. He asked me to come to help figure out how to hold this movement. How do we give it some infrastructure and some space for it to grow, to hold, to stay true to the work and to its mission? So, I said, "Okay, let me think about it."

I ended up there for what I thought was going to be a short time. I worked with him and the NAACP to hold this really significant, important work that was about building a fusion movement that nobody was talking about *for real* and bringing people together. Even back then we were seeing that everything was connected. So I went down there. I was like a traveling salesperson. I went there on Monday morning, and I flew back on Friday night. I might have made twenty bucks an hour and went back and forth. But it was going to be short term and I'd just retired. Here I am still with him.

I later directed the North Carolina NAACP, and we went through the Moral Mondays time and restructured the staffing of the NAACP and Moral Mondays. Then we founded Repairers of the Breach together. People all over the country were asking, how do you hold that Monday after Monday after Monday without a break, shifting the whole narrative about what we were doing. We were getting such a positive response to the work, but the NAACP had very strict rules about how Reverend Barber could move around the country. So we could not take our lessons and teach the work across the country. We founded Repairers of the Breach in the end of 2015, and we have been doing it ever since. We started with three people. Me, Reverend Barber and Charmeine Fletcher. We traveled all over the country talking, and it just started to grow.

The Poor People's Campaign: A National Call for Moral Revival

We met Reverend Liz Theoharis from the Kairos Center, at Union Theological Seminary, and that was a good connection. The folks at the Kairos Center had already had already been doing a lot of work around King and that led us to them. But by the time we moved into the Poor People's Campaign, we already had worked with Repairers of the Breach in twenty-five states. That was a grueling time, and it was also a wonderful time because we were deepening our understanding about the country. What needs to happen? How do you organize in a different way? How do you build a movement from the bottom up? So we were ready to go into a Poor People's Campaign. We understood the importance of bringing our work from Repairers into building a real Poor People's Campaign. That was not what we'd seen since King's death. The Poor People's Campaign is more than an anniversary remembrance. It is a concrete program that follows and enhances King's vision for the campaign. So, on the 50th anniversary, we started the Poor People's Campaign and partnered with the Kairos Center at Union Theological Seminary.

The Repairers of the Breach grew from three people to about twenty-nine people. Organizers are committed to building a movement from the bottom up, and committed to always insisting on a fusion model that does not separate the issues. At times particular issues arise. Now, the whole issue around *Roe* is out there.[31] In a movement like we're trying to build, certain things rise to the top, police murders for example, rise to the top. But our commitment is to put them in the context of everything else. You disaggregate the numbers. So it's asking, how many people that get killed are poor people, are Black people, and how does it impact families, and so forth. Then, with the Supreme Court decision that's coming out about *Roe*, it has to be looked at in an overall context, and where possible, in its historic context. If you don't, you lose a lot of the lessons about how to fight. If you don't look back at various struggles or various points of history where we've seen similar things, and lessons can be learned, then you cannot fight these battles as they come up. You can fight them, *but you are likely to make the same mistakes*. Our whole understanding of Reconstruction is that we have to rebuild, because we've been attacked two times already. That's how we ended up at the Poor People's Campaign.

Organizing from the Bottom Up

The Poor People's Campaign gives us a chance to win because it appreciates the need to put all of these struggles and issues together, and then *we all fight for it all*. We are all in this together because our issues are genuinely connected. That's what we want people to understand. We have to build from the bottom up. We can't start by having a room full of leaders trying to decide what to do for others. We have to ask the people on the bottom what must be done. That's what we do, and that's not what happens in D.C., and so sometimes we are not understood. But I'm telling you that this is the way to build something.

We've been able to shift the narrative. We've been able to go into West Virginia and expose Manchin because of this bottom-up approach which goes very well with my own understanding of the world. The majority of the people who are poor and who are marginalized are the people that ought to have a big say in how this country works. This approach fits perfectly with how I see the world, and it works and it makes sense and we're committed.

Reverend Barber says we're committed to "not being loud and wrong." There's a component of this that's policy driven, and research driven, and it is changing the narrative.

When we started the Poor People's Campaign, the bottom line was the government's definition of the number of people that were poor. They said forty million, some crazy number, too small. The reality is that there are nearly 140 million poor and low-income people in this country. This is based on a statistic that the government keeps but does not use. It's not based on pure income; it's based on what your level of poverty is given all the things that you need to stay alive. They keep that number, but they don't talk about that number. Since we started, we've been using that number, and people were saying that it didn't make sense. But now the Institute for Policy Studies, the Economic Policy Institute, even congresspeople are using the 140 million number. Biden used it.

We're able to shift the narrative on many things just by virtue of the way we are building this movement. This work has been demanding. I've been in this for a long time, and it challenges me in many ways. And it's the work that comes closest to really helping to create the conditions for this big social justice movement that the country requires. I'm so proud of this work, and I am so glad to be contributing to it. I look back and I've had some opportunities that most people don't get.

Leading from Behind

I laugh that my whole life has kind of been about helping to lead from the back. But it's worked for me. Ordinary folks like me can lead from the back, make a contribution, stay in the movement, and raise a family. That's what my life's been. So I'm very lucky to be working on the Poor People's Campaign as a strategic adviser. People care about what I think. I work very hard, and I think it's an important movement. I hope that people really appreciate the role that it plays now and that it can play. I'm really happy about that.

Naming Poverty

The Poor People's Campaign has opened the door and made it okay to say, "I'm poor." We have Sara Nelson, who I love, saying that flight attendants are poor, and they are. But unions don't often say that! We've got SEIU and other unions now saying they have members who are poor, *workers who are made poor* by their work conditions. So now there's this space made to not have to pretend that you're striving for the middle class. People strive to survive. It's just opened the door for people to be able to say, "Yeah, that's what I am." And this has opened the door for others to say, "Yep, if I have one huge emergency, I'm right there. If I have a big whatever and I can't pay my hospital bill, I'm right there with the poor. I'm all right today. Tomorrow, I might not be." The campaign has opened up space to have people thinking about that, and to have people doing something about it. It's great work, and we've got to keep bringing people to the campaign, keep bringing people to the thinking of the campaign.

I Believe We Can Win

We've just got to change this country. I believe it's going to happen. I believe we can win. I truly believe that, because I know that people will not be oppressed forever. They won't! People will not stay in that spot. It might take a while. It might not be in my lifetime, but we can win. I have confidence in the people's ability to say "no" at some point and to draw the line. That's going to happen because people can't live in a way that this country is headed. They cannot be oppressed forever. They cannot see their kids killed. They cannot, cannot, cannot! People will fight back and resist. The task for those of us trying to make change every day is to create a space for folks to teach us and for us to teach them, so that when it's time and people are in motion, we are right there and have been able to in some way set the stage for it.

THREE

Yomara Velez

**

I don't know if other organizers would say this,
but organizing was like therapy for me.
It was my outlet,
no matter how hard things got,
I wasn't a casualty.
That was, for me, everything.
I was like, I cannot be defeated by this,
I can't be taken down by this situation.
I have to fight, and as long as I was fighting,
I felt like I was safe.

*Yomara Velez is an organizer and daughter of immigrants from Puerto Rico
and Venezuela. She attended the University of Massachusetts as a single
mother and began organizing to demand access to higher education and
better living conditions for students in family housing. She has organized
around housing, police brutality, and environmental justice issues in
the South Bronx, and in 2002 she founded Sistas on the Rise (SOTR).
This collective of young mothers of color helped to create a new model of
organizing, grounded in transformative practices, that develops genuine
grassroots leadership and uplifts motherhood. She was an Open Society
Community Fellow and Union Square Award recipient. Since moving
to Atlanta, she has worked on immigration and economic justice issues,
including with the National Domestic Workers Alliance supporting the
development of local chapters across the United States. She is currently the
co-director of the Midwest Academy.*

*Yomara describes the importance of relationships, belonging to community,
and the significance of women mentors in her life. She reflects upon the
need for political education and the leadership of community members in
all aspects of organizing, and emphasizes the value of experimentation
and organic development of the work in a way that leaves room for error,
reflection, and learning. She shares her journey as a mother and an
organizer, and the ways in which she has created alternatives to oppressive
structures, including her commitment to homeschooling her children.*

Yomara currently lives in Atlanta.

I WAS BORN IN MASSACHUSETTS. SHORTLY AFTER I WAS born, my family relocated to Miami, where I went to preschool. Then we moved to Bayamón, Puerto Rico, and I did some of my elementary years there. When my father was laid off, my parents and I moved in with my aunt and her husband and son. I grew up with extended family, in a community where there were a lot of children around. My childhood in Puerto Rico was full of people with a lot of play time outside, running around and picking guavas from the trees. It was beautiful, and we had a little bit more freedom, I think, than children who grow up here in the States. When we moved back to the US, during the end of my elementary school years I went to a bilingual program for a couple of years while I learned English.

My mother's from Puerto Rico and my father's from Venezuela. We spent some months in Venezuela while my dad was trying to see what was possible there. My dad comes from a low-income family, *Afro Indígena Venezolanos*. He sold arepas in the streets out of a pail and then made his way to the US. My mother's family comes from the Adjuntas-Lares region, a rural area where they grow coffee. She came to the US with her mom when she was a teenager.

My first memories related to injustice, I remember being little and looking out the window at protests in Miami and my mom saying, "We need to stay in the house. People are outside rioting because they're upset." When I was five, a husband shot his wife and then shot his wife's mother on a balcony in Miami. There was a huge crowd, and I wanted my dad to put me on his shoulders so that I could see what was happening. I remember seeing the mother drop and then he killed himself. That memory has always stayed with me. My dad always raised us to be aware of our identity as mixed people: Puerto Rican, and Venezuelan of African and Indigenous descent. He would always say, "You're Afro Indígena, you need to be proud, and you're beautiful."

My dad learned English in this country. We always played a support role for him, making the phone calls, like the typical child of an immigrant. People would say, "Oh, I don't understand you," *although his English was clear.* My parents rooted and supported me in my identity and helped me navigate some of the traumatic things that I would see. Once, a police officer pulled my dad out of the car and banged him against the car, and I was like, "Why is she doing that? Why are these things happening?" I always asked questions. "Why are people rioting? Why did he shoot his wife? Why are they saying they don't understand you when you speak?" These things helped to develop my consciousness. Later, I was able to connect all of these things to a bigger system of oppression. It's not just *my* dad that gets banged against the car. It was not that they don't understand the accent when his English is clear, these are things that are bigger than my family, or my personal experience.

When we moved from Puerto Rico back to the US, I didn't know the language, and my parents were going through a tough financial situation. My dad had been laid off for a while and we were on welfare, living with my grandmother. The cold weather was really harsh, and I hated it. The snow was only pretty the first time, and then I was like, "Oh, this is not for me!" I've always been very quiet and shy, so I didn't speak on it as much, but I never wanted to be where I was.

My parents had moved to this little all-white town, Auburn, Massachusetts. I struggled because I had never been in an environment where I was considered *a minority*. As soon as I graduated high school, I left and moved in with my aunt in the Bronx, who was also very strict.

Motherhood and Marriage at an Early Age

When I got pregnant, as hard as it was, it also felt liberating. It was definitely my way out of a very restrictive environment. I got pregnant shortly after moving to New York, and my family forced me to marry my son's dad. My parents were Christian, and my mother would have had a heart attack if abortion was even a consideration. So I had the baby. We got married in Coney Island, Brooklyn. I cried that night; I was so upset with that whole situation. I moved from the Bronx to Washington Heights when I got married. I had been taking college classes when I got pregnant but dropped out. There were all these things that were not going well in the relationship, but my parents kept pushing me to work it out.

Applying for welfare in New York is the worst shit in the world. I remember getting up mad early, getting on that long line and waiting. If you forget one paper, they want you to come back, and then bring a different paper. It was such a nightmare. You spend your whole day sitting in the office. All the girls are mad, everybody's got attitude. The other issue was health care in New York. My prenatal care was at New York Hospital on the Upper East Side. All of the young mothers would go on "Teen Tuesday." Basically, they would just weigh you and ask, "How you feeling? OK, good. Great." That would be it. There was no education around birthing or any of that.

One time I dropped off a friend at UMass Amherst, and I remember thinking, "Wow, this campus is so beautiful." My friend asked, "Well, why don't you apply?" So, I applied to UMass, and I was shocked that I got in, but my financial aid wasn't good. I couldn't really afford to go. I went to visit the school and was like, "You know, I got in and I got this financial aid letter, but this is not going to work. I can't afford this money that you're telling me I need to pay." They told me that I could write a letter with my story to see if they'll give me more financial aid. I wrote the letter, and they came back with more financial aid.

College Opened Up a New Chapter in My Life

I felt UMass would provide a different environment for my son, and for me. I was so happy! UMass upped my financial aid, but I didn't have family housing. I went to the Black Student Advisory Organization, and met a woman there named Renee Lopes-Pocknett. She was Native American, she and organizing saved my life. She told me, "Oh, I was a young mother too. I came with my baby. I'm going to help you." She helped me find family housing, because they were telling me it was a two-year wait for the family housing. If it wasn't for her, I wouldn't have gone to school, because I wouldn't have had a place to live.

Renee became my de facto mom while I was there. She would ask me how I was doing, and she helped me with child care and got my son into where her daughter was going to daycare. She kept my morale strong. There were times when I just wanted to drop out, and she would say, "Oh, you can do it, keep going. You're almost there." I could see that she did it and now she was working at the school. I was like, "Oh, I want to try to do that too. I don't want to go back to New York without a plan, without a degree."

Welfare Reform

Welfare reform hit when I was at UMass. They took away my child-care voucher because parents in four-year colleges were no longer eligible.[32] My worker was telling me that I should withdraw and go to Holyoke Community College, finish there, and then transfer back to UMass! I said, "I'm not doing that. That sounds crazy. I have family housing. That doesn't make any sense." Once, the welfare office sat me down to watch a video about what *not* to do when you are in an interview. I'll never forget it. It had this girl wearing huge hoop earrings, and they were like, "Don't wear big earrings." All scenarios of what not to do: "Don't chew gum during your interview." There was so much that was so demeaning throughout that whole process that I can't imagine how anyone without a lot of community support gets through it!

Welfare reform also brought time limits. At one point I had to get off welfare so that I could "bank my time" for senior year, because I was afraid that I wouldn't be able to manage without being on welfare during my senior year. It was a nightmare. I was working three minimum-wage jobs and going to school. I didn't have child-care at one point. My friends were taking turns helping out. I came very close to dropping out. I was going to have a nervous break-down. Sometimes I'd have to steal food from the supermarket in my coat so we could eat. It was so overwhelming.

Once, I had studied for a test. I came in with my son Keanu and this white teacher said, "Who is this? What are you doing here with your kid?" I told her that I didn't have childcare. It was like straight out of a movie scene. She said, "Well, he can't be here." I told her that I needed to take the test, didn't have any childcare, and that he wouldn't disturb anyone. I said, "He's just going to sit in the back. Just let me take the test and I'm going to finish the test in no time and then we'll be out of here." She said, "No, you can't. You got to take your kid and you need to go." I was so angry! I was so ready for my test. I remember sitting at the bus stop with my son. He was so cute with his little book bag, and I was *just sobbing*. I took the bus to Renee's, sat on her couch, and cried and cried, "I'm just going to go." She helped me work through it, "No, no, you're almost there, don't go!"

Understanding My Situation in the Context of History

I found organizing when I was going through the welfare time limits because there were other moms at UMass that were also getting timed off. A lot of them left. We started an emergency fund to try to keep some of them. That's when I started organizing. I was lucky. I had Martín Espada as a teacher, and his class also carried me through. It was called Latinos in Film. He had somebody from the Young Lords come and talk to us. It was an aha moment, where I was able to see my struggles within a broader context. I was learning the history of the Puerto Rican movement in New York and was involved with an organization called Boricuas Unidos on campus. We were fund-raising for Iris Morales's film, *¡Palante, Siempre Palante! The Young Lords*. It was like a coming together of my own personal situation and understanding it in the context of history. I was clear. "This isn't going to go down like this. You're not going to tell me to withdraw from school and go to a community college so that my child can get a childcare voucher." I knew that I was getting set up. That was not the route I needed to take. That's when we started organizing around welfare reform. An organizer was on campus talking to people and I got involved and it changed my life. I was so happy. I was just like, "Oh my God, yes, let's fight!" I started facilitating meetings, and then I got more involved doing tenant organizing on campus, because there were a lot of problems around student housing. That's when it all started, and it hasn't stopped since.

I love organizing and I don't know what I would have done without it. Meeting other women who were experiencing the same thing, and providing support for each other, was really important, because a lot of us didn't have family that were immediately involved. Organizing meant creating an alternative family to provide for each other, and that was beautiful. When we graduated, my son was with me, and he wore my cap. It was monumental! The fact that we got to that point was amazing because of everything we had to go through to get there.

Back to the Bronx, Organizing

When I graduated, I came back to New York and worked part-time in Bed-Stuy at the Woodson Literacy Program, but it was far from the Bronx. I was still involved with Puerto Rican organizing and movement building as a volunteer. Mothers on the Move (MOM) was looking for an organizer, and I interviewed with them. I worked there with Lisa Ortega and Helen Schaub, and Sheila, Juan, and a bunch of organizers who had been organizing in the Bronx for a long time. During the interview process I remember them saying, "Oh no, we don't want no college campus organizer. That's not what we're looking for." I was like, "No! I've organized *for real*." They were like, "Well, what have you done?" I told them, "Well, I organized tenants, I door knocked!" They said, "Oh, you've door knocked. Well, we're going to take you door knocking right now, in Hunts Point."

They put me on the doors in Hunts Point. "Knock this building and see how you do." I knocked the building. I had my list of "yeses." I was knocking for a meeting that was coming up, and they were like, "Oh, OK. Yeah, she can door knock." Then, "Was she scared in Hunts Point? She wasn't scared. All right, well, maybe we'll give her a chance." Back then, the pay was pretty bad. I was getting paid less than eight hundred dollars every two weeks, but I was just really happy to have a full-time job. I learned so much at MOMs! It was the perfect place to start organizing because they had a very strong organizing culture. The organizing that I started doing with tenants was very systematic and you had to be accountable. I was the young one coming in and I was determined to deliver. There was a protocol that we would follow, and every week we had to report our numbers. It was a tough model, but it really gave me a strong foundation in terms of what it means to organize, and I wouldn't change it for the world. It prepared me for *anything and everything*. Every job after MOMs has been easy.

The more I got into organizing, the more I realized, "Oh, the people that come in through the community become organizers, and the people who become directors are the white people. All the directors were white, and all the organizers were Black and Brown. We're the ones that are in the field all day, and we're knocking on doors constantly, having late nights and weekend meetings, and they're in their office. I wanted to challenge that a little bit. I had a lot of questions about how nonprofits are structured and why are they structured that way. When I started learning about funders, I wanted to push us to do better around that too. Black and Brown people can't always just be the organizers. What is the plan for some of the organizers to also be in leadership positions? I think it still happens today. Regardless of what the race of the organizer is, the organizer is almost always in a supportive role and on the lower end of the salary scale. I don't feel organizing is valued the way that it should be.

At MOMs I was surrounded by people who had a highly developed political analysis, including the differentiation around organizing and service. The Bronx had a lot of organizations doing service work and housing development projects. MOMs' analysis was that those that are most impacted need to be the ones that are leading and shaping our campaigns. There was a lot of emphasis on developing *the community's analysis*. That meant that at our meetings, and with people we came across, we made sure that we were having conversations like, "These waste transfer stations come in to Hunts Point and we have the highest asthma rates in the city. Why is it that they're placing *another* waste transfer station in our community? How does race and class play into this?" Developing other people's leadership was one of the most important lessons that I learned from MOMs: "Yomara, who's facilitating the meeting today, because it can't be you." So, making sure you're prepping other people to facilitate the meeting, knowing what roles people are playing and how you are developing people throughout the membership, and why is that important? Why is it important for members *to own* this organization?

I met Iris Morales for the first time at MOMs. She walked in the office, and I was like, "Oh my God! I had a class with Martín Espada and learned about you!" She would talk to me, she would talk to our members and come through, and we would go have dinner. I would call her my elder, and she would be like, "I'm not an elder." Now I feel that way! The other day I was talking to someone, and they called me an elder, and I was like, "Whoa, slow your roll!" I am forever grateful to Iris for her support. Organizing at MOMs created a really amazing environment for me to connect with organizers in other cities. It gave me a broader view of all of the issues, how they connect with the diaspora, and how they connect with international movements.

Around that time, I started working at Rikers. I worked at MOMs in the daytime and then taught at Rikers in the evening. I was living

in the Bronx with my sis Maricruz, who was so supportive, my partner Raoul, and other friends. Together we figured it out. My son
would stay with them, and I would go to Rikers and teach GED
classes. It paid about thirty dollars an hour as a contractor. I was like,
"Oh, my God it's so much money!" After taxes, it was really not that
much, but it made it possible for me to stay afloat. I love teaching, so
it was perfect. Many of the guys were coming from Washington
Heights and the Bronx, and it was almost an extension of the work
that I was already doing in the Bronx.

I was in my twenties. I wouldn't want my kids doing half the stuff
I did. I'd be in a classroom with twenty students and no corrections
officer or anything. Even now when I think about it, I'm like, "Wow,
you were crazy!" I was going into all kinds of buildings in Hunts
Point, organizing at MOMs. I had no fear at all, about anything. I
would go into a building that only had two tenants in it, with a huge
amount of drug activity. I didn't even think about it twice. I always
speak of ancestors and feel like there's an invisible *something* around
me that takes care of me. There would be moments when I'm like,
"Oh, I'm going to die." But I made it through. When I wasn't at Rikers, I had tenant meetings all the time, including on the weekends. It
was all about organizing. That was my life, and it kept me focused.

Organizing Was Almost Like My Therapy

It's kind of weird. I don't know if other organizers would say this,
but organizing was like therapy for me. It was my outlet, no matter
how hard things got, I wasn't a casualty. That was, for me, everything. I was like, I cannot be defeated by this, I can't be taken down
by this situation. I have to fight, and as long as I was fighting, I felt
like I was safe. To me, to not fight would be to be vulnerable, and I
didn't want to be vulnerable like that. That was, for me, *everything*. I
talk to my kids a lot about that now, especially my oldest son: "All
the odds are against you, all the statistics said that you were basically
not going to be shit, and you need to work really hard to make that
wrong." Maybe it's a little extreme. Now I feel like he's definitely just
grinding all the time. But they can't tell our story for us, we've got to
create our own way and our own story. That was really what drove
me. Now, he's going to school to be a lawyer! It blows my mind. I'm

like, "Wow, you're really doing it." He grew up with a very strong foundation. There was always something happening. Something always needed to be done. There was never enough time, and I was always in a rush. He would door knock with me. He would take half the floor and I would take the other half and he would say, "This is Keanu. I want to let you know about the next meeting." He would always get more "yeses" than me because he was so cute. He grew up in the middle of all of that.

I was working at MOMs but transitioning to Youth Ministries for Peace and Justice (YMPJ), when Amadou Diallo was killed by the NYPD. We would have meetings at Richie Pérez's[33] office, at the Community Service Society, in the 20s on the East Side. It would be two in the morning and Keanu would be sleeping in the corner. I'd be like, "Baby we're almost leaving." Now, I look back and think, "Maybe that was too much *McDonald's and meetings*." It wasn't perfect and I probably wouldn't do it like that again. But it gave Keanu a lot to work with around his own purpose. Regardless of where we were or what we were doing, I always talked to him a lot about life and what we were seeing or living. "We don't have food, this is why. We are here in the rain right now. We're cold. This is why."

We moved to El Barrio. One day we came home and all the guys on the block were on the floor, face down and were getting arrested. We went upstairs, and Keanu was like, "Why were they on the floor like that?" We had a real conversation about why they were on the floor, and I told him, "You can't grow up to do this. I can't see you in these streets like this, you understand? You can't have a cop putting his hands on you and locking you up and taking your freedom. You just can't allow that to happen. That's not an option for you. I don't care what I need to do." I used to threaten him. "I'll send you to Venezuela! You'll go live in the *campo* in Venezuela. You're not going to do this." I was ultra-paranoid because as a single mom, I saw it all around me. I still see it. There are so many mothers struggling with their children and gang violence. One of the most painful things to see is kids owned by the system, because once you are at Rikers, *they own you*. I mean, you can free yourself through reading and all of that but you're still in those four walls, trapped. My biggest organizing project is making sure my sons make it.

Connecting with Revolutionary Puerto Rican History

It was everything to me to be connected to Richie and Iris. For my mother and for me, coming from Puerto Rico, there's always been a lot of love and a strong understanding of Puerto Rico as an identity, including the colonial status of Puerto Rico. Even though my mother wouldn't be a full-fledged *independentista*, she'd always say, "Oh no, we can't be part of the US." Meeting Richie and Iris connected me with revolutionary Puerto Rican history, with all of the work that they did, and how that connected to our existence in New York. That they were able to bring that understanding of colonialism, the impacts of colonialism, and the internalized colonialism in our community, was really important for me because it allowed me to understand how our liberation here is tied to liberation in Puerto Rico. It gave me a different framework to think about this. It isn't that we want to sit at your table, we want to create *our own table*. Even when we do reformist work we have to be thinking about liberation as our final destination. I'm glad I learned that first and not the other way around. I do reformist work now, but I can situate that within a context that's much broader. That is only possible because of the influence that Richie and Iris had. Richie had a big picture of where we were and how we got here. Even teaching at Rikers, I saw how the police manifests itself as the force within our communities to keep things in line and to protect property and wealth. Those are things that I learned because of them.

Moving into Environmental Justice Work

I started doing tenant and housing organizing at Mothers on the Move, and moved into environmental justice work. We were fighting AMR,[34] a waste transfer station, from coming into Hunts Point and were able to defeat it. From there, I moved on to work with Youth Ministries for Peace and Justice (YMPJ) and became their environmental justice project director. I was supervising and coordinating a lot of youth organizers working on environmental justice issues, and we also had the policing campaign. Our focus was cleaning up the Bronx River, having the Greenway built, and doing that while also addressing the whole issue of displacement, which was something that I feel I really contributed to coming in from doing housing work at Mothers on the Move. We wanted to make sure that development takes into account sustainability and gentrification. We connected with other groups in Brooklyn that had already been experiencing gentrification. Doing so helped us to think about what gentrification meant for our community, as well as learning about alternatives like Community Land Trusts.

We had a lot of success! A couple of years ago, I rode the 6 train through the Bronx, and was able to see the cement plant and some of the changes that had happened there. Environmental justice was a different type of work. I didn't really understand the complexities of working to restore brownfields, and we would work with a lot of scientists who would sometimes use very academic language. As an organizer you're always thinking, "How do we make issues accessible to yourself and the community?" Whenever folx were talking in a way that we didn't understand, I felt comfortable saying, "Can you stop right there? I'm not understanding exactly what you mean. I need you to explain it to me a different way." Early on we built that relationship with our partners. "You know, we may not know everything you know, but we as a community are experts in our own right, and we're going to guide you through this thing." We had a lot of community-based design sessions and community meetings where they would come in and explain what some of these things meant. Then the community could vision and say, "Well, this is what we think would be useful," or "This is what we would like to do." It was a very close partnership. Alexis, the YMPJ director, was very good at modeling this for us, asking clarifying questions, and centering community.

That's when we founded the Bronx River Alliance. When Alexis became pregnant, I stepped in to do more with the coalition. I got to go to Europe and presented on our project at the Salisbury Congress. I hate that kind of thing, but I got through it. It was me, Majora, Joan, and Jenny. We saw environmental justice projects that were being developed in Europe around brownfield redevelopment and shared community open spaces. YMPJ was beautiful. We did exchanges in Arizona with the Tohono O'odham youth there. We helped clear a garden so that they could plant traditional native crops. We brought our youth there, and then they brought their youth to us in the Bronx. We did exchanges with Palestinian youth; it was amazing. I learned so much from the leadership there. Coming from Mothers on the Move, it was a very different vibe. We accepted government money, and at Mothers on the Move it was like, "You never accept government money!" It opened me up to a different type of organizing.

Founding Sistas on the Rise

A couple of the youth I worked with became pregnant, and they were coming less and less to the program. That reminded me, "Oh, remember when you were pregnant and how that was? You should get back to organizing around that." So, I started Sistas on the Rise. We were doing volunteer meetings, using YMPJ's space. I had a whole community of support. Iris helped me take a vision and make it digestible for funders. She read my proposals and marked them all up. Everybody marked them all up! One person would say, "I love this part of the proposal. Keep this in!" Then the next person would be like, "This has to go!" There came a point where I told myself to silence all of that and just put in what I thought I needed to be put in, and send it out and see what happens. My students at Rikers named Sistas on the Rise (SOTR). I want people to know that. They told me, "This is so needed, you're gonna do great. You gotta push through and do it. Even if you don't get this grant, you're going to do it, right?" I was like, "Yeah, we're going to do it!"

I applied for an OSI grant.[35] I talked to a lot of people about it and had done focus groups with the young mothers to hear what they would want to see in an organization. I turned those focus groups into the proposal. When I got the call that I was a finalist for the grant, I couldn't sleep! I was a nervous wreck for the interview. On the way, I stopped at a Starbucks and got a cup of water so I could get chamomile tea to calm my nerves. Before I went in the building, I literally was smudging myself, smudging the proposal. I was calling on ancestors. It was a whole *to-do*! I went in and somebody else took the wheel because I didn't think I was going to even be able to talk. It was a group interview, and I had to almost defend my proposal and answer all these questions. That was the money that I needed to make that jump from YMPJ to Sistas on the Rise. I was very passionate, but I learned how to pace myself and not get angry and over-critical, that whole dynamic, right, of, "Oh, we're doing the real work, y'all over there ain't doing the real work." It's been a process of developing how I want to situate myself in this movement and what I want to contribute.

Edgar Rivera Colon, who was living in Hunts Point right across from the old Spofford,[36] had a little storefront in the building where he was living that wasn't being used. The ceiling had caved in, and the walls were a mess. They called me and were like, "Yomara, you can have this space for three hundred dollars a month." I was like, "What?! Three hundred a month. This is great!" All the youth came over and we painted. There was this brother that had just come out of Rikers. I didn't know him while I was at Rikers, but he lived in the building, and he would always stop by. He actually put up the ceiling. We fixed the space, but we didn't have any heat. It was crazy. We would put candles and warm our hands by the candles. We had no heat, and *we had babies*. But it was what it was. Eventually, we moved to a spot on Longwood. It used to be a laundromat, nice and big. We got dividers and people had little offices. It was very exciting.

We started organizing around the P schools—Pregnant and Parenting schools. I would sneak in like I was a student, and have lunch with the students asking, "How do you like the school? Are there any problems with the school?" We started identifying issues, getting their contact information, organizing. Eventually, we won all this money for the P schools. The students ended up getting credits for certain classes like P.E. that they weren't getting credit for, and social workers got put in place so they could do follow-up with them. A lot of students were missing class after giving birth, and those were counted as absences. We won something like a maternity leave policy for them. The most beautiful part of Sistas on the Rise was working with the youth and seeing them grow and come into being their powerful selves. Now all those babies are so grown. It's amazing to see.

Creating a Space by and for Women of Color

Sistas on the Rise wasn't perfect. We were young and figuring it out. We didn't want any hierarchical structures that reflected the systems we were living under, and we set it up as a collective. The decision-making committee would make decisions *together*. We tried to be a lot more reflective of what we were hoping to see in the world—a place where collective decision-making and collective planning were possible. We were a space for women of color, *by women of color*, and at that time, there weren't a lot of spaces that were talking about that. We would close our offices on Fridays, which in organizing was unheard of. We tried to ground our work in self-care and self-reflection. We would do feedback sessions where we would rotate these index cards. On one side it'd be, "These are your strengths, and these are things that you got to work on." We would write on each other's and then you'd get your card, and you could see, "*Oh, these are the things.*" We tried to develop a culture where feedback was a good thing and not seen as "Oh, you're not good enough or you need to get better at this." We were continuously challenging ourselves to grow and letting people know that it is *a process*. We worked on keeping a spirit of openness as organizers, one that was willing to hear different perspectives to inform our decisions.

We did political education. We would bring members to the Upper East Side and the Upper West Side, and they would take notes and photos of what they saw. Then we would do a walk in the South Bronx. We created visuals where they could express what they saw, and have discussions. The youth facilitated the process. When we met with the superintendent of the schools, it was all youth facilitated. They presented their demands. Every time the adults tried to look at me, I'd say, "They're the ones who are having this conversation with you." Once, we were meeting with the superintendent of the school system, and there was a huge argument outside. A pimp and a sex worker were arguing in front of our storefront, and I could see the people's faces from the Department of Education. They were scared. Sharim Algarin, my partner at SOTR, got out there and said, "You need to move it! You need to take that elsewhere, because they can't be seeing this situation right here in front of our storefront." Everybody was like, "Oh, shit." She was so badass. I'm so appreciative for all she and Leslie Spann did.

I laugh a lot because sometimes I feel like we try so hard to land on the right strategies that we don't leave enough room for mistakes, or just the organic development of the work. That's what was so beautiful about Sistas on the Rise. Here were women that came from the community. A lot of them didn't have a college degree. Some were very young. There was a lot of trauma, but they came to the space with a lot of intention and a lot of love, and it worked! We were able to fundraise, and none of us were professional fundraisers. That's not my background, but I got some pretty big grants to do the work. The women spoke about the work in a way that was real and tangible and from their lived experience. I think funders really appreciated that, even though some of them took a lot of rounds before they funded us. I was like, "How are you going to come here and see we don't have heat and still not fund us?!"

There needs to be room for members to decide on and to implement strategies that *might not work*. I think that now it's much harder to do that. Because we had a lot of freedom with Sistas on the Rise, we were able to say, "Oh, we're going to try to do this and see how it works." Sometimes it worked and sometimes it didn't, but it gave us room to evaluate and say, "Oh, we tried this, it didn't work. Why didn't it work? Let's have this debrief." It develops people differently when there's room to be their authentic selves. If a youth facilitated a meeting with the superintendent and it didn't go one hundred percent as hoped, *that's okay*. We will debrief and you'll do better next time. We would prepare people by saying, "This is your decision maker. He has decision-making power over some of the issues that you are having. You are going to have a conversation with him about your reality and what we need to see change. It's that simple. Stay where it's *real for people*, and you'll be okay." One of the most beautiful things about Sistas on the Rise was that it was *real*.

Navigating Organizing in the South

I met Keene in Brooklyn after a couple of years running Sistas on the Rise. He's from southwest Atlanta. We came to Atlanta when I attended a Ms. Foundation conference. We visited his friends, a lot of whom owned houses. There were communities of working-class people with a yard and a garden. I was like, "Wow, I really like this." There were trees. I thought it was really beautiful.

I've always struggled with housing in New York. But I always have some sort of divine ancestor looking out for me, and I was able to buy into an HDFC cheap, in El Barrio. My friend Marilyn helped me navigate the process. The unit needed a lot of work, but eventually it became home.

Our unit faced another building, so it never had natural light. It was very tiny and dark. I was like, "I want to live better than this. I want to have a garden." In Atlanta I could have that, and it was really affordable back then. I told Sharim, "I think I want to go. My time is coming up, and you all should take over Sistas on the Rise. It's your organization. It's never been about just one person. I think I'm going to try to go to the South."

My sisters are always so loving and supportive. Everybody was like, "Do it!" My community is the best that anyone could ever wish for. I don't know about other people, but my community—both in New York and here in Atlanta, *everywhere*—is the best. Without my community, I don't know where I would be. I came to Atlanta, and Keene and I started looking. I was shocked that we got pre-approved for a loan. I didn't think we would, because my credit score was not great, but that's when all of that mortgage craziness was happening, and they were giving people mortgages. We bought a house, I transitioned to Atlanta, and I continued doing some of the fundraising for Sistas on the Rise.

I started working here with 9to5, a national association of working women. Back then, the nonprofit infrastructure here was very small and there weren't a lot of jobs for an organizer. I interviewed for a help-line position answering the phones. In the interview they said, "You're really overqualified for this position. Why are you interviewing for this?" I was like, "Well, I need a part-time job because I'm still doing some work with Sistas on the Rise, so I need some flexibility to be able to write, and I need a job, and there's nothing else." Then I got another job, waitressing at a Mexican restaurant, and it was awful. I hardly made any money at all, but I made do between those three things.

When an organizing position opened up, I stepped into that and later became the lead organizer at 9to5. We were organizing to increase the minimum wage. They had a win prior to my arrival, but then the state passed exemption laws where all labor laws would go through the state and not the city, so it wasn't enforceable, and that undid the victory. We were trying to figure out what came next. I was focusing on restaurants and domestic and seasonal work because those were the people who were excluded from the state minimum wage.

Welfare reform was economic justice, but this was different. I learned a lot working the help line. We were working to pass the Healthy Families Act. It was a little bit of national work, a little bit of state work, and a really different landscape here in the South. I did a lot of work with 9to5 after I left, helping with organizational infrastructure and their organizing model. I facilitated planning sessions so they could have a solid evaluation of the work. I love planning work, and I did a lot of that with Sistas on the Rise, too. Then I started working with Adelina at the Georgia Latino Alliance for Human Rights (GLAHR) on immigration. At that time, GLAHR was a very small organization and wasn't receiving much funding. I'm on their board now, and I'm like, "Oh, my God, this is crazy!" The infrastructure in Georgia has grown a lot.

Living and organizing in the South was a whole different scenario. For one, there were no Puerto Ricans here. It was very much Black, white, and Mexican. All of a sudden, people didn't know *what I was*. I never had to explain who I am to people. Some people would be like, "Oh, you're Mexican," Or, you know, "You're white and Black." People didn't know where to place me. I had a very hard time adjusting. The first year was very, very hard. There were times when I went back to New York and would just hide out, couch surfing. I was like, "This is not for me." Also, I wasn't used to driving everywhere. I lived a block from Camaradas! I did every Thursday at Camaradas with Bomba![37] My culture—my people, my community, the neighborhood—has always been everything to me. In New York, you know everybody, you go up the building, they know who you are. You come here, it's like nobody knows who you are. They don't know what you've done. In organizing circles, it was "You just another Northerner trying to come down here to tell us how to organize." There was a huge culture of people moving here and trying to tell local organizers what they were doing wrong. Being in Georgia, I became a little more emotionally intelligent around the work.

The Tea Party was showing up at our rallies armed. I had never experienced anything like that. Adelina was getting death threats. You're in such close proximity with white supremacy and everything that you know is wrong with society. It's so real. One, you learn resilience. Two, you learn how to work collaboratively and in coalition. You learn quick that you need to be able to be open to working with other people and working in ways that maybe you weren't used to.

I didn't vote in New York, ever! I didn't believe in voting. I thought it was ridiculous for people to spend their time voting. That changed here, out of respect. Historically, learning about what people have gone through for your right to vote. I even got arrested during the Stacey Abrams campaign around voting rights. If you had told younger Yomara in New York that I would be getting arrested over a governor election, I would have been like, "You're crazy. That is not me." Or that I'd be gardening? A whole other Yomara was born in the South. The South put a lot of things in perspective, like the importance of coalition building, the importance of electoral politics, the importance of honoring ancestors, and even understanding the civil rights movement.

I'll never forget my first meeting. Everybody bowed their head and started praying. I was like, "Oh my God, what is going on?!" It was uncomfortable! I believe in prayer, but that's just not where I come from. We don't bow our heads in New York and start praying before a meeting. I was like, "You got to be respectful in the space. You're an outsider." I've always been an outsider one way or the other, but this really felt like coming in from another space. I had to learn about humility, humbling myself. "This is where I am, this is how the work is happening, and people need to feel appreciated, whether you agree with the strategy or not. You gotta show grace for people, people who are putting in time. You don't know everything."

Many strategies that I would have tried in New York didn't work here. For example, when we were organizing around the minimum wage, I did a whole mapping process to see who has power, who hasn't, and found someone to target. "Well, this guy's campaign donations are not that much. It's like five thousand dollars, maybe ten thousand." I said, "We just need to organize where he lives!" I went to North Georgia, outside of Atlanta, up in Buford, and I was door knocking. I mapped all the apartments. I thought, "We just need to hit up the apartments. These are working-class people. Once we talk to them, we're going to agitate them. They're going to come on board. We're going to mobilize them. We're going to have a base! Once we have a base, this base is going to meet with this guy, and this guy is going to fold! He's not going to hold up!" It's funny—I laugh now—that I really thought that! We even went to the guy's house, door knocked, and dropped off petition signatures there. He didn't come out. It ended pretty quickly.

But I'm not the one that should be knocking those doors. I'm not the messenger up there. It was very right-wing, very white, very Christian. Half the time nobody opened the door. It felt unsafe. I got maybe five names on a list after a whole day of door knocking. I found this little Christian bookstore, and I hung out there in the coffee shop. I felt that there would be a moment where I would be able to talk to someone, but nobody talked to me.

The strategy wasn't completely wrong. We just didn't have the right organizers in place. It wasn't me coming from the Bronx that was going to move this demographic. I told myself, "You better keep yourself in Atlanta and try to organize in Atlanta." So I got more involved in my neighborhood. I started a West End Park group and became the secretary. We did community cleanups. I learned to figure out the systems *that existed*, and from there tried to do some organizing. Sometimes it worked and sometimes it didn't. You try things and think they're great ideas, but they don't always quite land, and you learn from it.

I was able to build my community here through local organizing. We organized Standing Rock protests and had a huge turnout. We wanted to show solidarity in Atlanta, and decided to do a march, and we did some fundraising for Standing Rock. We drove from here to Standing Rock with other local folx from Atlanta, delivered supplies, and were able to help at the camp and spent a week there. It was powerful to be there and to see that Taino flag and a lot of different First Nations from across the Americas, not just the US. We took the protest to one of the banks that was financing the loans to build the pipeline and we set up an altar. It was a great way for people to support and hold at least one of the decision-makers accountable. They ended up closing off the bank branch because there were so many of us. It gave people an opportunity to be part of that movement, even if it was a smaller way to contribute. I met a whole bunch of people there and expanded my movement family. I've always, on my own time, done work that's movement work. It was less of an organizing effort that was prolonged and more of a moment to show solidarity with the people of Standing Rock.

I stopped doing paid organizing after GLAHR and decided to teach. I taught second and third grade at a local school in the neighborhood. We did a lot of organizing-*like* work that we incorporated into our curriculum. I had flexibility and beautiful students with progressive parents and grandparents, like Kathleen Cleaver's grandson. I was lucky that I got to teach in a way that aligned with my values. Now, I see a lot of these fights around critical race theory and that's heartbreaking. Meeting Kathleen Cleaver there was beautiful.[38] I went to her house for dinner. I had actually met her before in New York. Before Sistas on the Rise, a couple of us called ourselves Sisters en la Lucha. We did an event in New York at the Nuyorican Poet's Cafe and we created pins that had a picture and said, "This flag, you defend it. *Esta bandera se defiende*." I can't remember the exact wording, but we gave her one of those pins. Years later, I asked her, "Do you remember I gave you a pin five years ago at a panel that you did in NYC?" She said, "I still have that pin!" She showed it to me, and it blew me away! She gave me some books to read and talked to me a lot about the South, which was great. Fast forward, I'm in Atlanta and her grandson is in my class.

Domestic Worker Organizing

Ai-Jen[39] was talking about how the National Domestic Workers Alliance (NDWA) was interested in learning about domestic workers in the South. I was doing a lot of volunteer work with different groups. I didn't want to get paid for organizing anymore. Some of the losses we had around 287G were just really painful.[40] I had never in my life experienced a loss like that! I came into this with a lot of wins and felt that loss so profoundly. I needed time to heal from that one. I'd still volunteer with GLAHR, or sometimes did some paid contracting with them. Ai-Jen said, "We want to survey domestic workers in the South, and you're there, can you help us kind of navigate the South?" Lisa Adler was also here. She's now with the ACLU. Some of the leaders that I had developed at 9to5 had done domestic work, so I pulled them in to help with the project. They got stipends and did the surveys, and we were able to hold the project out of GLAHR. I was teaching, and connecting people here and there.

After the survey, NDWA started a project focusing around Black organizing in Atlanta. As the project wrapped up, I met with Ai-Jen because they were looking for someone to hold the work in NYC. I still had my HDFC, but you can only rent them out for a certain amount of time. I had been asking for extensions and extensions, and they were like, "No, no more extensions. You need to come back." Everything just aligned. I had a job offer. My son was heading to NYC for college. My time in Atlanta was done for the moment. I wasn't ready to sell my co-op because I wasn't ready to fully disconnect from New York. Selling that apartment meant I didn't have a home in El Barrio anymore.

I went back, and it was culture shock. I wasn't moving fast enough. It was as if I'd never lived in New York! East Harlem was changing so much, and I had to do a whole lot of adjusting. Then there was no natural light in that apartment. I had learned about gardening and tried to set up a garden on the fire escape. The super came for me and was like, "Move it or I'm gonna have to take it because of the fire codes." Coming back to New York was really hard for me, and cold! I just was not feeling it. I needed to go back to La Casita Azul where I grow my tomatoes.

The work in New York was really hard. It was after a victory—the passage of the New York State Domestic Worker's Bill of Rights. There was a lot of rebuilding that needed to happen around the domestic worker movement in New York. We worked closely with Adhikaar, Damayan, and Joyce at Domestic Workers United. We were developing and moving a post-victory strategy. We did a domestic worker convention in five languages. Over three hundred domestic workers and our affiliates showed up in full force. The line wrapped around the Columbia University campus. It was a key moment in the movement. I was feeling so good, but I just couldn't stay in New York. I was pregnant again, and the apartment was too small, and we had this house here. I told NDWA, "I gotta go back to the South, I can't stay here. I'll give you a couple of months' notice, but I have to make the transition." I had already been with them for about two years, and they came back and said, "No, we're going to build chapters and you can help build these chapters." They were thinking about what other roles I could play and I'm so grateful for that!

I have been here now for ten years! This work is really important. My abuelitas were domestic workers, and there's so much that still needs to happen. My ideal moment would be when we win a national bill, and are at the phase where we're trying *to implement* that national bill. That seemed like such a faraway dream when I first started, and here we are moving it forward! The fact that there's an actual bill now is really big. We went from no chapters to chapters in New York, California, Pennsylvania, and the DMV area: Washington D.C., Maryland, and Northern Virginia. We've paused because we want to make sure we're sustainable and intentional. We've been able to develop really great work in each state and have really great victories. I like victories, I hate losing. So being able to have wins, to see the Black domestic organizing work in the South solidify in our We Dream in Black chapters in Georgia, North Carolina, and Texas, and to see so many domestic workers transitioning into the directorships of the chapters, is really powerful. I am so excited every time I see a member come into this role. I supervise all of the chapter directors and they supervise their staff. It's great because I get to support with strategizing and campaign development in each state, but also work on infrastructure building. I get to pull from my experience as an organizer to support them.

In a way, I get to mother, even though that's probably not the appropriate way to say it. I don't want it to get taken out of context. I get to nurture other organizers, and I love that. I get to hear all the problems and hold space and smile and say, "It's going to be okay; we're going to get through this. You gotta keep going." I get to celebrate when they celebrate their victories, and I get to see victories in different cities and states. I meet with elected officials in all these different states and hear from them and see how every state is so different, and I get to work through really hard problems and in the process learn a lot and create a path to victory. Even though that's stressful, it's really stimulating to constantly be challenged.

NDWA has stretched me tremendously, in a lot of different ways. I'm so grateful for the work that I do there on behalf of our members. The win around the 2020 election was very big, in Atlanta especially. It took so many people and so many years of infrastructure building, and there were major players that have been here for a long time. I love what we're building here and in so many other states. I've been really lucky throughout these many decades of organizing to do this work from where I do it. I have the freedom, sometimes, to do it the way I do it, to learn from my mistakes, and to be around amazing matriarchs. When I sat on the board for SisterSong, I learned so much from hearing Loretta Ross and some of the other sisters and from our reproductive justice movement. I'm always kind of quiet, so I'd just sit and listen. I've always believed in reproductive justice, including for people who *want to mother*. It's not just about abortion. I've been lucky to have all these people be part of my extended family.

Creating Circles of Connection

I approach everything I do like an organizer. I tend to think about issues in a very community-minded way. I know that all of the experiences I've had, other people have had. I tend to create circles of connection so that we're not dealing with things in isolation or just relearning lessons that other people have learned. One day I was feeling like, "Wow, I don't necessarily have a retirement fund that is going to hold me when I'm older. I'm approaching my fifties now. Seeing my grandmother have to deal with dementia the way she did and being in a nursing home, and going to visit her there and just seeing how horrific the conditions were, and what happens in this country when you get old, made me realize how important it is to have money to help sustain you. I especially think about it with organizers. A lot of organizers go through years doing this work, and for a good portion of them, we're not really thinking about aging or "What happens when I retire?" I wondered if anybody else was thinking about it, what solutions they've come up with, and what their fears are around this. I wanted to know how we can support each other so that we feel less alone. Aging gets so lonely in this country. So I just posted the question on Facebook.

I did not expect that many responses, it really blew my mind. But it showed how, when you're *in tune* as an organizer, you know what are some of the unspoken things that are underneath the surface. It was like all these people had been thinking the same thing and didn't have anybody to be like, "Yo, I'm thinking this, and what are you doing?" Then I was like, "Well, I guess I'll create a survey to get people's contact information into a spreadsheet and figure out how to work the list little by little, and ask some key questions about what people are looking for and then try to align." It's funny because that survey has been in the back of my mind for weeks now. I don't know where it's going. I woke up this morning, and I was thinking about it, "Well, maybe I'll create a directory and people can connect with each other." I might do some smaller meetings with people that I have more in common with, and folks can self-organize if they want to. It's an interesting mix of people. I don't really know where that's heading but I think it'll be good.

The other thing I'm thinking about in terms of the future is *purposeful work*. Where do I want to spend the last years that I organize? What do I want to lend my energy to? What am I trying to build? Is it aligned with my purpose and my values? That's really important. When I think of what comes next for me in terms of organizing, I'm really interested in climate change. I'm really interested in more of the structural democracy question that we're facing in our country today.

Mothering

Mothering has always, from the very beginning, been part of my identity as an organizer. Through Sistas on the Rise we were trying to establish that organizing wasn't just for single people, that if you were a mother, you should be able to organize as well, and we challenged a lot of nonprofits to always provide childcare. If you met me when I was younger you always would see me with my son. Even to this day, when I go to the chapters, I have Kai with me. I bring Kai with me to do legislative visits. He sits in the corner and he's coloring or whatever he's doing. We are able to homeschool because my husband works an alternate schedule than I do, so we're not both working at the same time, and there's overlap. Our families and communities are already so broken, we don't need any more of that. We need to heal. We need to raise children who have a different experience and have a different vision of what's possible, and it starts with us.

Homeschooling is an extension of organizing for me. I'm not going to leave my community to go in search of a better education, which is what a lot of parents do. I'm not doing that. Luckily, homeschooling worked out, but it could have gone in many different directions. Diego is doing very well, and I think Kai will do very well. We're done dealing with poor-performing schools. I've always been about creating alternatives, so if you are not going to do right by me, I'm not going to put my child in your environment. There's a lot of work that needs to happen in Georgia, in our schools. That's another area where I would love to organize. Our educational standards are unacceptable. I homeschool because I believe that's the best thing I can do as a mother for my child. My child needs to learn about real history and his identity. I don't want him questioning himself, his ability to reach his dreams, or feeling uncomfortable in his own skin. He needs to build confidence in himself. That's really important to me. He needs to feel powerful and comfortable, and it is my job to facilitate that process.

We have found our balance. I always say that we do the best we can with what we have, and we're going to either fail and learn, *or we're going to fly*. It's hard. Homeschooling may not be for everyone. I get that, but it works for us. Isn't that what organizing is about? It's about creating the world that you want to live in. In my life, I create the world that I want to live in. Do I stress? Am I sad? Do I have problems? Absolutely! But I am living with intention and I'm happy within that context. I have learned so much, and I wouldn't do it any other way.

Knowing that I'm living my values and creating the type of life and world that I want to live in is my self-care. I'm not perfect, and I'm sure there's somebody out there that doesn't like me. But the core of me is pretty damn good, and I'm good with it. I'm good with me, and that's a beautiful thing. If you can be in this movement for this many years and look at yourself in the mirror and go, "I am good with me," then you are good to go.

FOUR

Betty Yu

✳

I got fully immersed in the organizing.
I realized that this was not just about *other people*.
It was about me and my family.
It was much bigger than just Chinatown.

Betty Yu is an award-winning multimedia artist, photographer, filmmaker, and activist born and raised in New York City to Chinese immigrant parents. Betty's art emerges from collective struggle, and she places it in the service of building collective power. As a cultural worker, she remains deeply connected to grassroots organizing and has over twenty years of community, media justice, and labor organizing experience. She is a co-founder of Chinatown Art Brigade, a cultural collective using art to advance anti-gentrification organizing. She teaches video, social practice, art, and activism at Pratt Institute, Hunter College, and The New School.

Betty's work has focused on workers' rights, immigration, gentrification, police violence, class, race, media justice, and other issues. She links anti-Asian violence and bias with the racism experienced by Black and Indigenous communities, and creates opportunities for education and solidarity. Her oral history reflects on how the issues impacting her family and community exist within a context of struggle for social justice, how she initially engaged in community organizing as a teenager, the meaning of belonging and accountability, the role of the arts in changing hearts and minds, the importance of collaboration with community, and the power of storytelling in popular education to shift narratives as part of an organizing strategy.

Betty currently resides in Sunset Park, Brooklyn.

I WAS BORN IN MANHATTAN BUT RAISED IN SUNSET PARK, Brooklyn. I always say that I was born and raised in Sunset Park, because that's in my blood. Sometimes I would go to Chinatown in Manhattan on the weekends when I had a doctor's appointment, or when meeting with relatives. Manhattan's Chinatown was my second home, for sure, but I was very insulated within the twelve blocks of my immediate neighborhood in Sunset Park.

My dad's family was from a small village in Taishan, China. They were peasant farmers who lived on the top of the hill of the village, meaning they had *a little* more money. They were afraid about what was going to happen after the founding of the People's Republic of China in 1949, so they fled and went to Hong Kong. My dad met my mom there, and my parents then immigrated to the US.

It's always complicated when people ask me what generation I'm in. I keep finding out that there are more generations of my family that have been in this country before my parents came, but due to the Chinese Exclusion Act,[41] they weren't able to *stay and build roots here*. I say I am a child of immigrants, which is true, but I also am fourth generation, if I take into account all the generations that have been here before me.

Sunset Park, Brooklyn

Our family settled in Sunset Park. A bunch of family members pooled money to buy a house and lived there together. Back then, some families were able save and buy a house with no mortgage. "Here you go. Here's the cash." That was a time when working-class families could actually *afford* to buy a house. It's *crazy* to think about that now in Brooklyn. Some folks were moving out as the Chinese were coming in. At that time, Sunset Park was mainly Latinx and Chinese with some white folks, particularly Norwegian, Swedish, and other Scandinavians. I remember some really racist stuff, but there were also some nice white people who I grew up with.

Sixth Avenue was a dividing line between the Latinx and the Chinatown parts of Sunset Park. We were one of the few Chinese families who would walk over to Fifth Avenue like it was no big deal. There was good pizza there and a lot of Italians on the other end. We went because of the good food and the shops. Growing up in the late

1970s and early eighties, I really loved having a completely multira-cial group of friends and upbringing. When you grow up with friends of all races, you kind of make fun of each other, but not in a way that's hurtful. It's like, "You're different, but it's funny." I used to think that everyone grew up like this, but a lot of Asian American activists I know who grew up in *really white neighborhoods* are like, "Oh, my God, now I'm in Chinatown I see people who look like me." It was many moons ago, but I didn't realize *then* that everyone didn't grow up like that, truly having the most multiracial experience where race was not even an issue. Of course, race has *everything* to do with our economic system, but at that time, I looked at a lot of things through a class di-vide more than anything else. That informed my politics as a teen-ager and as an early adult activist. I saw things more along the lines of class because of what my parents were going through—Chinese were exploiting Chinese all over Chinatown.

As my mom and dad had more kids, they had to work longer hours to make ends meet. I have three older sisters, and my grand-mother basically raised us. It was very hard for me. When I was younger, I didn't really get what was going on. Of course, when you're older, you understand that they were just trying to make ends meet and put food on the table. I appreciate that, but at the time I felt a lot of self-hatred. It wasn't so much about being Chinese, it was more about class. When people asked me what my parents did, I don't remember what I said, but I would make something up. That internal hatred of, "Oh, your parents are low-wage workers, not even working class." That kind of thing informs and shapes who I am today. I was so fortunate growing up in such a vibrant community. It definitely has made me who I am *to the core*, all my values and every-thing that I believe in, to this day.

Badass Women

People say that the Latinx part of Sunset Park was so rough in the 1980s, with gangs and all this stuff, but it didn't dawn on me to be afraid. I was brought up to be very, very tough. My grandmother would chase off all the other kids that would make fun of me because I was so small, and because I was Chinese. Even in her eighties she would chase them, saying, "I'm going to twist your neck off, get the hell out! Run away!" She was badass. I grew up with a bunch of badass women. My mom, Sau Kwan Leung Yu, worked thirteen to fifteen hours a day at a garment factory. She would come home, cook and clean, get five hours of sleep, and then get up the next day and go to work again. I had a very tough exterior growing up, and I'm so appreciative of that. When my grandmother passed at age 103 a couple of years ago, it was devastating.

NYC Public Schools—Lead in the Walls and Funding for the Arts

I went to a junior high school called Pershing at 49th Street and Tenth Avenue. It was the second worst school in Brooklyn at the time, and there were a lot of fights. I laugh about it now. Maybe people can relate if they grew up in the 1980s in a "rough" neighborhood. Girls put Vaseline on their faces, put their rings on, took their big door-knocker earrings off, and got ready to go at it. Boys just kind of went at it. Our school's claim to fame was that it still had lead in its walls. I remember it being a big story in the news because by that time they had removed it from most schools. It was a pretty bad school in that regard, but I turned out OK, and I had amazing friends.

I was so blessed to go to Edward R. Murrow High School in Midwood, Brooklyn. It was one of the schools in the public system most funded for the arts. I was exposed to photography, film, theater, creative writing, painting, and all kinds of things. I hung out with artsy kids. They experimented a lot, and I was in that realm. *It was amazing.* I think I was using that as a way to cope with not having a strong bond with my parents.

A Child of Garment Workers

I really didn't know my parents. When you talk to other Chinese folks of my generation with parents of that generation or older, they're like, "That's just how it is. They're stiff and don't show affection, all that." But it was more than that. I didn't have time with my family because *they were working all the time, even on weekends*. At that time, I was in high school and my sisters were older. By then they were in college or had moved out. I was really alone. I lived with my parents and my grandmother. In traditional Asian households, I don't speak for all, but in many East Asian and even South Asian households, the family tends to live with the grandmother or the in-laws of the father. There was a lot of fighting at home. It was even hard to get work done at home, honestly. Now, intellectually, I understand what was going on, but growing up I didn't. So I stayed out a lot with my friends and I spent *hours* in the photography dark-room, escaping. Photography was my outlet, and I won awards and things in high school. That was cool, and I got validation. When I was maybe fifteen, sixteen, I got really into the "raver scene." This was the early 1990s. The film *Kids* that came out by Larry Clark, I was literally the same age as those kids, and that was my life for a couple of years. I was just going through a lot of angst, for sure. My mom was really worried about me, asking my older sisters, "What the hell's going on with your younger sister? You've got to intervene. You've got to help me out."

Being Welcomed into Organizing

My sister Virginia passed away ten, eleven, years ago from an aneurysm. It was very sudden, and she left two wonderful little kids. *She was the one*—along with my other sisters— who pulled me out of whatever direction I was going in. She was going to college at SUNY Binghamton at the time, in upstate New York, for undergrad. She was telling me about an organization called Chinese Staff and Workers Association and this amazing organizing of garment and restaurant workers. I wasn't really that interested. She said, "You're a photographer, you can come down and photograph." I was probably sixteen at the time, and I went. There was a protest in front of Silver Palace, which had been the first unionized restaurant in Chinatown, back in 1980. This was in the mid-1990s. There were also protests against Jing Fong restaurant, which is the biggest restaurant on the East Coast.

Workers were getting paid seventy-five cents an hour. I heard about their working conditions and that also moved me to come out, to see what was going on and to support. To my surprise, I began taking photos. I was really into it. Before I knew it, I got involved, because honestly, I saw people that looked like me, who were my age, or younger, as well as older people. I had expected to see granola, white, hippie, Birkenstock-type activists. That was my image of an activist. I was like, "Oh, my God, everyone here is mostly Asian, and they're working-class folks like my parents and my sister and others." I met all these workers from Jing Fong and from garment factories, and they were all talking about their working conditions. It was all very familiar to me because I grew up in that.

I finally understood why my sister was involved. She was five years older than me. Once I got deeply involved, all the clubbing didn't seem to matter as much. *This* was something that clearly was reflective of my upbringing, and what I was going through as a child of immigrants who were robbed of time with their family because they were working such long hours. I started to realize that even in the unionized factories, conditions were not great. My mom and dad had to work *multiple jobs all the time* to just make ends meet. Soon after that, my mom started coming and got involved as well. My sister, mom, and I were really engaged at one point.

Seeing My Family in the Context of Broader Struggles

I started to piece all these things together in terms of what my parents were going through as garment workers and what conditions they were forced to work under. I began to see my role in helping to amplify that as well as helping to eradicate sweatshops and illegal garment working conditions. Not just for my parents, but for many thousands and thousands of people like them.

My commitment to that work solidified when my sister decided to join four other college students to stage a hunger strike in front of Jing Fong restaurant. They wanted to call attention to the lack of enforcement of labor laws, not just what was happening in Jing Fong. The Department of Labor is a couple of blocks away at City Hall, yet they turned a blind eye. I remember being there photographing and being in the picket pen with my sister. My mom would come, my grandmother would come, and all these people! I was really moved by people like my mom, who were garment workers, as well as the restaurant workers, coming and bringing water, flowers, and blankets *constantly*. It was incredible to see that, because just for showing your support you could get blacklisted from ever getting a job again if the owners knew who you were. The gangs were still a big thing at the time, *the Tongs*, and the other organized crime families. The Tongs would send the youth gangs out. They would stand across the street smoking and photographing people trying to intimidate them. People who were management from the restaurant were dangling roast pork in front of the student hunger strikers' faces. It was next-level disgusting. Chinese Staff and Workers had a whole security team, but people still got death threats. It was a scary, crazy time.

The Fifth Precinct is across the street from Jing Fong. One day, it was going to thunderstorm. The construction workers of Chinese Staff and Worker's Association, a division within Chinese Staff, wanted to build a little structure to cover people from the rain with a tarp. The cops came and took all the wood away, broke it down. Captain Chan, who people fucking rave about to this day because he's now the NYPD's chief of transportation, was the precinct captain at the time and *very much* in cahoots with the bosses and the Tongs. You see pictures of them together; it was very corrupt at that time, and probably is now. I documented all of this and made a short film.

I got fully immersed in the organizing. I realized that this was not just about *other people*. It was about me and my family. It was much bigger than just Chinatown. It was a historic event. Family in Hong Kong called us. They were like, "We saw you on TV. You guys were protesting!" It was kind of funny. We were like, "Oh, you saw it over there? OK!" I was still a teenager. My sister was on TV, on all the news stations. For about ten to fifteen years after that we would continue to be engaged in that work, particularly my mom. She became a leader in the workers' struggle to improve conditions in the garment factories. It was really meaningful for us to see our mom getting so impassioned and so involved in the organizing.[42]

Chinese Staff and Workers Association

Chinese Staff and Workers Association was the first workers' center in the US. They were founded in 1979 when the conditions in the restaurants in Chinatown were pretty bad and a lot of the restaurant workers in Chinatown wanted to join unions. The unions were majority white at the time, and Chinese workers were heavily discriminated against. They eventually started their own restaurant union, which was called 318 because it was formed on March 18 in the 1970s. Then it became Chinese Staff and Workers Association, a multi-trade worker center led by and for workers in Chinatown.

I was a volunteer. I was sixteen, seventeen, at the time and really involved, particularly with the Youth Video Workshop. They were talented folks—immigrant, and non-immigrant youth, creating monthly shows on Manhattan Neighborhood Network, our public access station.[43] MNN had grants to provide equipment and some monetary support for community groups to produce their own shows. The shows were about everyday people, workers basically. They were filming each other and documenting their fight to improve conditions, in the 1990s. I was really moved by that, because it was the first time I saw older and younger folks filming each other and learning to use the equipment. This was way before digital. I had learned some video editing in high school and got even more involved with the video workshop at Chinese Staff. When I was accepted into NYU for photography and then film, I helped to train folks on how to use the video equipment and things like that.

Telling Our Own Stories, Creating Our Own Media

It was really important for Chinese Staff to have their own television show and newsletters. All the four dailies in Chinatown were very pro-boss, pro-employer, and very anti-worker. They did *not* want to report what was actually happening or the resistance that was occurring. If it was reported, it was really skewed. "These workers are getting paid, they're brainwashed!" Our show was translated into English and Chinese and was an important piece of propaganda, *good propaganda*, where people were putting out what the truth was, on the ground, as opposed to relying on these newspapers.

After I graduated from college, I worked at Chinese Staff for about two years. I mainly organized garment workers and injured workers. A lot of garment, construction, and restaurant workers, and other trades as well, were getting injured on the job and couldn't get workers' comp. A lot of them were undocumented, but were *due* workers' comp. Helping folks to navigate the system was a small aspect, but it was really about fighting the Workers' Compensation Board for real structural changes, because people were getting like forty dollars a week. Who can live on that? We had a Brooklyn branch back then in Sunset Park, and I worked there for a couple of years. I then worked at Manhattan Neighborhood Network and was on the board of Chinese Staff for about ten years after that. I respect their work tremendously. They're one of the most badass, radical, militant worker groups in the country. I'm no longer involved with them, but that's my trajectory. It's only recently that I started to consider myself an artist because of all that is *attached* to being an artist. I know that we need to demystify the process and help others understand that art is a fundamental part of *movements* and that we're not just artists or art workers. I had a whole hang-up about that for a very long time.

When I was at Chinese Staff organizing, I was doing a lot of video documentation of what was happening. There was a big march in Albany with a bunch of Asian, Black, and Brown folks. I was one of the key people organizing it. Long story short, I got brutally arrested. It was on the cover of the *Albany Times*. The cop, Gallo, I think his name was, was like three hundred pounds. He violently flipped me on the ground and arrested me. My mother instinctively ran over to hug me. They arrested her, too, and a bunch of other people, including Wing Lam, who's the executive director and another organizer from Chinese Staff. We were taken to downtown Albany to get fingerprinted and put in the pen. I'll never forget all the cops there. Mind you, these were a bunch of older Black, Brown, and Asian folks, some in wheelchairs. They had all levels of cops on bikes, on foot, and on horses. We have footage of the horses knocking people down. I had people out there filming it.

I remember sitting in the precinct. My mom doesn't understand much English. The cops who were booking us were saying, "This is not New York City. This is Albany. Do you know where you are?" I was like, "Yeah, I know where we are." They said, "Stop watching so much Sharpton. Who do you think you are to come up from the city? You don't know where you are. You've never been up here, right?" Something to that degree. It was all immigrant folks of color leading the protests and the cops being like, "You're in the wrong place." That has definitely stayed with me to this day. That was 2003. It was crazy.

Cultural Work in Support of Organizing

We had a campaign around the police brutality piece of it, calling out the state police and state violence. I got really involved editing the video. Then there was a hunger strike of workers who were injured on the job and fighting for workers' compensation in front of Pataki's office. I realized how much joy I was getting out of working on that video. The editing was done by committee. It took over a year to make. We had many community screenings. I definitely got a lot out of it. There were people that spoke Spanish, spoke Chinese, spoke Polish. It was translation over translation, just a hot mess. Everyone gave input on the video and said it was great. I think we collectively did make a great video about the hunger strike and the police brutality and all of that.

That was when I realized I wanted to get back to filmmaking and storytelling through video. I was having a hard time as an organizer. I loved Chinese Staff and Workers and their militance, analysis, and ideas of what organizing should be. It was really demanding and exhausting, but extremely rewarding. Looking back twenty years later, *I got a lot out of it*, don't get me wrong. But I was burnt out, to be honest. I wanted to get into the media realm again. When I was offered a job at MNN, I took it. I remained involved with Chinese Staff because I believed initially, and I still do, but I wanted to support the work in a different way.

Resourcing Grassroots Organizing Through Media Education

At MNN we did a lot of productions and worked with groups like Picture the Homeless, Esperanza del Barrio, Chinese Staff and Workers Association, and tons of other amazing social justice groups. It was amazing because I still got to work supporting grassroots organizations in a meaningful way. I helped them tell their own stories, but I wasn't doing the organizing. We were very deliberate in our curation of whom we wanted to support, train, and provide these media-making tools to, even though we weren't saying it widely. I'm so proud of the hundreds of groups that were supported through the community media grants and the training at MNN. It was also there that I was exposed to media policy work. We were fighting to save public access because it was in danger of being defunded, but it was mainly old white dudes who ran the public access center. They had received funding in the 1970s and they never let go. There was little leadership changeover, and very few were really radical or political. I was disillusioned by that. Afterwards, I worked for a number of years doing media policy work at the Center for Media Justice (CMJ), an all people-of-color, media justice organization. Malkia Cyril was the founder and executive director. I got so much out of that, but it was frustrating, too. I was in grad school at the time. I would have to go to Oakland (California) often and take the red-eye back to NYC for class. I was working many hours, traveling to different places doing national organizing with the Media Action Grassroots Network, which was a part of the Center for Media Justice, and also trying to get my MFA.

Digital Rights Are Human Rights

CMJ was talking about *digital rights* as a basic human right. The digital divide was fundamental to people's livelihoods. It wasn't, "Oh, I want internet to play video games or to shoot the shit." It was *essential*. When I was involved, this is many years ago, there was still a huge digital divide. On First Nations reservations, internet access was really low. Of course, in the South, and in places in poorer rural communities, it was still pretty low.

I was traveling and meeting all kinds of amazing people. I really loved the people I worked with. I got to go to places like Jackson, Mississippi, as well as rural Mississippi, New Orleans, Georgia, and all throughout the South. I have so much respect for folks who are organizing in the South. I was very bicoastal in the sense that I believed that there were only radical folks on the East and the West Coast. A very privileged perspective, obviously! It wasn't until I was exposed to organizing in the South, and even in the Midwest, that I totally understood that folks of color, rural folks, and Native folks who were fighting for media justice were part of a larger framework around social justice movements. I learned a lot and got humbled a lot. Everywhere you go people are resisting locally. That's just the nature of it, especially in this capitalist country. Being on the ground, hearing people's stories, and how, against so many odds, they're struggling and fighting, has been really meaningful for me.

Organizing Lessons from Killeen, Texas

In 2012 or 2013, when I was working with the Center for Media Justice, I had to go to South by Southwest in Austin for some workshops. I was the typical militant person who was like, "There's no draft. If you enlist, you get what you deserve. Fuck anybody who enlisted. Fuck any soldier." I was really hard-nosed about it. Then I happened to meet a whole bunch of veterans. They had shortwave radio and were there to learn about how they could start their own low-power radio station because there was amazing organizing going on at the Fort Hood military base in Killeen, Texas, *the largest military installation in the world*.

The veterans I met invited me to visit Killeen. They had a coffeehouse called Under the Hood. They were like, "It's actually modeled after all the resistance and organizing in the late 1960s against the Vietnam War in Fort Hood." They told me about the film *Sir! No Sir!*, and explained that they were working with people from the Vietnam era who had passed on information about all the resistance and organizing during that period. So, actually, Under the Hood is a homage to the GI resistance that was happening in the coffeehouse that *the soldiers had* at the time.

After I visited, I wanted to make a film about what these folks were doing. They literally were across the street from the military base, and they got numerous threats! A lot of their communications were intercepted by the military. They were trying to do pirate radio and were literally confronting the military-industrial complex located across the street. Some of them were veterans who had stayed in the area, but they weren't enlisted anymore. Some were still in the military and would leave work and come to Under the Hood. I was really floored by that.

Collaborative Filmmaking

Three Tours was a film I worked on for about four years. It's a film about three veterans and their trajectory to healing and becoming anti-war activists. They each talk about their healing being inextricably tied to actually focusing on the damage they'd done in Iraq. These three served in Iraq, but they're also Afghanistan veterans as well. They talk about the *generations of trauma and devastation* that

101

they left there, depleted uranium, health conditions, everything. They talked about how their healing has to absolutely be tied to the reparations and rebuilding of lives there. I focused on their healing through activism, their art. It was my senior thesis for my MFA program, but it became much more than getting my degree and graduating.

I was very collaborative with Ryan, Nicole, and Ramón, and the organization they were involved in, Iraq Veterans Against the War, and was very much in connection with them all the time while making this film. Nicole Goodwin is an amazing African American queer artist and poet. She enlisted right before 9/11, and then she had a kid. She didn't think she was going to go overseas because this was before 9/11. Her kid was three months old when she had to go to Iraq. She talked about her experiences having to be a guard at a prison in Iraq and the torture that she was hearing about, including purposely feeding prisoners spoiled food, and stuff like that. Just the trauma that was there—and that it was happening to people that *were Brown*—made the wheels start to turn in her head. "What the fuck? Why am I here?" In addition, she experienced some sexual trauma while she was there in the military. Then Ramón Mejía, who is Mexican American, was a part of the first wave of a people who went to Iraq from Kuwait overnight. He has these beautiful photographs that I incorporated into the film. He was a machine gun operator. He talked about the burning pits everywhere, and kids who were literally made orphans overnight, running around. Then Ryan Holleran, who was at the *tail end*, right before the exit under Obama, talked about coming out of the closet to his buddies, and how, from that point on, they treated him differently. This is right when I think Obama lifted "Don't ask, don't tell." There were some folks who were very supportive, but most weren't.

People always ask me, "Why did you make this film?" I'm like, "If I looked different, would someone ask me that?" I forget where I screened this, maybe in Albuquerque. I was like, "If I was a white man would you be asking me this? Or a white woman?" My work is not just about my ethnicity or my race. Yes, that informs who I am, but I'm capable of making stories about other people if we do it the right way.

Transformative Organizing

Iraq Veterans Against the War now call themselves About Face Veterans Against the War. I was moved by their transformative organizing. (I know that these words get thrown around so much. I always try to avoid these heady, big words that don't really mean a lot in the non-activist world, because people are like, "What the fuck are you talking about? Can you use real-people speak?") I stay in touch with my friends from when I was thirteen or fourteen. I don't just surround myself with activists and organizers, because we're in our own little world sometimes.

The organizing that About Face Veterans Against the War does among veterans is so powerful. Different movements can learn so much about their healing process. In the height of when I was making the film, suicide rates among veterans were really high. They were really high after the Vietnam War, too, but in terms of the Iraq War, they were the highest. There was also the highest rate of homelessness among veterans at that time. I interviewed more than twenty, thirty, veterans and only one person checked in with me at the time, which is fine. I appreciate him so much. He was like, "How are *you* doing? You're hearing some stories." I just broke down and started bawling at the stories they were telling. I asked them questions. Whatever they wanted to tell me, they told me. It was heavy. A few of them that I interviewed took their own lives in the years after that.

I think the amount of healing that they do *personally*, and how it flows out into the world as organizers and as activists is really meaningful. During Standing Rock, they used their training to put their bodies in the service of a movement led by folks of color. That has been very, very impressive, and was for me, personally, a really transformative experience. I'm still in touch with all of them. I love them so much. For me, personally, that was a really transformative experience. When we talk about transformative organizing, and what they've done . . . How do you figure out how to live with that? How do you heal from that? Their staff was white and now it's not. They've done a lot of internal work, in coming to reckon with that, asking themselves why is it that most of the folks that were in leadership were white veterans, and what that says and what that means. It's a constant struggle, and I really respect them for that.

The Chinatown Art Brigade

One huge turning point in my life as an artist and a cultural worker was when I helped co-found Chinatown Art Brigade in 2015 with Tomie Arai and ManSee Kong. ManSee was heavily involved for many, many years as a staff organizer with CAAAV: Organizing Asian Communities. She's an amazing filmmaker. Tomie Arai is a muralist, a fine artist, a visual artist, *a superstar*, a well-known, amazing person who also did support work with CAAAV for years.

I started to get involved with CAAAV in 2013 or 2014. I got a lot more involved with the organization during the case of Peter Liang, a Chinese cop who was born and raised in Chinatown. Liang killed Akai Gurley, a Black man who took the stairway because the elevators *never work* in NYCHA, in the Pink Houses. There's a huge fracture in the community, to this day. CAAAV was really one of the first a pan-Asian groups in Chinatown that had a lot of Chinese members in it to come out and stand with Akai Gurley and build strong relationships with his family, calling for justice.

In 2015, we were approached by one of the organizers at CAAAV who said, "We know how to do the organizing on the ground with tenants. We do that work really well, but we want to start to animate people's stories. We want to use arts and culture in a really meaningful way. Would you be interested in working with tenants in some way to really amplify the work?" They approached the three of us, and although we didn't know each other well, it really worked out.

We formed Chinatown Art Brigade, a collective of activists, artists, tenants, Chinatown residents, and scholars. During the first couple of years, I learned *so much* in terms of what it means to be a collective. We also worked with *another collective*, the Chinatown Tenants Union of CAAAV. We were still trying to figure stuff out, and we were working with this collective of mainly Chinese-speaking immigrant tenants, most of them monolingual. It was an amazing learning experience, and we made the road by walking, to be honest.

We did a couple of months of intense workshops with Chinatown Tenants Union and other folks. We had created a week-by-week curriculum: "This is what we're going to do from week to week." Some of the tenants were like, "What the hell is this? This doesn't make any sense." It was too heady and intellectual. It was also clearly prescribed *for them* instead of actually embracing their knowledge and their experience and knowing what was best in terms of how to communicate the stories *that they lived*. We should have created the framework of how to go about these workshops together. So everything went out the window. We radically changed the whole curriculum, working *with them* and figuring out what made sense. We started these story circles that were modeled after Junebug Productions, which is part of the Free Southern Theater. They created a whole model of story circles, specifically around active listening. Each person in the circle spoke for three minutes, with a few prompts. Either you could tell a story about the time that you felt belonging or the opposite of that, dis-belonging. Everyone else listened until everyone had spoken.

There were tears in the room. It was very heavy, very emotional. One person, Mr. Chen, shared a story about how he had been in this country for seventeen years, I think. He hadn't gone back to China to see his son because he's undocumented and he's afraid he would not be able to come back. He talked about uprooting himself and leaving China when there was a lack of economic opportunities. Then in Chinatown, I don't know how many times he had moved because of increased rents. He talked a lot about dispossession, displacement, and that he doesn't know what a sense of belonging means, even though he's from China and has lived here for many years. There was a lot of emotion. These tenants had known each other for ten years or more, but never actually got to know each other's real stories. That was shocking to me, honestly. You get thrown in there and you do the organizing, but you actually don't even know each other! I realized at that time how the story piece of cultural organizing is *really powerful*. I forget one woman's name, but she responded to Mr. Chen, telling him, "I didn't know that about you, and I've known you forever!" That was really meaningful. As artists in Chinatown Art Brigade, we shared too. We made ourselves vulnerable. I think that's important as well. It's not just that we wanted to hear this poor story from the tenant or the worker. There was an equal playing field, and we were all in it together. That set the path for the project.

The Power of Imagining

We imagined a future with an abundance of housing, *an ideal future*. We mapped that out. We did place-keeping walks around Chinatown, and people talked about resilient places that were still there, and places that are no longer there because of gentrification. We would stop at different locations for people to have a moment to speak their truth, or chalk the ground to write something or sketch something, whatever it was. These workshops culminated in a collection of images—photographs, sketches, and drawings. We eventually turned the material into projections on the walls of Chinatown at night that we did with The Illuminator, a group that does large-scale projections.

The tenants had changed the lyrics of a famous Chinese song into lyrics about holding landlords accountable and tenants' rights. It was a very familiar song, so random people joined and started singing karaoke together. People stopped and stood on the sidewalk staring at the wall of images and text we'd projected, in Spanish, Chinese, and English. That was a moment! Cathy Dang was the executive director of CAAAV at the time. She was like, "It was an amazing opportunity because people stopped, and they looked up. Organizers were able to talk to them and engage with them about what this was really about." A lot of people were interested. "Who's doing this? What is this?" It was an opportunity to talk to people about CAAAV, the Tenants Union, the gentrification that was happening in Chinatown. Folks were about to learn about the Chinatown Working Group, and all these plans that were out there to protect the community, and how folks could get involved. We did that several times. It was really meaningful.

Connecting Gentrification, Incarceration, and Labor Exploitation

In 2017 or 2018, Mayor de Blasio announced that he wanted to shut down the jail on Rikers Island and open up four borough-based jails, minus Staten Island. The Manhattan one would be in Chinatown, next to the Tombs.[44] People were in an uproar. There were Chinatown folks whose politics were coming from a "Not in My Backyard," anti-Black, and racially coded place. "No jail. I don't want my kids walking around and having these people walk the streets or the family members that are visiting them." Pretty racist shit. But other people were, whether they were abolitionists or just folks who said, "No. Rikers should close. We shouldn't have these jails." Opposition to locating the borough-based jail in Chinatown ran the gamut.

There were hearings. They had to have a whole "scope of hearing" process. The same process that a developer would need to do if they wanted to build a condo in a neighborhood, a ULURP (Uniform Land Use Review Procedure) process.[45] Folks *flooded the hearings* and the town hall meetings. There were lines around the block. All kinds of folks came out. For de Blasio, the whole thing was, Oh, these new jails are going to have UV lights and light therapy, and we're going to rehabilitate people. Folks and family members don't have to go into Rikers now! They can just go take a train, and blah blah blah, all that stuff. Folks in opposition were coming from all over the place politically, but some have come around and now see that this is not rehabilitation. There should be no such thing as human cages.

In 2018, we found out there was a secret meeting between the mayor, some local nonprofits, and Margaret Chin, the local city council member. Chin is *awful* on housing and likes to say she's a criminal justice reform person, but she's not. The Museum of Chinese in America (MOCA) was also in that meeting. We found out later that MOCA would receive 35 million dollars as part of a "community give-back" plan to build the jail in Chinatown. "Since we're building a jail here, we're going to give you something back." It was hush-hush for a while. We knew it happened because we had heard word and did some research. We found a newspaper article, but it hadn't really gotten much public attention yet. Chinatown Art Brigade was the first group to say this publicly and to protest MOCA about this.

At first, no one believed MOCA would get this $35 million community give-back as part of the plan to build the jail. Then, fast-forward, the NYC Borough-Based Jail Agreement came out from de Blasio's office saying in black and white, "MOCA is going to receive 35 million dollars." MOCA had become *so corporate*. Jonathan Chu, the biggest real estate developer in Chinatown, was on their board. It's run by someone who used to work at Goldman Sachs. I mean, it's far gone. Chinatown Art Brigade helped organize an emergency protest in front of MOCA, calling them out for receiving this money and selling out. They're now saying, "No. The 35 million dollars is coming from somewhere else." I'm like, "Fuck that shit, it's black and white. You can't fool us. We're not idiots, you know?" The protests have been great. MOCA's executive director, Nancy Yao Maasbach, at one point came out and tried to give *tote bags* to workers who had been fired from Jing Fong who were there protesting MOCA. The workers threw the tote bags on the ground and stepped on them. Then she told the media, "Oh, they're getting paid to be out here." *These are the workers that got fired from Jing Fong.* Chinatown Art Brigade was one of the first groups to call out the art-washing.[46] They said, "This is all right here. Incarceration, freakin' gentrification, all of this racist policy. All of this is encompassed here in this institution."

Since then, there's been a lot of protesting. Chinese Staff and Workers and a lot of other groups have made the connection, which is great. Jing Fong, which we protested back in 1995, is the only remaining unionized restaurant in Chinatown. Jonathan Chu, the co-chair of the board of MOCA, owns the land that Jing Fong is on, and evicted them during COVID. He also got all this COVID relief money, and still fired one hundred unionized workers. So that battle continues, and the restaurant union, Chinese Staff, and all the folks are making these connections between labor exploitation, gentrification, and incarceration, which is great.

The Fight to Stop Industry City in Sunset Park

When Chinatown Art Brigade started, we were focusing on China-town in Manhattan. It inspired me to look at what was happening in my own backyard, where I grew up in Sunset Park, Brooklyn. The same exact thing was happening. A billion-dollar complex called Industry City was coming in, with developers using a lot of the same tactics. The government once again was sanctioning *all of it.*

Ten years ago, Industry City was built. Warehouses that used to be garment factories, candy factories, shipping yard facilities, and all of that throughout the early 1900s, were mostly sitting idle after de-industrialization happened in the 1960s. Industry City came in and was like, "Oh, industrial waterfront! Let's make this an artist-maker space, because artists love that." Developers had put $1 billion into the project, but there was another component in 2019 to expand. They wanted to *rezone* so that they could actually build out *more* beyond the six buildings they have. They wanted to privatize the streets around them as well.

Right before COVID, I was invited to a community board meeting to show my interviews with residents of the Chinatown and the Latinx parts of Sunset Park about Industry City. The stories they shared and what they had in common was that these developers *are not here for us*. In 2020, there was a hearing about the rezoning. Everyone was like, "How are we going to have this hearing on Zoom? Who's going to come?" The Sunset Park organizers lined up folks to the point where it was *the longest recorded hearing in city council history*, a nine-hour hearing. It was mostly people who said, "No, you can't let them rezone!" Carlos Menchaca, the city council member, was flip-flopping. He was *pushed* to do the right thing. Otherwise, I don't know if he would have.

They defeated the rezoning. Industry City is still there, but it's huge that they stopped them from expanding, because their footprint already has caused so much damage. Industry City's been there for the last ten years. The amount of tenant harassment and evictions that have happened in that time has been massive! I will say that UPROSE, a group in Sunset Park, along with Sunset Park Not for Sale, and Protect Sunset Park, were a few of the groups and coalitions that really made it happen. I probably played a *very small* role in that, but I want to continue to document people's stories. Some people think, "Oh, it ended right?" But we know it's very complicated. Now they're trying to do "spot rezoning." The developers are trying to find little blocks here and there to build condos. That's happening all over Sunset Park. When they can't get a whole rezoning and one big, huge complex, they try to do spot rezoning. That's a tactic a lot of developers are using in neighborhoods like Sunset Park, because what they have to go through to get the permission for that is much more limited.

Museum Spaces as Sites for Organizing

I was very excited when Queens Museum reached out to me about being a part of an exhibition about home called, "After the Plaster Foundation, or, 'Where can we live?'" The museum is between Flushing and Corona, Queens, in a majority immigrant, working-class community. I really wanted to focus on what was happening in

Flushing, and the curators were super supportive of that. We had been supporting struggles that were happening there because rezoning and speculation had been going on for a while. The speculation accelerated, especially with all the money coming in from China. International, transnational, and domestic companies were investing in these huge behemoth condos and raising real estate values.

There was also an acceleration of organizing in 2019. Coalitions were forming to stop a plan backed by developers to rezone the waterfront. I had been in touch with some groups and knew MinKwon and one of their organizers, Seonae Byeon. Seonae used to be an organizer with CAAAV, and she moved over to MinKwon. I met with Seonae and a bunch of other organizers, as well as Bobby Nathan. Everyone knows Bobby—he's the unofficial people's mayor of Flushing. He's been in Flushing since the 1980s, and he was schooling me about a lot of the historically Black parts of Flushing, which I didn't know about, even before *he* got there. These were Black folks who were *already displaced*. Freed Black communities had formed in Queens and had lived there until the 1960s, when folks were pushed out.

I worked with MinKwon and wanted them to be able to use the piece I was filming for the exhibit as an organizing tool. I worked with them over a period of time, and they told me, "Yeah, it will be helpful to show the whole process of gentrification and how it is happening here." Bobby said, "Let's go into the buildings. Let's show what's happening, let's show how these landlords are making *minor adjustments* and saying that they're *huge adjustments* to get these capital improvement grants and then they can raise the rents. Yes, there was the rezoning that we have to fight, but you have to also see what's happening *day to day* with these tenants, with folks like me." Bobby, for instance, was at risk of being pushed out of his apartment, and he fought back. He was organizing in his building, and was like, "Yeah, I got displaced." I wanted to show that end of it as well.

I also really wanted to capture the multiracial aspect of the organizing. Ideally, I would have captured more stories from the South Asian community, and even from the African American community, especially in NYCHA housing. I could have done a better job, honestly, but COVID happened literally in the middle, and I had to patchwork what I had already filmed. I didn't have a time to do a lot of reshooting, just pickup shots and stuff like that. I did work with folks at MinKwon in terms of showing them the edits, but I literally stopped filming the day before shutdown.[47] I was like, "Fuck, OK. This is what I have." I grabbed like six or seven real estate magazines. I've never *seen* that many real estate magazines for one neighborhood, and I made a collage out of it. For a while we didn't know if the exhibit was going to happen at all, and then the curator said, "It's going to happen." It was a time of utter chaos. The show opened in the fall of 2020.

During COVID, it was really hard. Bobby doesn't have a cell phone, only a landline, and I could never reach him. I didn't really have a chance to check with him too much, and he got very sick with COVID. When I invited him to the show, he was like, "Yeah, I got really sick. I was incommunicado." But he was really happy with the piece, and I was super happy about that. I always want people to feel good about the work.

In an ideal world, the process would have been a lot more collaborative, but they began sharing the video a lot, as an organizing tool. Their suggestion was, "Let's put a time line out to show *exactly* the trajectory of this fight." We worked on the time line together, beginning with naming Queens and New York City Munsee Lenape land. It can never be said enough that as much as we do in the fight around housing justice or anti-gentrification or even immigrant rights work, we can never, *ever* forget the folks who are most disenfranchised. This is all Lenape land. The original Lenape homelands covered part of what is today known as New York City, Philadelphia, New Jersey, and part of the state of Delaware. Some Lenape are still here in New York. Most of them were forced west—to Oklahoma and Wisconsin. Saying "*This is all Lenape land*" is something I've made a practice of doing in my work as a collective with Chinatown Art Brigade, and in my own work as an artist. Saying it is always grounding.

I did the research for the time line with a bunch of other folks. Tarry Hum, who's a scholar and an amazing human, is the chair of the Urban Studies Department at Queens College. She does a lot of anti-gentrification work and helped with the time line. I made sure to check in with people who knew much more than me. The time line was a part of the exhibition and for MinKwon to use in their work.

Distinguishing Cultural Work and Organizing

People always say, "Oh, but you do organizing." I'm like, "Well, yeah, *cultural organizing*. I work with a lot of community groups." But I'm very clear. I have so much respect for on-the-ground community organizers, and that's not what I *do*. I *support* that. The word organizer gets thrown around so loosely. It's a huge pet peeve of mine. Maybe it's my age. Maybe I'm just old-school and I just have to get over it.

Sometimes I ponder the limits of *digital organizing*. You send out a big email blast and you're like, "Sign this petition," or you post something. I'm like, shit, that ain't no organizing. I've been challenged, and I get that that's a real tool. It's a catalyst for folks, but to what end? Are you changing hearts and minds? Are you doing consciousness raising? Are you bringing people together in a meaningful way? Or is it just like "click this" and you sign this, and you don't even have to see people face-to-face? *That isn't transformative organizing to me.* I have a very specific definition of organizing in my mind. It takes a lot. It's fucking hard work. That kind of organizing I have so much respect for. That's the kind of work I want to support through my cultural work. I want to be clear about my role, and be confident in it. I'm not like, "Oh, I didn't cut it as organizer." I just realized I wasn't the best at it, and it burned me out. I want to give support in a different way.

Imagining the World We Are Fighting For

Apex Art reached out to me about being a guest curator for a show. I was like, "Oh, wow! I've never done this before, but I would love to." Before COVID, my idea was to do something focused on *imaginings and futures*. Of course, now, during COVID, I think a lot of people feel that imagining a different world is essential, it's a lifeline. A lot of our organizing in housing justice and in other issues is frustrating. We know what we're *fighting against*. Obviously, folks are doing that day-to-day work, and I have so much respect for that. *But what are we fighting for?* What that meant for me was the flip of gentrification. What do we imagine to be an ideal future? What do we hope for? What does it *look like*? What does gentrification have to do with Defunding the Police? What does it have to do with capitalism? What does it have to do with all these things that we're fighting against? What does it look like on the other end?

I called the exhibit "Imagining De-Gentrified Futures." I always love opportunities to collaborate with other people or work with other artists who I really admire. I asked some artists whose work I really respect to collaborate with me on a manifesto I always had a vision of doing. I called it *Radical Housing Manifesto*. I wanted it to be a collection of people in New York and their visions of what that could be. I gave them a set of questions and wanted folks to picture what it would be like when we're on the other side. It was cool. Everyone interpreted it differently, and that was part of the exhibit as well. I also had my own work, which was imagining a de-gentrified future, starting with my own block in Sunset Park. Of course, that was also delayed because of COVID. There were seven months when I didn't know if it was going to happen, and then it happened in the fall of 2020. Everything happened at once. It kept me busy. There was just so much horrible shit happening in the world, at least I had something to focus on. I was really thankful to be distracted, in a good way. I worked on that at the same time as the Queens Museum project, so it was a little bit crazy.

Cultural Work as a Catalyst for Change

A big part of the work for me is the educational component. I sometimes get criticized for being too didactic, but I come from more of an organizing background. These pieces are tools for education and a catalyst for change. That's just what my work is. As a part of "Imagining De-Gentrified Futures," we held artist talks and we had folks do a reading. I invited Sam Stein, who wrote *Capital City*. Tarry Hum and Sam Stein's pieces about gentrification were also part of my Queens Museum Resource Guide. We read one of his chapters and we talked about it. That was really important for me to have that component. As a part of Queens Museum, we had an activist panel as well, where anti-gentrification organizers in Flushing talked about the work.

The only way it makes sense for me to do this work is to have a platform where people can learn about how they can get involved. The cultural work is just one end of it, maybe to pique people's interest, but the art has to be part of a larger organizing strategy. Although I'm not an organizer, I understand that. You can share this work and pique their interest. But then what? It's always important for me to have another component of the work where people can directly hear from people who are organizing, who are doing this work. Art plays a very limited role, but it can be meaningful if it's done in the right way.

There are a lot of artists out there who started out as socially engaged artists, and then they make it to another level and it's like, "Why the hell are you doing this? What's the point of this? Is it really about the community, or is it about yourself?" We all have egos. We all have to make a living. I get that. But never forget why you're actually doing this in the first place. I was offered to do something in Chinatown, and the money was coming from Margaret Chin's office in Chinatown, from the city council. I was like, "There's no way I'm doing that." Hell, even people I trusted, they were like, "Maybe you can use it as a way to subvert." I was like, "No, I can't do that. I can't. I can't do that." It's too close to the organizing, and her not being accountable to the community.

Combating Anti-Asian Hate in the Age of COVID

I started *We Were Here: Unmasking Yellow Peril*, during the pandemic. Through photography I was documenting how gentrification has impacted my parents. Then COVID happened, and I couldn't see them anymore, although we did some stuff over Zoom and Facetime.

The first anti-Asian hate incident was near Sunset Park. A man poured hot acid on a woman, burning her face. It happened not too far from where my parents live. That affected me deeply, and I was sitting with a lot of that. I had all these archives from my grandpa. He was an amateur photographer, a Chinese hand-laundry worker, an organizer, and a founder of one of the first organizations organizing Chinese workers, called the Chinese Hand Laundry Alliance of New York. I didn't find out about him or his life until the last ten years.

I had all these photo albums with me. That was when I started to see the obvious parallels between the exclusion of the past, what's happening now, the xenophobia, and the anti-Asian hate. The language is very similar, "yellow peril," "sick man of Asia." When COVID started, the *Wall Street Journal* wrote this disgusting article called "China Is the Real Sick Man of Asia." Those terms were used way back in the day by Germany and Europe when they were dividing up the parts of Asia they were going to try and take over. All these same exact terms came back! I did some deep diving into research about a lot of this. It hit me deeply because I realized that this is all my own personal family history. My great-grandfather coming to work in Nevada and not being able to stay because Chinatowns were being burned down. Chinese people were lynched on the West Coast. That affected me deeply. I used a lot of that early COVID time and created an interactive website around that.

That was the groundwork for the participatory project I did when we were finally able to see each other. I did a whole storytelling project, with a few events in Flushing, in particular. I interviewed folks about the anti-Asian hate crimes. I wanted to bring out the nuances, so I asked them about what they thought of police and the increased policing. I asked them about what the future would look like. What does community safety look like? People gave really beautiful answers, not cookie cutter, not the same. Some loved the cops, and some were like, "No, I don't know. I don't think they're going to keep us safe." Then I did a projection in Flushing of the stories.

This project is really meaningful to me, but it's also sensitive. I'm opposed to even saying "anti-Asian hate," because that has become synonymous with increased policing, which I'm against, and a lot of the folks I work with are against. The NYPD Asian Hate Crimes Task Force was launched, and at one point the streets of Chinatown were so militarized with cops. The narrative is that Asians love cops and that we just want the cops to be there to protect us from the boogeyman, whoever the boogeyman is.

Asian and Black Solidarity

This project has inspired me to bring out deeper histories of Asian and Black solidarity that go way back, even past the 1960s, to bring out histories of redlined communities and why Black and Asian communities often live side by side. There's a *reason* for that. The same with Latinx communities. I want to draw out those nuances in this project because the mainstream representation of the Asian community right now is very monolithic. People don't know that Chinese Americans are fighting the new jail plan in Chinatown. More of them are coming from an abolition perspective. There's a new wave of younger folks, way younger than me, who are really fired up and they have really great analysis and, wow, they have so much energy! So I want to tap into that, too.

People with new ideas give me hope. Even though I say, "Oh, you guys, the kids." I learn a lot from them. That's what gives me hope. My parents give me hope. I have to stay positive, because there was a very dark time there during COVID, but I'm trying to stay on the positive path. Otherwise, yeah, I'll just fall flat on my face and not do anything!

There's a balance. There's the anger and there's the passion, but then what keeps you going? Hope keeps me going. I'm not super old, but there are people who have completely left the work or are totally bitter. I get that. They're totally jaded, and I don't want to become that person, *at all*. I try to just learn from other folks and stay grounded. It's constant learning. The reason why I work on these projects that are filled with being in community, whether it's a community organization or community of individuals, is because I'm a lifelong student, a perpetual learner, and I absorb people's stories in a way that changes and that impacts me in a real way.

FIVE

Loretta Ross

✳✳

I had a chance to lean *into* a global discourse,
by constantly asking the question,
"Why aren't more women like me participating in it?"
It became very lonely to be the only person
who had this point of view,
racial identity,
and intersection of analyses.
My organizing was born out of a fierce determination
not to be the only one who looked like me,
thought like me,
experienced the same things I had experienced,
so that if I could have an impact on things,
I'd have more people to have an impact *with*.

Loretta Ross is an award-winning organizer, movement builder, educator, author, and innovator. Her work centers on the intersections of gender, race, and human rights, and has been particularly dedicated to end violence against women. Shaped in part by her own experiences as a single mother, Loretta has launched and co-founded groundbreaking organizations, coalitions, and formations with a Black feminist lens to ensure the inclusion of Black women in feminist leadership and organizing. She co-created the term and theory of reproductive justice, and her work includes anti-Klan organizing in which she presciently linked struggles against white supremacist ideology and organizations with the need to organize for gender justice and reproductive rights. Loretta currently teaches at Smith College in the Program for the Study of Women and Gender, and co-curated the college's Feminist Oral History Project. She is the author and editor of several articles and books. Her latest is Calling In the Calling Out Culture.

In her oral history, Loretta reflects on the relationships between gender equality, racism, and self-determination. She details her work to build collective power among women of color globally, including her own choice to stay in movements after her close friend and political comrade was assassinated and the organizations she worked in were subjected to political surveillance and repression. Loretta shares her analysis about the need for social justice movements to welcome folks in, and the need to educate in order to build relationships and solidarity while taking into account the life circumstances of all involved, particularly women of color. Loretta also shares her own experience as a survivor of rape and incest, and her ongoing work to heal from trauma.

She currently resides in Holyoke, Massachusetts.

I WAS BORN IN TEMPLE, TEXAS, DELIVERED BY A MIDWIFE at home, on a Sunday, August 16, 1953. I was the sixth child of eight, in a blended family. Mom had been married previously, so she had five kids by her first marriage. I was the first kid from her second marriage.

Dad was in the military. He was stationed at Fort Hood, Texas, and Temple is nearby. My dad was a hard-partying G.I., and my mama was a devout Christian woman. I always wondered how the hell they ever got together, because Dad never went to church, and Mom couldn't stay out of church! They stayed together until their death, but I always thought that they were a mismatched couple. Dad adopted my mother's children from her previous marriage, and we weren't ever allowed to treat each other as half-brothers and -sisters, even though they had a different last name. We became a fairly successfully blended family. Some families grew up playing Monopoly, but Dad taught card playing to all of his kids. That was our family activity. Mama thought it was a sin, so she never joined. I learned how to play competitive pinochle from my dad, and that's my hobby of choice. Prior to COVID, I used to travel around the country playing in pinochle tournaments.

Mom was a very complicated, loving person, but because she was a victim of childhood sexual abuse, she had huge problems with intimacy. She was abused by an uncle from age eight to sixteen. A local college had offered her a scholarship, but she turned it down because she would have had to remain living at home with that uncle in the house. So she chose to get married rather than go to college. She had told me herself about the childhood sexual abuse, but I didn't know about the college scholarship until she had died. It explains a lot about why my mother was such a frustrated scholar. She read all the time. Mom had eight kids in a three-bedroom house, and she still had a ton of books. I've always mourned the fact that she never got a chance to use that wonderfully inquisitive mind of hers and go to college. In a way, I felt she experienced it vicariously through me going to college.

My mom never hugged her children. Her fear of intimacy was so deep that what felt inexplicable to us growing up, became totally explainable once I understood more of her life's journey. Mom had no problems demonstrating love by how she cared for us and how she'd sacrifice anything for us, but physical intimacy was an issue. One of the things that makes me sad is that she never got any healing for her childhood sexual abuse. She told me when I was thirty-five that it happened to her, which made a lot of unexplained things fall into place. Lorene Dolores Burton was her maiden name.

One thing that is special about my family is that we have family genealogical records on my mother's side that go back to 1844, which is pretty remarkable for descendants of an enslaved family. Writing family names in Bibles and staying on the same land in central Texas since 1867 provided an intact lineage that was provable. As a result, I grew up with a deep sense of family knowledge and feeling of rootedness. Not many American families, Black or white, can say that. Even though we were always moving, I always knew that Temple, Texas, was the family seat, the family land. I've always thought that it was a privilege to have that much knowledge of one's family.

Dad's full name is Alexander Elijah Ross. He was born in 1918. When Dad was about sixteen years old, in the midst of the Depression, he dropped out of high school and joined the US Army. He stayed in the military for twenty-six years. We kept getting moved around, because he was a weapons specialist, and his job was to teach people how to use different guns and other weaponry. He loved to party and had lots of Army buddies and loved taking me to the Non Commissioned Officers Club, to show me off. I think he taught me how to play pinochle so that I could be a ringer and help him win bets on me—a nine- or ten-year-old girl who could kick these Army guys' asses. Dad loved that. Me and Dad were really, really close.

Awakening to Gender Inequality

Even though ours was a very patriarchal household, there were such sharp boundaries! Dad was responsible for everything from the garage on out, and Mama ruled the roost. Keeping Dad's ability to work was a high priority. Because he was first in the military, then he went to work for the Post Office, there were always uniforms involved. Guess whose job it was to wash and iron the uniforms and make sure they were crisp and clean every day? It was always the girls' job. The boys never had to do any of that! Whether it was cooking food, or getting his uniforms together, or doing the laundry or whatever it took, our job was to support that provider. I actually didn't resent that part of it. It was cooking for my asshole brothers that got on my nerves!

One day I was sick and couldn't go to school. My mother made me get up and fix breakfast for my brother, and I remember spitting in his eggs because he was fine! *I'm the one sick and you're well, and I'm getting up to cook for you?* I don't know how old I was at the time, but I know how mean I was. I think Mom got exhausted by raising eight kids. By the time we came along, she was through with cooking. Her job was to teach me and my older sister, Carol, how to do it. That probably increased my resentment because there was not a concomitant effort put into teaching the boys how to cook. Dad was my role model, not Mom. The life my mother envisioned for me was not the life I wanted. She thought that she had arrived at the pinnacle of success because she was a Black woman who was the only housewife in a neighborhood of thirty families. What Betty Friedan was running from, my mother was running towards! She thought it was the ultimate dream to be a housewife, to have credit cards, to have a husband bringing in the money. She couldn't fathom why neither Carol nor I wanted that lifestyle. I was filled with horror at the thought.

My baby sister, Toni, was born thirteen months after me, with a very compromised immunological system. Within six months of her birth, she contracted polio. Then she got muscular dystrophy and spinal meningitis, all before two years of age. Mom, who had been a domestic worker in the workforce, quit her job so that she could take care of Toni and she groomed me to take care of Toni when she no longer could do so. *Oh, hell to the no.* First of all, I resented being adultified at age three, that's a little early to constantly be told, "Well Loretta, you're going to do this when I can't do it anymore because Toni's going to need you." I just hardened my heart to that possibility. I thought I was going to do more than be Toni's forever caretaker. What a different life I would have had if I had followed my mother's script.

My sister Carol was my de facto mother, because once Toni was born, keeping her alive consumed all of my mother's time and attention. Toni was born in the military and remained Uncle Sam's dependent until she died! My mother failed to avail herself of all the resources that were available to her, because she was really invested in that martyrdom thing. Even as a child I saw something wrong with that and all I knew was that I wanted to escape.

My Sister Carol

I was four or five years old before I realized that my older sister Carol wasn't actually my mom! I used to walk around calling her Mom until she said, "Loretta, I'm not your mother, I'm your sister." But she *felt* like Mom to me all of my life. She died last year from breast cancer. When my son was born, she co-parented with me, so did Mom and Dad, too. When Mom was being obstinate over anything like consenting for me to get birth control or an abortion, Carol was there to step in the breach.

My sister Carol was the one who figured out that I had been raped at age eleven. Mom had started a Girl Scout troop for Black girls, because back in the 1950s we weren't allowed to join the white Girl Scout troop. We'd gone out to an amusement park, and I got separated from the troop, and this guy drove by in a car, and asked me if I wanted a ride to go find my troop. He had no intention of helping me. He took me into some woods and raped me. I was eleven years old. He was a GI, and I trusted GIs because that's what I'd been raised around.

After he raped me, he asked me where I lived and dropped me off at my street corner. I remember walking down the street and into the garage. Carol was in the garage, and she saw me. I had on these white, blue jeans with blood running down between my legs and leaves all in my hair. Carol took me into the shower and helped me clean up and everything. Mom didn't even notice. I think I walked right past her. I'm still wondering why she left me at the park. She brought all the other girls home, and I wasn't there. I don't know if Mom and Carol talked about the condition in which I came home, but nobody ever asked me where I'd been. How could a girl disappear from a Girl Scout outing and there's no uproar? That's a big fucking mystery to me. I suspect that Mom knew what happened, but she didn't have what it took to have that conversation. Carol and

I talked about it many years later, but not at the time. Carol wasn't going to talk about it until I was ready. Any trauma that happened to me, she waited until I was ready to talk about it, and then she was always there for me.

Motherhood at Fourteen and Choosing to Keep My Son

Mom was always a bit manic around anything that had to do with sex or sexuality. When I needed birth control, she was adamantly opposed. When my cousin got me pregnant, she thought I had enticed him. She was into blaming herself, and, of course, blaming me. I got pregnant the summer between ninth and tenth grade, by a cousin who used to ply me with alcohol so he could have sex with me. I didn't even have the sense to call it rape back then. I thought I was consenting. He was twenty-seven, and I was fourteen.

I was in tenth grade when I received an early admission and a scholarship to Radcliffe College. It was 1968, and the white colleges—particularly the elite ones—were desperate for the crème de la crème of the Black students because their financial arrangements depended on them having a certain percentage of students of color. My high school counselor at this predominantly white school I went to in San Antonio had graduated from Radcliffe, and she had recommended me for early admission and a full scholarship to Radcliffe. I should add that I was one of three Black kids in the honors class, what they call the AP class now. My family and I decided that the best way to handle the pregnancy was to place me in a Salvation Army home for unwed mothers.

It was like living on a prison compound. Back then it was very typical for young unwed women to go through pregnancy in secret, give their newborn baby up for adoption, and then melt back into their life like nothing untoward had happened. That was the plan, and I fully agreed with it. Parenting my cousin's baby at fourteen was not my idea of how to become a mother. I was the only Black girl at this home for unwed mothers. We slept in big dormitory-style rooms, a lot of cots, no privacy. The building was surrounded by these high, high walls with barbed-wire fencing. It was in San Antonio, way on the other side of town from where we lived. Basically, the message was, "If you follow our orders, and you do what we say, then you can go back to your life like nothing ever happened." I was all right with that script until they brought my son to me in the hospital. Then everything flipped.

My mother, because of her trauma, couldn't come to the hospital when I had the baby. She didn't show up at the hospital when I was in labor or anything. My sister Carol did, but not my mom. The only time my mom came to the hospital was when I refused to go through with the adoption. I became resentful that the only time she showed up was after I didn't follow orders. I had made up my mind before she showed up, but it kind of hardened my decision to keep my baby. My dad and my sister said to her, "You know, Lorene, that's Loretta's decision. You don't get to decide that for her." Of course, a week after I got home with the baby, my mother's fawning all over this kid like me being pregnant was her damn idea! Then I had to elbow her out of the way, "I'm the mother, not you!" My father had to intervene again, "That's not your baby, Lorene, that's Loretta's baby!"

Striking a Blow for Gender and Racial Equality

I was a good student, but the rest of my high school years were miserable. I had started the girls' drill team in the tenth grade. Before that, they had a boys' drill team, but they didn't have a girls' one. I guess that was my first blow for gender equality! Part of it, too, was racial. Because it was a predominantly white high school, no Black girls were *ever* going to make the cheerleading team. That just wasn't even within the realm of possibilities in the 1960s. Starting the drill team and insisting upon these elaborate routines with rifle stocks and dance steps meant that there was a place for the Black and the Mexican girls. I used to fiercely disqualify all the white girls who couldn't keep up with our dance steps. I keep saying maybe that was my early leadership, but I think it was my early establishing of a fiefdom that was run by women of color. The drill team was where we had *our thing*. There were white girls who tried out for it, but they didn't know our dance steps. I used my power inappropriately, not to teach them, but to disqualify them. "You can go try out for the cheerleading team. We can't try out for that, y'all go do that."

When I got back from having the baby, they told me I could no longer command the very drill team that I had started. I could lead them in practice, but not in competition. I had been a member of the national Junior Engineering Technical Society, but suddenly I was no longer qualified because I'd had a baby. I could no longer be in the honors club for AP students. My counselor, who had recommended me for Radcliffe, wrote them and told them I had a baby. Radcliffe wrote me back and said, "Well, somehow we've just run out of scholarship money. We can still let you in, but it'll cost you twelve thousand dollars a year." That foreclosed Radcliff for me. Then the mockery and gossiping of my classmates, the mean girls dumping on me. I wasn't the only girl that had gotten pregnant, *but I was the one that brought the baby home*. All I wanted to do was to graduate and go to college.

After Howard was born, I was poised between being a child and having adult responsibilities. I still wanted to go to prom. I still wanted to do the things that are typical of eleventh and twelfth grade of high school. Having a baby didn't mean I didn't want to do those high school things anymore. When I first came back to high school and had the reputation of having a baby, all the boys treated me like I was the next available slut that they wanted to fuck because I wasn't a virgin anymore. There was a lot of fending off of that. When my boyfriend Frank and I started dating in the eleventh grade, I felt relieved because he never treated me like the next available slut. We stayed together through the eleventh and twelfth grade and first year of college. He went to Annapolis, and I went to Howard University. We thought our relationship could endure that fifty-mile span. It didn't, but we still remain dear to each other to this day. Everybody thought Frank was Howard's father, which he wasn't. He played along with it, and to my son's death, everybody thought Frank was his dad. They enjoyed a great relationship the entirety of my son's life.

Howard University

I graduated at sixteen and went to Howard in September 1970 on a Greyhound bus with two hundred dollars. I thought that I needed to look a certain way to go to college. I actually purchased my first wig, trying to look like Diana Ross or something. My mother's cousin, Lois Hoyle, was a dressmaker, and she labored all summer to make me a whole wardrobe of tailored outfits that she thought were the proper thing for a girl to wear to college. I got to college, and nobody was wearing none of that shit! This was the nineteen-sixties and seventies. The hippie look was what was in. It was not at all what I imagined a college wardrobe would be. I retired those things to the back of my closet and pulled them out only for weddings and funerals.

Howard was a hotbed of Black student activism, radical ideas, and Black power in 1968. After the assassination of Dr. King there was a riot, and in 1969 students occupied the administration building for about a hundred days. The new college president, Dr. James Cheek, was the dashiki-wearing Black president with the Afro who was really a Black Republican. His job was to quash all the student protests. I remember attending a meeting my first year, and next thing I knew, I was voted vice president of the freshman class. I don't even remember running for the fucking office! I had a tendency, whenever I was in a meeting, to take notes. Quite often the fact that you had information meant that somebody thought you were leadership. *The Autobiography of Malcolm X* and *The Black Woman* by Toni Cade were more important to me than anything I was reading in those chemistry and physics textbooks. That's when my Black consciousness started to emerge.

My First Experience with Tear Gas

Howard University bought the Meridian Hill Hotel and converted it to a dormitory. That's where I lived, at 16th and Euclid Street. When a rebellion started happening along 16th Street where the dormitory was, the university locked the doors so no one could get in. When we went to the roof and saw the police shooting tear gas down in the street, we started pelting the police with whatever we had. Then they shot a tear gas canister up to the roof. The roof of the building was only six floors high. There were about one hundred people up there, all coughing and gasping, trying to escape down this narrow stairwell to get away from it. I felt so radical to be pelting the police with shit from the rooftop of my dormitory. That was my first experience with tear gas. Then it just took off after that. We felt wronged by the police and mad at the university for locking us into the dormitory. We were mouthy, outraged young people. Our favorite word back then was *relevant*. Everybody had to be *relevant*. The worst thing somebody would call you was *irrelevant*.

The beauty of Washington, D.C., was that we made a real sincere effort to close the "town and gown" gap. Part of it was geography. Our dormitory, Meridian Hill, was a mile from the campus. By definition, we were living *in community*. When you lived in Meridian Hill, you were hanging out at the park with all the community people right across the street. We renamed it Malcolm X Park. You were going to the grocery store in the neighborhood. Even though I was a college student at Howard University, the center of my social life wasn't *on* campus. I went to campus to go to classes, but my social life was in the city.

Gentrification, the D.C. Study Group, and the Citywide Coalition on Housing

I dropped out of college and moved into a studio apartment with my son at 1801 Clydesdale, down in Adams Morgan. I was working as a secretary and got home one night to a notice taped to our doors. The owner of the apartment building had ordered all of us to vacate within ninety days! This was regardless of whether we had leases or not, because they were converting the apartment complex to condominiums. It was ideally suited and overlooked the National Zoo. When we were in my bedroom we could actually hear the lions roar.

The only place big enough for us all to meet was the laundry room in the basement of the building. I went to find out what the hell was happening. I pulled out the pad, started taking notes, and the next thing I knew, I was tenant president. This was happening in two neighborhoods, Capitol Hill and Adams Morgan, because of their proximity to white Washington, D.C. I started investigating what we could do about it and heard about a group of people meeting at St. Philip's Church. I attended a meeting there and met other people undergoing similar evictions. This was 1973, during the early gentrification of the capital. Tenants were already involved in trying to pass D.C.'s rent control bill to stop these evictions, which eventually passed in 1974.

The organizing we were part of was the beginning of the Citywide Housing Coalition, a coalition of tenant groups who were facing these evictions. It was there that I met Dr. Jimmy Garrett, a professor at Howard University's political science department. He recruited us from the housing work, but he also worked with the Southern African Support Project and a prison abolition group. He started the D.C. Study Group as a Marxist-Leninist study group and was fired from Howard for being a Marxist-Leninist. Jimmy recruited college students, city residents, and all these other people to help form a housing movement against gentrification. We would meet every Sunday at Jimmy and his girlfriend Hope's house, and study Black theory, Black history, Marxist theory.

We were an all-Black group and one of several M-L groups in D.C. that included the Communist Party, the Communist Workers Party, the Socialist Workers Party, and other formations. We kept getting recruited by them because these other formations were all white and the thought of attracting Black M-L adherents was very attractive to them. But they were too damn sectarian for us, at least for me! I was like, "Y'all are fighting to death over dead white men, and you don't even have a good analysis of race and gender, so why the hell would we want to work with y'all?" Jimmy was pretty good at helping us understand the contradictions, which was one of our favorite words during all of this. We would work with all of them, but we wouldn't allow ourselves to get recruited by any of them.

Our Southern African Support Project grew into the Free South Africa Movement, which became fairly famous because a group of women left the D.C. Study Group, mainly because of Jimmy's sexual harassment. He didn't visit that on me, but he did on a lot of other people. Jimmy was in a live-in relationship with Hope, but that didn't stop him from sleeping with other women. There was a group of women who really didn't like that shit, and so they split off from the Study Group and formed the Southern African Support Community, renaming it the Free South Africa Movement. That's Imani Countess, Sylvia, and others, and they stayed very much involved in the anti-apartheid work after that.

The Assassination of Yulanda Ward

I met Yulanda Ward, a student of Dr. Jimmy Garrett, in 1979. It was the same year that I started working at the Rape Crisis Center. I invited her to join the board of the Rape Crisis Center, and she became vice president. Jimmy might have had a faculty adviser role, but Yulanda was our political leadership. She was twenty years old, and just so damn smart and profound. I think she was an emerging lesbian because she always dressed very butch, but I never quite knew her sexuality. Her gender seemed fluid, but we didn't have all these terms we have now. She was from Houston, Texas. After we had a meeting, she was the one leading discussions of what we were going to do next. She's the one that kept us organized, knew what meetings to go to, and what strategies we would implement. She was our lead organizer.[48]

Less than two years later—on November 2, 1980—she was assassinated. That really shook us up. I was naïve enough to think that the work that we were doing wasn't dangerous! We were the legal people. We did petitions and lobbying of City Hall. We didn't even go to City Hall meetings to shout and fight! The most outrageous thing we did was to have rallies in parks. The Black Liberation movement was active at the time, the Black Panther Party, the Assata Shakur stuff, the people who were doing armed struggle. But that's not who we were! We never thought we were particularly threatening to anybody. But our calculations were wrong.

D.C. was a party town, and I was a hard partier. Every Halloween, a friend of mine named Heavy Wheaton had a party at his house in southeast D.C. In 1980, I chose not to go because I wanted to stay with my boyfriend instead. I was in an open relationship, and another boyfriend, Ernest, came and knocked on the door and told me that Yulanda had been killed. That sent shock waves through us. We were trying to process why one woman with three men heading to a party got killed in a supposed robbery where nobody got robbed. They still had their wallets, their money, and their watches, including Yulanda. The police kept telling us that it was a drug deal gone bad. In the Citywide Housing Coalition, the only drug we used was marijuana, and Yulanda didn't smoke! The three guys who were with Yulanda when she was assassinated said that four men approached them and walked past them. They all spoke. Then the four men turned around, put guns to the back of their heads, and made them lay down on separate parked cars. The guys said that while their heads were down on the cars, they heard a shot ring out and the men ran. They looked up, and Yulanda was dead on the ground, a bullet to the back of the head. What the police were saying about a drug deal gone bad didn't make sense. The guys said the gunmen didn't ask them for money, or their wallets or anything. They murdered Yulanda and ran.

We formed the Yulanda Ward Memorial Fund in an attempt to find out what had happened to Yulanda. By calling it a political assassination, which most people didn't believe, we started analyzing all the things that had happened to us in the year preceding her killing. There had been twelve break-ins of the homes and offices of members of Citywide Housing Coalition. We thought nothing of it, because we lived in a Black neighborhood where these things happened. By the time we put together the twelve unrelated crimes that the six or seven of us had experienced, we saw a pattern. Then, Evelyn Queen,[49] who was the US attorney handling our case, started persistently demanding all the records of the Citywide Housing Coalition, all the records of the D.C. Rape Crisis Center, all the records of the Southern African Support Project. We kept asking, "Why are you investigating us? We didn't kill Yulanda! And no, we're not turning over confidential records of the D.C. Rape Crisis Center. You ever heard of the word confidentiality? We're not turning over all these rape survivor records to you. They didn't kill Yulanda!" The other thing that was suspicious was the waves of four Black men they kept arresting. They arrested three different groups of four Black men, accusing them all of having done the crime and then releasing them because they were all innocent.

The purpose of the Yulanda Ward Memorial Fund was to hire our own investigator. We ended up hiring this white boy, Brett, whose last name I cannot remember, but who was fairly well known as a movement investigator because he had investigated the case of Terrence Johnson. Terrence Johnson had been picked up on a traffic stop in Prince George's County, Maryland. While he was incarcerated, a police officer entered his cell. A scuffle ensued and Terrence ended up killing the cop with his own gun. Terrence got convicted of murdering a police officer. Brett investigated Terrence's case and eventually got Terrence cleared and released from prison. Unfortunately, Terrence committed suicide about ten years after he was released. He'd stayed in prison for so long it totally scarred his life. A young promising college student who had his life fucked up because of police brutality.

Brett, a white guy, started walking the streets of Black southeast D.C. He found one guy who said that he knew about the murders, but he hadn't participated in it. It turns out the guy was one of the four. When Brett revealed to the police who one of the four was, they ended up rounding up the other three and put them on trial for Yulanda's murder. All the way up to the trial, the men kept claiming they didn't do it. Meanwhile, the subpoenas for our records kept coming. Then Evelyn Queen served a warrant for our arrest at the D.C. Rape Crisis Center for refusing to cooperate with the grand jury. I wasn't there the day she showed up to serve the warrant but Hope Young and Nkenge were. While the grand jury was impaneled, they ended up going to jail for refusing to comply with the subpoena. Sweet Honey in the Rock did a benefit concert for us and helped raise a lot of money to pay for Brett's investigation.

Finally, the day of the trial arrived. We were all eager to go to court. By this time the Citywide Housing Coalition was falling apart. A lot of people became frightened and didn't want to do the work anymore. Several of us, though, myself included, were eager to go to court to find out *what the hell happened*. We wanted to know why Yulanda had been assassinated. Was it her prison work, was it her housing work, was it her work at the Rape Crisis Center? We did not know why Yulanda was killed! The day of the trial came, and we were suddenly told, "Oh, they all confessed last night. There will be no trial." Now, these guys went from nine months of saying they didn't do it, to suddenly confessing the night before the trial? Then we were told that they couldn't identify the suspects for us because of Yulanda's prison abolition work, that they needed to be incarcerated secretly around the country in the federal system so that none of the people Yulanda worked with could retaliate against them. You see how crazy all of this shit sounds, but the experience of COINTEL-PRO was fresh for many of us organizing at that time.

Choosing to Stay in the Movement

I had met Nkenge Touré through Citywide; she's the one who recruited me to the Rape Crisis Center. It was my first paid movement job. I remember when Nkenge asked me to come to the Center. I told her, "I don't want to go work with those white women." She said, "Stop. Would I lead you wrong?" I was intimidated by her being in the Black Panthers. I felt like a dilettante. Nkenge and I had been through all of this at the Rape Crisis Center and had become really good friends by that time. The board of the Rape Crisis Center was agitated and nervous because they didn't like the warrants, subpoenas, attention, and demand for the Rape Crisis Center records. Some members of the board said that we needed to cooperate with the police. The rest of us said, *Hell no!* I had to decide whether I was going to go forward with this work or do something else with my life, because I was scared. I was a single mother with a seven-year-old child to raise. I decided to go forward, but it was *a decision*. It was no longer just going where life and circumstances led me. It was an active decision after Yulanda got killed.

The Dalkon Shield and Sterile at Twenty-Three

My personal life was also complicated. In 1971, while still a student at Howard University, I had an abortion and had accepted implantation of the Dalkon Shield.[50] By 1973, it had exploded my fallopian tubes. That led to a full hysterectomy in 1976, and in 1979 I won a lawsuit. I was twenty-three years old and sterile. That complicated my relationships. I was already a single parent and carrying the baggage of an existing child as well as the baggage of being sterile. For a long time afterwards, I wouldn't even date men. I was so traumatized and alienated. Right after the hysterectomy, my first two relationships were with women.

My first relationship with a man after that was with Ernest Patterson, and we stayed together for twelve years. My son has had several fathers in his life but never his real one. The men that I've had quality relationships with have all managed to play very significant roles in his life. They were all at his funeral.

Building a National and Global Movement of Women of Color

In 1980, Deidre, the counseling director at the D.C. Rape Crisis Center, Nkenge, and I organized the first National Conference of Third World Women and Violence. It was Deidre's idea and was the first national meeting of women of color who worked in the anti-rape, anti-domestic-violence, and anti-street-harassment movement. We were all doing little pockets of work across the country but had never congregated together. Nineteen-eighty was pretty seminal in terms of building that movement of women of color. This may be an overstatement, but I like to think that we were the foremothers of INCITE! Women of Color Against Violence Against Women, twenty years later. Many of the relationships that I have now with women of color feminists we developed in 1980. Nkenge and I did a lot of organizing together around the UN World Decade for Women, including attending conferences in Copenhagen, Nairobi, and Beijing. I didn't get to Mexico City, but mobilizing Black women to participate in international fora was what we did.

The United Nations declared 1975 to be the first International Year of the Woman, "to remind the international community that discrimination against women continues to be a persistent problem in much of the world" and held a conference in Mexico City to organize around those themes. At that conference, activists pressured the United Nations to develop a World Decade for Women. The UN agreed and planned to commemorate it with conferences every five years from 1975 to 1990. Mexico City was the first, in '75. The next conferences were to take place in Copenhagen in 1980, Nairobi in 1985, and then Beijing in 1990. Those were the four world conferences for women that took place. I was lucky enough to get to the 1980 one, and the reason is that I had just gotten my settlement for the Dalkon shield lawsuit. That allowed me not only to go to Copenhagen, but also to fund other women to go with me.

The phrase "Zionism is racism" was included in the document that emerged at the conclusion of the first conference in 1975. As a result, there was a real risk that the entire World Decade for Women would be deemed anti-Semitic. One of the ways that our organizing was affected was that every time we'd try to get together, the whole question of Palestine and Israel kept erupting and overturning meetings. "If you don't support Israel, you're anti-Semitic, therefore the feminist movement is anti-Semitic," was a persistent line we had to deal with. It just got to be a big fucking mess. By the time we got to the planning meeting at the American Association of University

Women about what was going to happen at the Nairobi conference, an agreement was reached that no one would mention Israel or Palestinians at this planning meeting.

But wouldn't Bella Abzug use her opportunity on the damn stage to break the agreement? "We've got to support the right of Israel to exist and not let these terrorists take over." So here I am, Loretta Ross, taking on Bella Abzug from the crowd. "Bella, I thought we weren't talking about this shit. You can't use your platform from the stage to violate the agreement. Because if we're going to talk about Israel we need some Palestinian women in the room, and since we don't have any Palestinian women in the room, you need to shut the fuck up." I didn't say it quite that baldly, but that's the gist of what I conveyed. It was wrong what Bella was doing. You don't get to use your privilege and platform to violate the agreement and misrepresent all that we had achieved to that point.

In Copenhagen for the Second World Conference on Women in 1980, the struggle against apartheid was still going on in South Africa, and South Africa had sent an all-white delegation to Copenhagen. There was a furious debate about seating the all-white delegation of women from South Africa. African women from the continent were protesting, and of course as a Black African American woman, I joined them. What disappointed me was that the United States government had funded the US delegation to go to Copenhagen, and the only Black people on the delegation were from the National Council of Negro Women, a well-respected organization, Dorothy Height's organization. They wouldn't join us in protesting the seating of the all-white South African delegation. It felt very lonely challenging the National Council of Negro Women, the premier Black women's organization, whose representatives were on the official US delegation. I felt that their timidity was not well representing Black women in the US or how we felt about apartheid. It felt like I was being disrespectful or naïve criticizing our best representatives.

I left Copenhagen determined that there was going to be a much more diverse set of Black women at the next damn conference in Nairobi in five years, and I was going to organize to get as many Black women there as possible. I told myself, "I ain't gonna be here by myself next time!" I needed some allies in these global discussions. There is a radical Black women's perspective that was not being represented in these global discourses. As I get older, I'm getting clearer on my motives, and they aren't always so altruistic. There is need and vulnerability that also drive it. I was also being exposed to other global struggles at these conferences and learned about the East Timorese women's issues for the first time in Copenhagen, for example, and what was going on in the Philippines with the Marcos dictatorship, and what was going on in Nicaragua with the Contras. There was just so much you learned by being in dialog with global feminists that you didn't have easy access to here in the United States. My whole framework became globalized after Copenhagen.

The International Council of African Women

Nkenge and I formed the International Council of African Women once I got back from Copenhagen, and we spent the next five years organizing Black women to go to Nairobi for the 1985 conference. Eleven hundred Black women went, and we like to think we had some small impact on that. We didn't organize all eleven hundred women, but we spent five years spreading the information, identifying funding, challenging funders for not sending women of color to represent the US internationally, so that it was mostly white women going, which gave a partial view of what US feminism looked like. That's what the organizing was like. You're holding pre-conference meetings and gatherings with people so that they can understand the issues that are involved. You visit the UN so that you can participate in the conversations there and get the necessary credentials and clearances. Many of the NGOs or non-governmental organizations working on women's rights were headquartered at 777 UN Plaza, so we spent a lot of time there. We worked with different churches to raise money and tried to get cities to form their own delegations. We produced a lot of guides: "How do you organize your family to support your first international trip? How do you have local fundraisers? What can you sell that you can let go of?" Or "How can you write your first proposal to a foundation? Can you use another nonprofit as a fiduciary agent so you can get the grant?" I mean, it was do whatever you can do, including selling pussy, to get there. For about twenty years, I organized women of color to go to these global gatherings.

The Origins of the Term Women of Color

President Carter gave five million dollars for the US Conference on Women in 1977. I was not at that conference, nor the Mexico City conference, but a lot of older Black women that I worked with were at that 1977 conference. These Black women were dissatisfied with the plan of action that the majority-white delegation of women had put together, and which they were planning on taking to Copenhagen. They had two or three pages of what they called "minority women's issues." A group of older Black women, some of whom had worked with Dorothy Height and Mary McLeod Bethune, prepared a document called the Black Women's Agenda. They wanted the delegates at the Houston conference to vote to substitute it for the minority women's plank that Ellie Smeal and Bella and all of them had put together. When they got to Houston with this Black Women's Agenda, other minority women wanted to be included. Obviously, if they included Latinas and Asian Americans and Native Americans, it was no longer the Black Women's Agenda. It was in those negotiations that they developed the term Women of Color, and it became the Women of Color Agenda. It got unanimously passed by the delegates at the conference. Coretta Scott King actually read it out loud. Gloria Steinem was the one that told me that Coretta had read it.

I was doing a training in Seattle somewhere and somebody said, "I don't like the term women of color, that ain't me." I said, "Do you know where the term came from?" So I gave her this history. I did not create that term, but I love the way that they defined it as a statement of solidarity, not identity. You're born Black or Native American or whatever you're born, African American, Asian, whatever. But when you choose to stand in solidarity with other oppressed women, you are a woman of color. A lot of people think it's the biological designation when in fact it's a political designation.

I was a beneficiary of the times. When the UN held the First World Conference for Women in 1975, and then declared the Decade for Women in 1976, that coincided with an activist growth spurt for me. I'm certainly not responsible that more of the world's attention was directed towards women's issues. That was the context in which I had a chance to lean *into* a global discourse by constantly asking the question "Why aren't more women like me participating in it?" It became very lonely to be the only person who had this point of view, racial identity, and intersection of analyses. My organizing was born out of a fierce determination not to be the only one who looked like me, thought like me, experienced the same things I had experienced, so that if I could have an impact on things, I'd have more people to have an impact *with*.

The NOW Years

Donna Brazile was my roommate in Nairobi. I had spent close to five years organizing Black women to go to Nairobi. I was chatting one night with Donna and telling her I didn't have a job to support myself. I am a fast typist and supported myself by typing people's theses and dissertations to keep the money flowing while I did my organizing. She suggested I go to NOW and see if there were any opportunities there.

I worked my way into a job with NOW by pointing out what I thought in terms of organizing women of color and how NOW could benefit from that. Ellie Smeal was the president, Molly Yard was the political director, and NOW was the premier feminist organization in America. I didn't know anything about hardball politics, dealing extensively with Congress, being on a first-name basis with the Speakers of the House, and all those kinds of things. What I also learned, much to my surprise, was what a long history NOW had of engaging with women of color. I learned about Pauli Murray, who co-wrote NOW's Statement of Purpose. I learned about Eileen Hernandez, who had resigned in protest, calling NOW a racist organization. I learned that NOW had a revolving door. It had no problem attracting women of color, it had problems keeping them! Typically, white-led organizations have a desire to diversify and piss-poor-ass skills in actually doing it, because they don't address those internal practices and habits that keep all new people disempowered, not just women of color. Power is hoarded, information is weaponized. There's a scarcity mindset where people believe if they share what they have, they're going to lose something.

NOW has a culture that replicates the patriarchy that it's trying to overthrow. It's somewhat intentional, because it's grooming women to participate in power politics. One example of replicating the patriarchy was that we would work hard all day, and quite routinely the inner circle would go out after work and have drinks together. They would unfailingly invite me to those after-hours settings. It wasn't a matter of feeling uninvited or that they were secret or anything, but going out with them ran up against some structural barriers in my life.

I was a single mom and was getting home entirely too late for parenting a ten-year-old, much less staying out until ten or eleven every night in order to participate in the highest level of decision-making. I think that men have, for the most part, other people to take care of their home responsibilities that quite often single mothers don't have. My colleagues didn't see it as a problem until I pointed it out to them. That's what I mean by replicating those *systems* of the patriarchy. Many important discussions and decisions were made in those after-hours gatherings over cocktails or when they went golfing together or to Sweet Honey in the Rock concerts together, and it created barriers *structurally* that were not intentional on their part, but still had that impact of excluding people who couldn't do it that way. Why is it almost a de facto requirement of being a feminist leader to work sixteen hours, eighteen hours a day? How does it have a disparate effect on people who can't do that? It means that we're not at the seats of power, we're being impacted by decisions that we're not participating in making.

If you're Black and you don't have a clear enough analysis, it feels like racism. If you're queer, it feels like homophobia. But in fact, it may be based on structures and habits that people haven't interrogated or thought about. I learned that at NOW. I learned that because it was so hard as a young feminist to distinguish the normal brutality that white women treated each other with versus that directed at me! I'd say, "Was this racism or them just being white?" I had to sharpen my power of discernment so that I wasn't overreacting to things that weren't even about race. The habit of making midnight decisions wasn't even about race! But it had *the effect* of leaving all the divergent staff out of it. If you can't be at those networking and information-sharing opportunities, then you miss out on things.

Depending on what your background is, your identity and triggers are, you may misinterpret what's actually going on, and you can't fix something with a bad diagnosis.[51]

The Center for Democratic Renewal

I went into activism through the portal of feminism rather than race. Race was always an issue within feminism, but my grounding in how I saw the world always had a very strong gender lens, because my first work was in the anti-rape movement. My job at the Center for Democratic Renewal (CDR) was my first real interaction with the civil rights movement *in a formal way*. I had known of the civil rights movement and partnered with them in several things, but I hadn't been a witness to their inner workings.

I'm always surprised when I find out new information that's hidden in plain sight. The civil rights movement was lovingly patriarchal as opposed to harshly patriarchal, unlike the radical Black movement of which I'd also been a part. Customs that are *cultural*, like, if two men and two women ride in a car together, the default was for the two men to sit up front and talk to each other, and the two women would sit in the back and talk to each other. That was the cultural default, just like it was a cultural default that if the woman did all the cooking, she'd still fix the guys' plates before she fixed her own. Cultural defaults that I grew up with but didn't interrogate weren't made visible to me in many ways until I went into the civil rights movement. I learned that the people who were monitoring hate groups didn't include a *gender component*. There were a few people, like Jean Hardisty, Suzanne Pharr, and Mab Segrest, who talked about how the walls between the far right and the anti-abortion movement were so porous as to be nonexistent, but that was not a dominant narrative at the time.

The sacrifices that people made for justice only became clear to me in the civil rights movement when I did that work. Of course, I'd heard about the assassination of Martin Luther King Jr. and the obvious headline kind of stuff. *But how routine the sacrifices were!* For instance, in Blakely, Georgia, we were called in to investigate how the fire department was run by a chief who was in the Ku Klux Klan. A Black child had died at a house fire after the fire department, which was only two blocks away, delayed responding because the family was Black. It was so routine! That horror and those sacrifices don't make national newspaper headlines but are as customary as women experiencing rape and domestic violence. Seeing that up front and close brought the struggle around racial justice to an urgency and immediacy that I hadn't felt before I worked at CDR. I felt urgent and immediate about domestic violence, rape, sexual assault, and gender discrimination and all of that, but I was too young to have sat at segregated lunch counters. I had an intellectual analysis around racial justice, but not a visceral one. The kinds of very routine calls we got at CDR weren't visible to me until I did that kind of work, and remained invisible to the majority of Americans who were not on those very quiet front lines.

From Civil Rights to Human Rights

I am constantly surprised by what I don't know, and when I find I don't know something I always assume that others don't know it either. When Reverend Vivian told me that Dr. King meant to build a *human rights* movement, not just a civil rights movement, I was shocked! How could have I, considering myself a "woke" person, to use today's term, not have known that?! That's when C. T., Shulamith Koenig, Abdullahi An-Na'im, and I formed the National Center for Human Rights Education. My first response was, we've got to tell people about this, because if I don't know, millions of people don't know either.

People can't change the circumstances that they don't know about, and people can't fight for rights they don't know they have! They need to know that they are entitled to these things. It's kind of like teaching slaves to read. You don't know what they're going to do with the knowledge, but you're damn glad you did it. That's how I see education. I don't know what people do with the knowledge I'm privileged to share with them, but I never regret having shared it. I never regret that I'm compelled to help people know how to analyze the circumstances of their lives so that they can take action or not. Sometimes people don't want to take action, but I know they can't act if they don't know.

SisterSong

Prior to the formation of SisterSong, there had been four attempts to organize a national coalition of women of color to work on reproductive health and rights issues. Those attempts failed for various reasons, but the thing that they had in common was lack of funding. We call Luz Rodriguez the mother of SisterSong because her vision caused SisterSong to develop, and the things that she put in place are why it's still around. At the time, SisterSong's structure had a representational matrix where four Black, four Native American, four Asian American, and four Asian Pacific Islander women's organizations were represented. When Luz was no longer representing the Latina Roundtable for Reproductive Rights, the Latina caucus basically kicked her to the curb, and that's how she got almost forgotten, not because of anything she had actually done or not done. When I became national coordinator I intentionally sought to bring Luz back into the fold. She's the reason we're here! We created a modified federation structure where individuals could join SisterSong, because there are more women of color *not in organizations* than are in organizations. That structural change meant I was able to bring Luz back into the fold. I have nothing but praise and love for Luz because she was gracious and all of that, but I imagine how it had to hurt, to be exiled from your own creation. A lot of people mistakenly think I'm the founder of SisterSong because I was the most visible person for a number of years, when in fact it was Luz. I just had a chance to grow her baby up.

White Supremacy in the Age of Trump

I didn't go back to college until I was forty-eight years old and graduated with a bachelor's degree in 2007, when I was fifty-five. A friend of mine, Marlene Gerber Freed, was going on sabbatical from Hampshire College and asked if I would substitute for her. She knew I loved to teach because she and I had co-written the book *Undivided Rights: Women of Color Organize for Reproductive Justice*. I never imagined that such an opportunity would come my way without a PhD. As a matter of fact, that's why I had enrolled in a PhD program at Emory, because I wanted to teach. I leapt at the opportunity and went to Hampshire.

That was 2016, the year Trump came down that golden escalator. It occurred to me that I could teach about reproductive justice, but it was white supremacy and fascism I really need to think about in that historical moment, especially with the experience at CDR doing anti-fascist work. I conceptualized—and continue to teach to this day—a course called White Supremacy in the Age of Trump. That was about the same time that I began to use social media. My grandson somehow never could answer the telephone. He finally said, "Well, Grandma, if you want to talk to me, get on Facebook." So I signed up for an account.

On Facebook, I noticed how mean people were being to each other! They post something and then there's all these reactions to it. A woman who worked at Planned Parenthood, a young Asian American woman, Marissa Graciosa, and I were organizing a program to honor Gloria Steinem and Wilma Mankiller at Smith. I asked Marissa about this, and she said, "Oh, you mean the call-outs?" My immediate reaction was, "This has gone on so much that y'all even have a name for it!?" I wanted to know what was being done about it! I felt that we're never going to defeat fascism when we're behaving like this with each other! I was not on faculty at Smith yet. I was actually in the middle of a writing fellowship at Mount Holyoke College at the Five College Women's Studies Research Center, writing the next two *Reproductive Justice* books: the book I wrote with Ricki, *Reproductive Justice: An Introduction*; and *Radical Reproductive Justice* with Lynn Roberts and Erika Derkas, Whitney Peoples, and Pamela Bridgewater Toure.[52]

I asked the president of Smith for money to organize a forum for students to talk about the "call-out" culture and what they wanted to do about it. Kathleen gave me $20,000, which wasn't a lot of money, but it was enough to organize one hundred students and feed them and hire a facilitator for them to talk about call-out culture. I've been working on it ever since, analyzing its prevalence and the fact that every piece of literature I read about it has no solutions to offer! I've learned some things I'd like to share. It wasn't that we didn't fight back in the women's movement in the 1970s. We'd call it "trashing." From my experiences at NOW, I learned how to discern threats, routine neglect, and intentional racism. I felt that those kinds of experiences could add value to understanding what "call-out" culture is and how to shift people away from exclusion and negativity and toward inclusion and affirmation.

Howard

In 2016 my son Howard died of a heart attack. That was traumatic, to say the least, and I put the "calling-out/calling-in" work aside. I didn't write for a couple of years because I was just devastated. That was the worst pain I'd ever experienced in my life, without a doubt. Howard had moved away from home to go college when he was eighteen. We never lived together again. His mature adult development took place in Texas while I was living in Georgia. Other than me flying home for visits, I didn't really get a chance to see the fullness of his development. Howard turned out to be a great man. He was forty-seven when he died. I didn't even realize how great he was until his funeral and the testimonials that people kept offering about the ways that he had had an impact on their lives. I was astonished by what I learned about my son at his funeral, which probably doesn't speak well of me. He had become an engineer, and I knew that he tutored kids in math and science to help them graduate, but the kids coming up and testifying about what an impact he'd had on their lives, it was just amazing.

Strangers kept walking up to me at his funeral, about three of them, telling me they were my son's brothers, and sisters. *I was like, what?* My son was an only child! But apparently, my son had painstakingly found out who his half-brothers and sisters were and had bonded them into a family. He'd never told me because he knew it would hurt me to know that his pedophile father was actually a serial pedophile. He had made two other fourteen-year-olds pregnant and was married at the time with three kids. My son had a whole bevy of half-brothers and half-sisters that he sought out because he hated being an only child. Unbeknownst to me, he formed family outside of me. He would go to their weddings and their family reunions and all kinds of activities. They all came to me at his funeral and told me about the twenty years that he had with them that he never disclosed to me. He turned out to be a special guy.

Learning Self-Care

I'm still that traumatized fourteen-year-old. I'm just getting better and better at managing. Self-care is not my default, but I'm getting better at it. If there's anything that I've observed about my life story, it is about resisting those imprinted patterns of self-doubt, negativity, and feelings of undeservingness. Trauma lingers in your heart and soul. Healing is not an event you just arrive at, and it's done. It's a process. As I walked back from the brink of suicide with therapeutic help, I had to recognize that passive suicide is part of my pattern. It never actually goes away. It's a daily struggle to *choose* whether to be better at taking care of myself. A daily struggle to *choose* whether to live or listen to that inner narrative that was branded in my heart or to make different choices. We all have our different paths and journeys, but the significance of what I do is always framed by knowing that what I went through at fourteen should not happen to another child. I can see its long-lasting impact. I can see the external conditions that caused it to happen, that allowed it to happen.

Most of all, I could see the impact on my son, because every child deserves unconditional love from his mother, and he never had that. I loved him, but I hated his circumstances. The more he grew to resemble his father, the more tested I was to stay in the role of his mother and not have it as a constant reminder of my pain. We had a fraught relationship, and we worked really hard to love each other—really, really hard. He knew from the beginning that keeping him was my choice. He knew he had narrowly escaped adoption. Whatever insecurity I had implanted in him, I wanted him to be clear that I kept him because I wanted to. I wanted him to know that whatever hard times we might face, we went through this shit together.

I love going on right-wing talk shows, though I don't do it as much as I used to. When they talk about victims of rape just giving the baby up for adoption, I drive my story right into that bullshit narrative because *I've got the lived experience your ass can only theorize about.* They never invite me back because I win their audiences away from them. In that way, my son Howard continues to give and serve.

Calling-In

In 2018, I started working on my manuscript again, and discovered the writing of Ngọc Loan Trân.[53] Loan was the first person I encountered talking about "calling-in." I seized upon it, knowing that we can build a movement on this. I kept working on my manuscript. Then COVID happened. I was on the faculty at Smith, and a friend

144

asked me if she could get a copy of the syllabus for my course on White Supremacy in the Age of Trump. She put it online, and the next thing I know, I get overwhelmed with requests from people wanting to take the course online. I responded saying, "Well, I'll do it if you help me, because I don't know how to do anything with technology." It was the first one I offered online. I announced on my Facebook page that I'd be doing the online course and within forty-eight hours, five hundred people had signed up. It was two weeks after George Floyd was murdered, which I'm convinced was driving it because we had a country that was wanting to know what the hell to do about white supremacy. I had "calling-in" as one of the modules.

People really gravitated towards the "calling-in" piece. In September 2020, I started offering an online "calling-in" lecture series, and now I'm in the sixth one. We've got two hundred to three hundred people registered every Tuesday night that come to learn about calling-in techniques. I offered the courses for five dollars a lecture because I wanted to do popular education and make it very accessible to people. I figured five dollars is a low enough bar that a lot of people can access it. When I did the "calling-in" class in September, there was a woman who was friends with Jessica Bennett at the *New York Times*. She told Jessica, "You need to check out what this woman is doing with this 'calling-in' stuff." So Jessica contacted me and asked if she could watch me teach the techniques. There are student privacy issues raised by having a reporter watch them in class, but we worked through the bureaucracy. Jessica's story ran in the *Times* in November 2020. When it did, I was immediately besieged by offers from literary agents and publishers. Simon & Schuster won a bidding war with an offer that included an advance that was well over a million dollars! I'm calling the book *Calling In the Calling Out Culture: Detoxing Our Movement*. When I decided to make that class cost only five dollars, I had no idea how it would lead to a million-dollar publishing deal. That was not my plan, but it proved what I believe in my heart, that when you serve your people, all your dreams will come true.

I just bought my second home up here in Holyoke, and in the same period, Smith gave me tenure after only being here two years and only with a bachelor's degree! I mean, really!? But Smith's president wants the college to be a nucleus for fighting white supremacy and "calling-in." She's one of these liberal white women that's scared of saying the wrong thing and putting her foot in her mouth because she does all the time. But at the same time, she's not letting her fears stop her. I really admire her for that, because not a lot of people stand up despite being afraid.

Creating a Mutual Support Network

The first thing I did when I accepted the Simon and Schuster offer was hire a financial planner, because you shouldn't get major checks and still end up robbing Peter to pay Paul. The last check I got for $100,000 was to be the co-director of the March for Women's Lives. I didn't even cash the damn thing. I just countersigned it over to my organization. I'm not regretting that I did, but at the same time, I'm like, "Loretta, at what point are you going to admit that you don't have a retirement plan? Yeah, you're going to be one of those poor people on Social Security that have to work at Wal-Mart if you don't watch out." I made a commitment to myself that if I ever got handed a bunch of money again, I was going to be smarter about it.

The only thing that I truly squander money on is books and music. I'm like the Imelda Marcos of libraries, because I have three of them in my house and I can't seem to stop buying more books. The other thing I do is give money away. I feel guilty because I'm in such a privileged position in relationship to people I love, and I'm talking about other women in the movement. There's a lot of people in the movement who have done work for years who didn't have big checks written to them. So we're a mutual support network. I feel privileged to be in a position to be able to effortlessly help a lot of people. I'm having a ball. I never thought I would be in this position, but it's a great place to be. You know, there's a song by Taj Mahal: "I'm just waiting for the world to change." So just keep on doing the work, waiting for the world to change.

SIX

Terese Howard

⁂

If you're sitting on a piece of cardboard,
if you're covering yourself with a blanket
or anything, you're breaking the law.
I felt very responsible to fight that.
That was really when I dove in headfirst
to fight the camping ban from passing.
I started to organize with the folks at the encampment,
bringing folks to different city meetings
and getting more aware of the
homeless-industrial complex
and what was going on.

Terese Howard is an organizer and educator who has been organizing with houseless people for civil and human rights since 2011. Raised largely "off the grid" in rural Colorado, she grew up unschooled, developed an interest in philosophy early on, and began organizing when her college shifted to a conservative Christian culture. While still a student, she was arrested protesting Columbus Day in Denver, moved off campus into a collective house, and established the Free School Denver. She became involved in Denver's Occupy movement at its onset, and is a founder of Denver Homeless Out Loud (DHOL), which was founded to defend the rights of people without housing who are targeted by the police. In 2022 she founded a new organization, Housekeys Action Network Denver, focused on organizing with homeless folks to guarantee housing for all.

Terese describes the anarchist values that inform her organizing and her life: mutual aid, the sharing of resources, solidarity, the need to create horizontal structures within movement, and recognizing that we are in relationship with one another and the planet. Her reflections on her work reveal a methodology based on the significance of relationships, particularly within the context of organizing with unhoused folks, and the need to build solidarity and skills across organizations and movement.

Terese currently lives in Denver.

I WAS BORN IN 1985 IN SPOKANE, WASHINGTON. IT WAS ME, my sister Claire, and my parents, Evan and Cheri. My sister Claire is two years older. We lived in Spokane first, and then when I was age six to ten, San Francisco. We moved to Montrose, Colorado, when I was ten. Montrose is a smallish town in western Colorado. My family is Christian. I no longer identify with Christianity, but it was a part of our life to practice Christian spirituality.

My parents are strong believers in unschooling, a version of homeschooling based on the ability to learn through living,[54] with a lot of autonomy and self-direction from the kids. My sister and I grew up with that educational background, which I really value a lot. Of course, there are different things I have weaknesses in, because I didn't get very good at math and am not very speedy at tests. But I think it was a really great way to go through childhood and on-ward—feeling empowered to do what you believe in, make it happen, and take initiative.

Through church, gymnastics, homeschool group activities, and all the different things we were doing with the community, I had a lot of power to get shit done. If I said to my parents that I thought something could be done differently, their response would be, "Cool! Well, let's make it happen." Then my parents would help facilitate an environment that enabled me to make that happen. I would take the initiative to make my own classes, organize the people, and stuff like that. I was really lucky to have an incredible family.

My parents' philosophy of education and child-rearing came from a few different kinds of foundational beliefs, including that children are *real people* who have innate wisdom and things to contribute. They valued creativity and questioning authority, and not just going to a school where you would be told what to do without questioning things. We lived with very little money. My parents made an intentional trade-off of time for money so that they could be more present, and we'd have more freedom to do the things that we believed in. It also came from some of my parents' upbringing, and definitely a lot of privilege was involved. My parents both came from white, middle-class families, and they both had really good educations and certain safety nets to fall back on. Some of those privileges are definitely a big part of what I think made it easier for our family.

Growing Up Off the Grid

We were living pretty much off the grid, more like living in the 1800s than the present. For example, we didn't have a washer and dryer. My mom didn't like those kinds of technologies. She didn't feel they were appropriate, so we did laundry by hand. We had two big buckets and this thing we called the "coocha-coocha," a little plunger-type thing that you shake the laundry up with. One time, we saw one of those at a museum from the 1800s. A lot of the stuff around my parents' house where we grew up was intentionally low-tech, hand-cranked, and simple, like a composting toilet. There was a lot of environmental consciousness there, and a different pace of life.

We grew up with very little money, and it was an intentional commitment by my parents when they got married to live under the poverty level. My parents wanted to live in a way that gave them more time. So, my mom didn't work in a *paid job*, since she worked caring for my sister and me, and was doing all the things that saved money but take time, like growing your own food and washing your stuff by hand and taking care of goats and all that kind of stuff. My mom's work was related to *saving* money insofar as her work related to money. We lived off of less money, and that's been a continued important part of my life. There are certain types of experiences that you have when you don't have money. In spite of *why* our family didn't have money, which was sort of different than a lot of families, there were common experiences.

Unschooling

Since we were unschooled, and my dad would do a lot of his work from home, we were together a lot as a family. I would decide, "I want to study Plato" or whatever, and my dad would be my sort of teacher for that, and we would read. I would read a book, he would read a book, and then we would talk about it. So we'd have regular kind of pseudo-classes. It was pretty great. My dad studied philosophy growing up, and he had most of the books that I wanted to read. I actually don't think I really had to check much out from the library. He was in school getting his PhD in Christian spirituality until I was fourteen or something. He also painted houses part-time, did some church jobs, including being a pastor, and taught college classes like

150

intro to philosophy and intro to religion. He has also written books. It was very handy to have a dad that was focused and educated in philosophy. I could have conversations with him and really learn a lot.

In my teenage years and my early twenties, I got into philosophy with a bit of religion entangled with it. I still wasn't even really looking at the world's problems, I was just looking at metaphysical and epistemological issues. I kind of went through the gamut. Coming from a Christian background, I had a lot of questions, like How do you know if God is real? Who is God? What does it mean to know God? Then I shifted to lots of other questions more related to *How do you know, period?* What is existence? I felt driven to ask all of the basic philosophical questions and to understand all of the possible answers and ways of looking at them. I went from being super into Plato, to being super into Descartes, to being super into Heidegger, to being super into Nietzsche. I shifted from philosopher to philosopher, landing in a postmodern, phenomenology- and ethics-based world that I identified with more. It started with those kinds of questions, and then it shifted to questions about politics and social and cultural shifts, and social systems.

Montrose is a pretty small, white, rural place, more middle-class but definitely with some poor folks. I wasn't exposed to all of the problems of the world then, that came later. But in my childhood, I remember feeling a sense of responsibility for the world. There were little things. If there was a person at our church who didn't have, or who was struggling with, money or something, I would want to buy them things, or whatever. It wasn't until my early twenties that I really dove in headfirst around questions of injustice. That's when I got involved with a Columbus Day protest, got arrested, and suddenly became more aware about all kinds of things—police, jails, racism, and colonialism. I then built on that with more of a focus on what responsibility looks like on a larger social scale, rather than just a smaller community or individual scale.

Taking On Conservative Christianity

I went to a small Christian college in Lakewood, which is right outside of Denver. It's now a pretty fucked-up school. It's very conservative, but at the time, it wasn't quite as bad. It got bad while I was there. My friends and I began organizing around some of the issues at the school. I was starting to look at what it means to push back against a system, how to do that, and the politics of it. The university had brought in a new president who was a former Republican senator. He was pushing the school in this very horrible, conservative Christian direction. He had a "strategic objectives" document for the university that said things like "Promote family values and Western civilization and limited government." It really, really got dramatic.

My two best friends and I became close through being critical of Christianity, and having a lot of interest in philosophy and art. My two friends, more so than me, were artists and literature kinds of people. We were a little threesome, and were definitely the eyeballs at the school. We started to push back against the university, organizing against the president and the strategic objectives, and connecting with Food Not Bombs and some of the collective houses in Denver. All at once we started diving more into political questions and started to get heavily involved in the anarchist community. My friends and I really identified with anarchism a lot. It was both philosophical and political for me at that time. We were starting to meet people in downtown Denver and seeing the issues there with police actions and the racist shit that was going on, like gentrification in the neighborhood and environmental stuff. This was all within a period of a few months in my junior year of college, around 2006 to 2007.

The Inhumanity of Jail

Just after going into my senior year in 2007, my two friends and I moved to downtown Denver and started a collective house with some other people. There was a lot of intentionality around being a collective and having a mutual-aid economy, collective process and decision-making, and our relationship with the environment, and all that. We were influenced a lot by anarchist thinking. Then we got this flier for a Columbus Day protest and my friend Krystan was like, "Oh, let's go to this." She and I went bright and early in the morning. I really knew very little about it, but we pretty much got sucked in and felt, "Oh yeah, this is clearly what's right. Columbus was fucked, and this narrative, this history, needs to stop. We can't be telling these lies and celebrating such a genocidal person." That made sense. There was this huge protest with a few hundred people organized by AIM (the American Indian Movement) here in Denver. We joined in and ended up sitting in one of the circles and holding ground, blocking the celebration of Columbus, and got arrested.

Being in jail was a very significant experience for me. Not having gone to public school, very rarely in my life was I in an environment where you're controlled like that. Now, I have been in many environments that are similar to jail, like shelters, shelter lines, and food lines. Those systems are similar to jail. I was overwhelmed by the horror of having that sort of an authority, who had no care for our humanity, on top of me.

During that protest and the arrests, there was an excessive police presence and extreme use of force. They were painfully bending people's wrists back to try to get us to break up from the group and move us out of the area. They didn't end up doing that to me, but they did that to other people. I was seeing that and hearing people screaming in pain. Those cops were moving people in defense of the Columbus celebration. That was really striking. We were being herded like cattle from place to place. There were some things in jail that stood out. The food is not food. I mean, God, it was horrible. You're treated less than human. They're calling people out by number, not by name.

In a cell across from my friend was a person banging on the door, yelling and yelling. The guard just kept on making fun of her and not coming to check on her. Then she had a seizure or something and fell, and there was blood coming out from under the door. My friend Krystan saw this person fall. Everybody started screaming until they actually went over there to get her out of there and get her to the medical wing—not the hospital. In my area, there was a woman who was pregnant and was screaming for help. They ended up taking her out because she was in labor. I don't know what happened, but that kind of shit definitely made it clear that jail is really about torturing people, not anything else.

Bridging Two Worlds

All this was during my senior year in college. We were living downtown in a collective house with a bunch of people from the crust punk anarchist community. We were doing Food Not Bombs and a Free School that I started organizing. We were also doing protests, dealing with cops, getting arrested, organizing with AIM, and doing Indigenous solidarity stuff with an anarchist focus. Then we would go back to this conservative private Christian school in Lakewood, where everybody was in a completely different world. They were completely oblivious to this other world that we were living in. Their goals were to make a lot of money, get married, live in nice houses, and whatever. I think it was a bit emotional for me during that time with all of the turmoil and back and forth. We biked everywhere. I didn't have a car until very recently. It was about an hour bike ride every day to school and then back to downtown Denver, but I ended up sticking with my two friends. They both quit school, but I ended up staying. It was a clash of worlds, but you know, both worlds are real, so it was good in a way.

There was a lot of staff transition that last year. That was part of why we were doing a lot of protests at school. One of the professors was fired for not aligning with the school's values. This was a moderate person who was teaching global studies. They weren't radical or anything, they were like a Democrat, but that was no longer going to fly. There were a few cool professors that I had really good relationships with, who were open. I don't know if you could identify them as progressive, but they were open and educated and critical. It was good to have that, so I could actually study the things that I wanted to do and have the kind of support from professors that had the time and intention to care about working with me. I also had some professors that really liked me and my friends a lot because we were the only ones who were pushing back against the school. I was still very deep in these philosophical, political, and theological questions, so it was important to me to continue to study. I was writing a paper on Levinas and Heidegger and the understanding of God as *other*. I was very committed to school. It was really important to me to learn. I was also going to Metro, which was a big public university, at the same time. I created my own degree and combined schools so that I could get what I wanted out of it. I was going to two schools at once. I was doing Metro downtown, and then I was also doing that Christian school for three of the four years. I tend to be very committed to what I start. That's kind of a pattern in my life. I typically stick with things through their lifetime, for the most part.

Organizing Free School Denver

Free School Denver was a project I organized once I finished college. It was basically a free network of classes, discussions, and learning environments. The "free" refers to both the economic sense of free and the social sense of freedom. It's based a lot on anarchist principles and ideas about sharing knowledge. One of my housemates in the collective house where I was living at that time was the one who said, "We've got to do this, we've got to get this started." So we, along with a couple of friends, dove in and started Free School Denver. It was pretty sweet. There were a lot of different classes that people would host. Anybody who had knowledge or skills on a particular topic could share it. We'd make a calendar with all the different classes and put it out in the community, and people would show up. We hosted a lot of the classes at the collective house where we lived. We'd have classes on gardening, anarchism, feminism, drawing, how to make menstrual pads, and more. It was a really awesome part of building community and sharing knowledge. I organized that for three or four years. I also started the Graduate School of Howard for myself. This was basically grad school, but not an actual paid school because I didn't see a reason to pay for school. I created a bunch of classes for myself and wrote out syllabi and lesson plans and stuff and then just studied, primarily philosophy and politics. I was reading the history of anarchism and communism and writing papers. I did that for a couple of years, until 2010.

Solidarity

I was also doing a lot of Indigenous solidarity work, going to reservations, and doing stuff in the community there, organizing fundraisers. Some of the folks that we got to know through the Columbus Day protest stuff were from the Black Mesa Chapter of the Navajo nation. We would go there partly to help the elders and folks that needed help. We built hogans, dug holes for porta-potties, and worked on projects that needed to be done on the land. We were also helping to support different protests. There was a bunch of stuff going on with the oil company that was mining—destroying the land, and the water, in particular—and we were part of the protests around that.

During a lot of these years, it was my good friend Krystan and I. Sally came some of the years, too, as did my other good friend from college, and a bunch of other friends and people who we were organizing within the anarchist and collective community. The key leaders were folks from AIM or were from that area, and we would go down with them. It is important to just do what's needed. We have different skills, of course, but when what's needed is digging holes and you have the ability to dig holes, it seems important to use your privilege to do that. In that context, I think that solidarity means responding in a way that's positive and helpful as somebody who's not as directly affected by a particular situation.

Then, I decided to go traveling with my friend Krystan. I thought that would be a different experience. We went traveling across the US, partly together, partly just myself. I mostly did Craigslist rideshare, a little bit of hitchhiking, or whatever, to get around the US and explore a bit, see some new stuff. I was trying to do research about what *Indigenousness* means while I was traveling but found that didn't work out so well. I wanted to do all these interviews with people, but I found that traveling and trying to find appropriate people to interview involves more legwork, and needs to done ahead of time to really make it effective. After going traveling, I came back and decided to go to real grad school for a moment and I started school at the University of Colorado, Denver. That was in 2011.

Occupy Denver and Tensions Between Housed and Houseless Folks

The kickoff of the Occupy movement in Denver was on September 24, 2011, and I quickly got really absorbed. I did a lot with organizing the General Assemblies and helped train facilitation and consensus processes. I had a lot of experience with and cared a lot about consensus process–type things, which are rooted in anarchist values.

The Occupy movement quickly became a space in downtown Denver where a lot of houseless folks were living. It's very logical. It was literally what houseless folks were already doing, living outside. With Occupy, there was a spot where everybody was living downtown.

There were tents and people were bringing food and all that. Plus, it was a movement that houseless people cared about, because it was about income inequality and so on. So a lot of houseless folks came to be part of the Occupy movement. There was a big raid in October, and cops just swept up the whole camp. Some folks moved across the street. But after that big raid, the *housed* population of occupiers, people with housing but who were actually physically living at the encampment, decreased significantly. Then it just continued to decrease and stayed very low. It was primarily houseless folks that were physically holding down the Occupy encampment. For me, it was really important to organize with the folks that were living there, and to try and bridge some of the gaps that were going on.

There was a lot of tension between some of the housed folks who would come down and the houseless folks that were living there. There was a lot of division between focusing on the here and now by the houseless occupiers, and a focus on the future and federal-level policies from the housed occupiers. Housed folks who were part of the Occupy movement focused on things like pushing back on the policies that created the one percent, and the need to be focused on these economic issues and policies, and not just occupying public space. They would just come down for protests, or meetings, or to organize actions. *But they weren't living there.* Then the houseless folks living there were like, "Well, it's called Occupy Denver, and we're occupying this space and we're the ones holding it down and keeping the visibility and actually *in the struggle*, because we're houseless and you just come down here for these meetings. You don't even live here." So those kinds of tensions. We worked on those things through the General Assemblies and through meetings, but there were definitely ongoing challenges.

Getting Educated by Folks Experiencing Houselessness

I decided the best way that it would work for me, and what I felt like was a good balance, was basically to stay at the Occupy encampment two or three days and nights a week, and at my house three or four nights a week. That was how I made it work in terms of mental and physical stability. It's exhausting, as anybody who is houseless knows. *It's exhausting living outside.* I had the privilege of having a home to go to, so I would go home some and then also stay out there. It was really important for me to stay out at least a few nights a week so that I was having a more direct experience of what the folks that were living there were experiencing—being intentional about being amongst the community that we're working with and being a part of that visibility. The relationships that formed were important. Experiencing all of the little nuances that come with actually staying out all night and all day were also important. Things like how to stay warm when it's freezing cold, getting up and helping to deal with fights that happen in the middle of the night, getting used to the noise and the lights, finding a bathroom and making sure you have water with you, how to *find* water, and all of the realities of living without housing that were a part of the reality of living at the Occupy encampment.

One thing I learned was the significance of body heat. There was a group of houseless folks that were living at the encampment that called themselves the Family of Love. We couldn't have tents, because the cops would come immediately the minute they saw anything looked like a tent. We had to make everything with tarps without it looking like a tent. There was a particular way of folding a tarp in half, folding it over, stuffing in a bunch of blankets, stuffing a bunch of people in it, and then propping it up with these traffic cones. We called it a hot pocket. We had like sixteen people in this Family of Love, inside this tarp structure, this *hot pocket*. One night that I stayed out there it was literally sixteen degrees below zero. It was freezing cold, and we were *sweating*. It was so hot. We had sixteen people all lined up inside all these blankets and this tarp, set up with these props. We were sweating because of that much body heat. That's one thing I learned, there's definitely some significance in body heat. Other things too, lots of them.

Organizing with Anarchist Values

Some of the anarchist values that were important at Occupy Denver were creating non-authoritarian structures. We didn't want to create structures of governance where you have one authority who is the final decision-maker and the other people just sort of bow down to that, or even majority-rules type processes where you have fifty-one percent of people that are supportive and forty-nine that aren't, and you go with the fifty-one percent. Other values around horizontal organization—where you don't have all these top-down leadership structures like hierarchical organizations do—were important. We were committed to having more side-by-side leadership structures where people made decisions together, as opposed to having an authority that makes all the decisions. That is where consensus process comes in. Decisions are made collectively with affected bodies. The people who are within that collective body are able *to consent* to decisions and not be forced into them through the use of authority. Those are some of the anarchist values we were working with.

Other values included creating a mutual aid economy as opposed to a capitalist economy. The idea that we share resources through mutual aid as opposed to competing for resources was important. We sought to create a sense of mutual benefit where everybody openly shares resources, as opposed to somebody owning the resources and then giving them out or having them bought and exchanged. This is tied to a critique of property, such as we don't own the Earth. We are stewards and in relationship, and so it's about finding ways to share resources.

At Occupy, I got more connected to folks who were without housing in Denver. It was a natural flow. We were building relationships, and as a movement, I felt that we should not just be focusing on the bigger policy stuff, but also on the concrete reality of the fact that this economic inequality is right in front of us, and *in the realities* of the large number of folks that are homeless in the encampment as a result.

Organizing with Houseless Folks to Fight the Camping Ban
Roughly nine or ten months into the Occupy Denver movement, the mayor and the downtown Denver Business Partnership decided to use that as political cover to pass a camping ban. It came out that one of the council people, Albus Brooks, was going to be introducing a camping ban which would illegalize use of any form of protection from the elements other than your clothing. If you're sitting on a piece of cardboard, if you're covering yourself with a blanket or anything, you're breaking the law. I felt very responsible to fight

that. That was really when I dove in headfirst to fight the camping ban from passing. I started to organize with the folks at the encampment, bringing folks to different city meetings, and getting more aware of the homeless-industrial complex and what was going on.

We fought the camping ban and lost. The ban passed in a four-to-nine vote in the city council. They started enforcing it and that's what cleared out the Occupy encampment. I didn't feel it was right to just give up: "Oh, well, it passed, we're done." I felt that I—and we as a movement—had a responsibility to keep this fight going. After the camping ban, the housed folks at Occupy lost the option of maintaining a visible encampment. For the houseless folks, sleeping outside wasn't an option, it was their daily reality. Especially after everyone was pushed out of the one highly visible encampment, all the people that we had connections with scattered. It was like, well, fuck, how do we stay connected? Those folks are still a part of the movement, they're just scattered now.

Denver Homeless Out Loud

It wasn't until about six months later, in September 2012, that some police data came out saying that the police were connecting people to services because of the camping ban. I knew we needed to hit the streets to talk with houseless folks about what was really going on and keep this fight moving forward based on what we're hearing. I sent an email to a lot of the people who were involved in fighting the camping ban, saying I wanted to do a survey with houseless folks about how the ban was really affecting them. A couple of people replied. That's the core group that was the start of Denver Homeless Out Loud and how I moved forward with the work.

Our very first meeting was actually just a conference call. It was me and an older woman named Billie Bramhall, who has since passed away. She was eighty-something when she was a part of our group and was a super awesome, radical lady who'd been organizing for years. Another person, Antony, was also on that first call. He was a really great, really smart guy, who knew a lot of web stuff, a lot of technical stuff. Darren O'Connor was there and stayed involved for a little while. Those were the four people on our first conference call. Then it was just me and Billie and Antony for the next couple of

160

meetings. The three of us kind of got things rolling. Then we got connected with Tony Robinson at the University of Denver. He was super excited about helping out with the survey design for the report and the more academic side, so that was a really important partnership. Then we started getting other folks, including Marcus Hyde, Ben Dunning, and others who joined up pretty early on. Within the first few meetings we got things rolling!

I think Ben was the only person who was houseless at the time. Marcus had been houseless in the past. We started to get more houseless folks involved at the early stages. But it really wasn't until after we did a survey and put out a report about the effect of the camping ban, and we took it to city council and they ignored us, that we started to talk about how we wanted to build out our work from there. We were like, what's our next step? What was really important at that stage was that we wanted to be organizing with houseless folks, we wanted to be more connected *on ground*. So we started doing a lot of things to be more intentional about that, like meeting in a park, doing a lot of flyering, doing more outreach, and getting more of a broad connection on the streets. Yeah, for the good majority of Denver Homeless Out Loud's life—until things changed drastically and went down the tubes in the past year—it was a pretty good mix of housed, formerly houseless, and currently houseless. That mix varied at different times, but we always had a mix.

Denver Homeless Out Loud started very organically. We followed a lot of the same sorts of organizational structures as the Occupy movement: a collective, consensus process with anarchist principles. We had weekly meetings and used consensus process to make decisions. We registered with the secretary of state as "a non-reporting, non-exempt nonprofit," which is just basically a legal entity that isn't a 501(c)(3), but which functions pretty similarly. We became that kind of an entity early on, and about nine months in we hooked up with WRAP (Western Regional Advocacy Project). We collaborated and talked more with Paul and other folks at WRAP. Then WRAP became our fiscal sponsor. Financially, from that first September 2012 meeting to February 2013, we operated off two thousand dollars. That included printing our report in large quantities and giving them out. We operated almost entirely with pretty much no money and lots of donations, with people contributing what they could for a long time. Then we started getting grants, but we were very low-budget for a very long time. For a number of years, we were operating at about twenty thousand dollars a year, and then started to up it a little bit to about sixty thousand, but we operated with a very small amount of money.

Documenting Conditions as an Organizing Methodology

Over the years, we've done a lot of surveys and reports. The camping ban survey was our first one, and it was very striking. One of the things that really stood out was that sixty-four percent of people we talked to had moved to a more hidden or secluded area where they felt less safe as a result of the camping ban. Very clearly, the majority response was to move and be less safe, more hidden. It's something that we knew, but was really reaffirmed. Another thing that really stood out was that thirty-nine percent of people we surveyed had at some point chosen to not cover themselves in order to avoid police contact. This was in the middle of winter, in Denver. We were surveying in November and December, during the *freezing cold*, and people were choosing to not use a blanket in order to avoid having police come and tell them to move on, or ticket them, or whatnot. That was very telling about the unseen effects of the ban. The majority of the results of that camping ban survey, and what we continued to find in other surveys, showed that a lot of the real harms of these laws are unseen by the general public. Unless you're really on ground with folks or on ground yourself, you don't see these effects.

It was important for me to continue to do this work for a couple of reasons. Partly, I felt a continued responsibility to keep up the fight, to keep organizing. Then, that second part, which is a big priority of mine and a driving principle, is the value and importance of being guided by *directly affected people*. It's so critical that we're hearing from and basing the fight for what's needed on what folks— those who are unhoused and personally impacted by these sorts of laws—are saying. I felt that I just had to keep doing this because it's not happening, and it needs to be done.

Being Accountable to the Streets

If we organize based on widespread guidance from directly affected people, then it's not about whoever the leader is and their particular experience with homelessness. There have been plenty of groups that have had a token homeless leader and are still not accountable. You need to talk to a shit ton of people, and you've got to be on ground, all the time in order to identify and push forward the priorities and needs identified by people who are directed impacted. That requires the experience and wisdom and heart and soul from lots of different people in lots of different positions but, in particular, those with connection to or concrete existence in houselessness.

There is absolutely a role for housed folks and unhoused folks to collaborate, to work together, to make this possible. But it is so important that the big picture of what we're fighting for—and the priorities of what we need to focus on—come from the streets. This way we know what's really needed.

There are absolutely huge challenges organizing with houseless folks. This is partly why it's so important that folks with housing and folks without housing work together. The challenges of organizing while living without housing are vast. You usually don't have consistent access to internet. You're constantly looking for a place to sleep. You have to protect your property. You have to find places to eat. Your life is just overwhelmed with the stresses of homelessness, and so trying to add going to regular meetings, answering a bunch of emails, doing web design, doing a lot of street outreach, gathering surveys and data, and trying to add all of that into your daily life on the street is pretty fucking hard. I mean, I can't say that from full direct experience. I can say that from a couple of different perspectives. One is limited time. For years, until very recently, I regularly spent time on the streets for whole days and nights up to a week, in order to have that experience, connection, and solidarity, and to record cops and deal with other things. So I can say, God, even just for a week, it is exhausting to try to live on the streets and go to a bunch of meetings and answer emails, and blah, blah, blah.

I can also see it from watching some of the folks that we did organize with at Denver Homeless Out Loud who were without housing and doing all of that. *So much power to them.* I am so impressed

with those folks and how they were able to do that level of organizing while homeless, one of whom was Ray Lyall, a co-organizer with
me at Denver Homeless Out Loud for about seven years. He was
just a super hard fighter who would be sleeping out on the dirt and
then he would come in the morning to go to a meeting, or go out to
do outreach, or work on our website, and all that kind of stuff. He
was an example of somebody who really did that while homeless.
Just this past week, he passed away, and yeah, I honor him! There
have been a few others, but it is *so fucking hard* to do that while
homeless.

When we think about what it looks like to organize as a community, to fight for our rights and needs for everybody—with or without housing—*it means all of us* staying true to our values and
commitments about how we gather our direction. We have to constantly ask ourselves: *Are we getting this from the streets? Are people from
the streets reading this? Are their voices being heard? Are they involved in
this?* It's about constantly asking those questions, beating yourself up
about it, and not giving up, and as hard as it is, making it possible to
open doors in *every way possible.* It's about making sure that when
we're having meetings, there are *always* houseless folks there, and
that we're never making decisions in a vacuum, that we're talking to
hundreds of people on the streets. We're not just talking to a couple
of people that are at our meetings. All of these things.

Linking and Learning with Other Houseless-Led Groups
We became members of WRAP about a year in, and the connection
was important on so many levels. The research and assistance that
we've gotten through WRAP enabled us to do many of the reports
that we did and to dig more into the law. Our partnership with
WRAP is what enabled us to run the Right To Rest Act[55] here in
Denver for four years, and then later a ballot initiative, the Right To
Survive. WRAP's work enabled us to have an actual bill, to do more
research, and then have all of the art that we can use in everything
we do. It gave us a sense that we weren't alone. It gave us a sounding
board from other organizations to know what's going on in different
states, and to get ideas from other organizations. We learned so
much from going to Portland, working with Right To Survive, and

learning from Ibrahim Mubarak. *It is very critical to have that network and base of organizations to collaborate with.* That's what helped us get the tiny home village going.

The tiny house village started because we wanted to take the making of houses into our own hands. Some of our members were carpenters and people with building experience. Basically, we said, "Well, fuck it, let's just build houses." That was a lot of the foundation, along with a desire for building community, having community space and more autonomy. We organized for a number of years to fight to legalize the houses. We were doing a bunch of things, including direct actions. We built a bunch of tiny homes in a vacant plot that used to be public housing. The public housing was demolished and then it was sold off for market-rate housing. Just before they started building the market-rate housing, we built a bunch of tiny homes on that plot of land. We did the pre-setup and then built them really fast, in a few hours. We had a whole community of houseless folks who were ready to live there. Then seventy cops came in riot gear and helicopters and arrested us. Then they stole our homes. They dragged them off and destroyed our homes.

Fighting to Legalize Our Tiny Home Village

So, from then forward, for a couple of years, as a community, we held an encampment outside the fence. Ray Lyall was actually one of the key people in that, and then Jerry Burton continued it, just around the corner. It ultimately got to a point where it looked like things might get legalized. Then there were a bunch more sweeps,[56] and we marched on City Hall. They took Jerry's blankets, and it was caught on camera. It got a lot of attention, and we pushed back on the mayor. We were able to use the footage as leverage, and we filed a lawsuit against the city. All of this led to the moment when the mayor had to take action. The easy, quick answer was, "I don't want to stop criminalizing folks, so I'm going to let them do a tiny village." That was when they became legal.

We got a bunch of other organizations, like Interfaith Alliance, Beloved Community Church, and other groups, and we all worked together to get the first tiny house village up and running. There were a lot of beautiful things about it. We interviewed folks that needed housing and then chose the initial residents. Ray was one of them. There was a core of folks that moved in. It was an organizing opportunity to push the message forward and to fight for land, visibility, and rights. It is now legal, and we do have villages that are decent places and are better than the streets. A lot has changed, and we've learned a lot over the years. As Denver Homeless Out Loud (DHOL), we started it with all of these other groups. We were the initial ones that fought for it, for years. Then during the last few months or so, other groups came on board. We started a new entity called Colorado Village Collaborative, which runs the villages. It's not the same sort of community hub that we had dreamed it would be. The organization that now runs the village is taking things in a different direction. I have a lot of disagreements and issues about the direction, but it is a form of community and it's something that we were able to legalize.

Denver Homeless Out Loud

For nine years, my life was DHOL. I spent seventy hours a week doing DHOL work, being on the streets, helping to set up encampments, dealing with cops, running legislation, and doing outreach and surveys. We never had paid staff. We were organic, volunteer, all consensus-based, totally open. Sure, we had our problems, definitely our fair share of problems. Lots of challenges come with that kind of an open model where literally anybody who shows up can be a part of the decision-making body. So lots of challenges, for sure, and high stress. But we also had a lot of strengths, because we had a lot of different folks who were without housing participating in different ways, and a lot of organic passion with folks who just cared and wanted to fight for our rights. Over the years, there's been a lot of folks who've come and gone. One other person and I were the only ones who were with it the whole time. Lots of people were there for many years, and yes, there is a lot to learn from the strengths and weaknesses of our organizing model.

An Organizing Model Changes

At a certain point, I decided I wanted to have a baby. That was going to be a shift in my life, and I wasn't going to be able to dedicate seventy hours a week to being on the streets and such. I also wanted to shift the organizing model a little bit to have the ability to have more people do the work and be more committed, so I didn't have to feel like I was having to carry all the load. So we decided to shift into a paid-staff model. We became our own 501(c)(3) and hired our first staff person just a couple of months before I stepped out on maternity leave and had my baby. At this point, all of the organization's structures began changing, some of which we had agreed on changing, and other changes started to be made as I left on maternity leave.

We had had weekly meetings where we were intentionally organizing with houseless folks. Sometimes they went well, sometimes they didn't go well, but they were always the space where we would organize with folks and make decisions. Those disappeared. It was like, "No, we're not going to do those right now." There was a board that we started to put in place because we had to have a board if we wanted to be a 501(c)(3), but it didn't actually happen. We used to have a membership model, and then it was, "We don't need this membership model, we have staff."

After three months of maternity leave there was already a trajectory to make a lot of these changes. Honestly, I look back and see that I went along with things that I don't agree with now. How did I even let them make some of those changes? Some of the things were in motion while I was still there. I thought it was more about giving something a shot, or that changes were temporary, or that we were shifting what we were working on. But it was all just this way of breaking down the organization and turning it into the type of group where four staff were making all the decisions, with no accountability to the streets.

It was getting to a point where I was concerned about what was going on, but I hadn't tried to address it head-on. Then this one staff person just decided to just flip on me. She was hired to take on my work doing street outreach, but she wasn't doing any street outreach. She would say, "I was in the streets that day." But you can hit the streets and not actually be gathering info, the sort of things that street outreach is supposed to be about, where you're getting that direction and documenting that and so on, and she wasn't doing any of that. It came to a head when she decided that she wanted to have all of the power and wanted to push me out, and she found a way to do that. We went through all of these mediations, and it was just not happening. It became very clear to me that she was going to hold power however she could.

I had a six-month-old, and I was just getting used to having a baby, and she used that time as the opportunity to take over the organization. So I decided that I needed to step away, because it was either that or fight endlessly in this ridiculous way. They're no longer the organization that we were. They're not who DHOL was. They have not continued the legacy of DHOL. During the time that I was there with her, they were continually just always talking shit about DHOL's past, like, "We're different now." And just breaking down everything that we were in terms of truly being accountable to the streets and organizing with the community to fight hard to stand up against what's going on. So it's pretty shitty, and I'm very sad about it all, but I ended up just trying to move on.

Lessons Learned

I've moved on and started a new organization, and I'm super excited about what we've got going on. It's really an opportunity to learn from the past and the things that went well, and also to do things a little differently. The organization is called Housekeys Action Network Denver (HAND), and it is going great so far. We're brand-new, only a month old. It's exciting to be able to continue the fight in a way that is still accountable to the streets, and have more ability to have staff, including more houseless folks in paid positions, and also to have a broader base.

One of the lessons that I'm bringing forward is being exquisitely clear about what street outreach involves and what it means to be accountable to the streets. Previously, I was just vague about it and never really told the person we hired exactly what street entails. It isn't about just watching stuff and helping people or whatever, but documenting input, giving information, getting information, and activating and involving people in the work. So it's getting a lot clearer about that and how we use that documented input to build our priorities as an organization. I have to give a lot of credit to WRAP and to the San Francisco Coalition on Homelessness for some inspiration in this as well. They helped me clarify the process of looking back at outreach to direct priorities. I've also gotten a lot clearer at looking how we're using our time, energy, and resources.

There are a lot of lessons. Having open doors for houseless people in the work had been really important for all of DHOL's life until now, and it's really important for us at Housekeys Action Network Denver. Looking at how to do that is super important. At DHOL we had a lot more of an organic fluid openness, which had its strengths but also had its weaknesses. So at HAND, we now have funding to pay people to be a part of our outreach team. It's been a great opportunity to have an open door of involvement with houseless folks, and have it be something that is paid and is supported so that people are more able to, and apt to be, a part of that work. That gives us a team of folks who are *on ground* every day, doing outreach, and also more involved in the other layers of work. They're also able to be more involved in the advocacy side of things, such as coming to our community meetings, offering input, helping to evaluate our findings to make decisions about what kinds of policies we want to work on, and speaking to the powers that be. They are more *a part of* all these different aspects of the work. I'm excited about this way of opening doors for more involvement. I definitely learned a lot about the importance of always asking, "Who's at the table? Who are we listening to? Who are we hearing from? Who are we accountable to? Where are these priorities coming from?" It's important to ask yourself those kinds of questions all the time in all of the work.

When you're organizing a big action, it is also important to find out what people who are currently without housing need and want. For example, we're organizing a big ten-year anniversary of the camping ban. One of our members, Jerry, who's actually from DHOL and has now gotten involved in HAND, is reminding us, "Are houseless folks going to be there speaking, and do we have tents and sleeping bags to give out as a thank-you for coming?" Those kinds of things are something that we learned in DHOL that are so important to continue. There are other changes too, like learning better boundaries, and how to keep a little bit more structure so that we can be less stressed out and a little bit more effective with doing fewer things at once. I could go on and on.

The Importance of Being Nimble

It's been critical for me in this work to be very nimble in responding to what we're hearing and what's coming from the streets. That means not only having a plan, but being able to change that plan based on new information, not getting so, "This is what we're doing, this is our plan," so we don't hear from the streets. If there's a camp, and there's a person at the camp that really wants to lead a press conference or an action or whatever, then we need to be able to shift that energy. Having the ability to use our resources and our skills to support the energy, the fire, the leadership, and the passion that's coming from people who are directly affected is really important. I think that's an important piece of what it means to be accountable to the streets and organized in collaboration as housed and unhoused folks.

Housekeys Action Network Denver

As HAND, we're primarily focused on housing. We're getting caught up in other issues as well, but the primary goal is to fight for housing for all. We recognize that we're talking about a system that has created mass homelessness and that fucks people over who are in all sorts of different situations. It's a fight for our future, and not just for the people who are currently without housing. People who are currently without housing, people who have been without housing, and people who might be without housing are all a part of this fight together. It really is everybody who's really poor or oppressed in all sorts of different ways.

SEVEN

Malkia
Devich-Cyril

**

I also understood activism
beyond Black activism—
the intersections.
I did not think that America was something
that *just happened*.
I thought of America as a place
where a set of laws and rules
were constructed
to result in a racial hierarchy,
and that required deconstruction,
and that we were—as a family—consistently involved
with the construction and deconstruction of the nation
at the local and national level.

Malkia Devich-Cyril is an organizer, activist, movement builder, writer, poet, educator, and public speaker. As a social justice leader in the areas of Black liberation and digital rights, their work connects racialized capitalism to the digital economy. They are the founding director of MediaJustice (MJ), co-founder of the Media Action Grassroots Network, and an award-winning pioneer of digital rights as human and civil rights. After more than twenty years of media justice leadership, Devich-Cyril now serves as a Senior Fellow at both Media Justice and the Philanthropic Initiative for Racial Equity, while spearheading new projects to transform public narratives on race, power, and collective grief in a digital age.

Malkia's oral history reflects on the responsibility of lineage, conferred by their mother, a leader of the Harlem Chapter of the Black Panther Party. Related to this is the theme of belonging—to family, community, and movement—and the importance of narrative struggle to make meaning and build power to change material conditions. At the time of this interview Malkia was formulating an analysis around the relationship between grief, grievance, and governance as a critical strategy to win freedom.

Malkia, who also goes by Mac, currently lives in Oakland, California.

I WAS BORN IN THE CLINTON HILL NEIGHBORHOOD OF
Brooklyn in 1974, at Cumberland Hospital, which has since been
shut down and no longer exists. My mother's name is Janet Cyril,
but she's known as Mama Janet. My mother was a leader in the New
York branch of the Black Panther Party. My father is Michael D.
Hill. He was also involved with the Black Panther Party, but he
joined in Oakland, California. They were not together at the time
that I was born. I've never met him, and I don't know much about
him, but recently, after forty-seven years on the planet, I spoke to
my father for the first time, by phone. I don't yet know how my parents met, or what drew them to each other except for the fact that
they were both Black people who loved art and wanted to be free.

My mother's family is from Jamaica, but she was born in Brooklyn and spent a significant portion of her childhood living in Anchorage, Alaska. Her father was in the military and her mother was a
scientist, an educator, and a musician in the Anchorage Symphony
Orchestra. Though she was the eldest of five, by the time my mother
joined the Black Panther Party she was already estranged from her
family after having been abandoned in San Diego as a teenager. In
some ways, she grew up alone. I think about what it must have been
like for my mother when she gave birth to me. She was twenty-nine,
in sickle cell crisis, and requiring an emergency C-section. I was less
than four pounds when I was born. Two and a half years later, she
had my sister Sala with a different man. It was the same, except my
sister had the added challenge of being born with scarlet fever. Our
beginnings were hard, but my mother and her circle of women comrades and friends brought sunlight into shadowed places.

All of My Politics Come from My Mother

Because of my mom, because of this circle of women, we were able to
grow up in a brownstone house in Bedford-Stuyvesant, Brooklyn.
Because of my mother and her sister-friends Sandy, Ila, Debbie,
Freddie, and so many more, my sister and I attended a nursery school
these women founded. My mom was the type of parent that at every
stage of life, whatever we were doing, *she* was doing. When we were a
little bit older, my mother joined the board of Brooklyn's Science

Skills Center so that we could strengthen our science and math skills and be safe after school.

When I came out as queer I had just turned thirteen, and my mother joined the board of the Hedrick Martin Institute, which was the first organization for gay and lesbian youth in the country, so that she could help me navigate that part of my life. My mom was involved in everything that my sister and I did, at all times—even when we didn't want her to be. All of my politics come from my mother. My love of the arts, of writing, of the people and community organizing—it all comes from her. My mom died in 2005 from sickle cell anemia when I was in my late twenties.

Growing Up in Bedford-Stuyvesant

In the 1980s, Bedford-Stuyvesant, where I grew up, was definitely a place that was overrun with crack cocaine. It was hit hard by the AIDS epidemic, too. It was one of the largest and poorest Black communities in Brooklyn, I think one of the largest Black communities in the country at the time. Gentrification has displaced so many of the people I grew up with. I go back now, and I don't recognize my street, my neighborhood. Except for my house, one of the few still owned by Black people, where my sister Sala is steward. And the tall clock building, the one my mother always told me would help me locate myself—it still does. Right next to the clock tower is where I attended Hanson Place for first and second grades. Interestingly, it was actually a Seventh Day Adventist school, even though my mom, I think, considered herself more of an atheist. It was where they had a lot of Jamaican students, so I think she sent us there for that reason. It was one way to keep us connected to our Caribbean heritage.

An In-Between Space

Because my mom was born in Brooklyn, and my sister and I were born in Brooklyn, and my grandmother grew up in Brooklyn, my connection to being Caribbean was distant. My sister's father was from Trinidad, and some of his people were from Venezuela. So I knew that we were not from the US South. *What I knew* was that I didn't know the cultural mores of the Black South. *What I knew* was that we didn't eat food from the Black South. *What I knew* was that my mother's parents didn't come from Mississippi or Louisiana or the Carolinas. I didn't go down South in the summer. This is what many of my friends did, the ones who were not Caribbean. But what I *also* knew was that every Christmas and every Memorial Day, we went to my Aunt Cissy's house in Jamaica, Queens, and I couldn't understand a word they said.

I couldn't understand their accents and dialects, but everyone else at the party seemed to be able to. My sister and I would just kind of huddle off to the side, listening. I loved the sound and the cadence, but I was embarrassed that I didn't sound the same. So I didn't identify as an immigrant or as part of an immigrant community until much later in my life, because I didn't understand. I kind of was in an in-between space. I didn't think I was like them, but I also knew I wasn't like the Black American friends that I had, and their families.

A Globalist Childhood

I didn't know how to think about myself in terms of my relationship to America. I felt like an outsider on every level. I didn't identify with the immigrant experience. I didn't identify with the citizen experience. Even my understanding of chattel slavery was not one that was connected to the American South, but one that was connected to the West Indies. My Aunt Carol, a historian, traced our family lineage from the first African in our line in America, an Ashanti woman. My mother taught us all of this, about how actually the vast majority of Africans were enslaved in the West Indies, and that when you think about the experience of chattel slavery in the Western Hemisphere, it's primarily *outside* of the United States—but the way it's been framed is that it's all *inside* the United States. So I grew up feeling like an outsider.

I also grew up having a globalist understanding of the world because of that. I *felt* like an outsider, but I *understood* that I was from the Caribbean. At the same time, my mom had this understanding of herself as part of an immigrant community, even though she too was an outsider in some ways. Our home was filled with people from other countries. She always had people visiting from India, Black

175

people from England, she had people visiting from Latin America, from Africa, all throughout the continent of Africa. Our home was filled with people whose relationship to the United States was one of direct colonialism, and listening to their stories helped shape my understanding of who I am.

The Meaning of Citizenship

I understood from a very young age that citizenship was privilege conferred, sometimes by force, not something you just get born into. I understood that for Black people in the US, even if you had the citizenship paperwork, that didn't make you a citizen. I had an understanding of citizenship. I had an awareness of citizenship. I also had an awareness of migration because my mom traveled the world. We lived in Martinique, Trinidad, and Saint Lucia when my sister and I were young. My mother, Mama Janet, and her group of sister-friends traveled the Black diaspora, and it taught me something about the vastness of the world, the vastness of Blackness. Growing up in that in-between space, growing up in such a unique household, it simultaneously made me feel like an outsider and also gave me a lot of clarity about power and identity from a very young age.

COINTELPRO

By 1974, the Black Panther Party was under severe attack, and had been for quite some time. Some might say it had dissolved by then, although my mom would not say that. My mother said, "Once a Panther, always a Panther." I think that experience of collective action, power, and trauma isn't easily erased. So when I was born, many of her friends were engaged in court battles. Some had fled to other countries in exile, fleeing either trumped-up charges or other circumstances. There was a great feeling, I recall from a very young age, a great feeling of fear. A suspicion of the government, a heightened sense of security, of being in a culture of security, but also this feeling of *connection to a movement as a birthright*. I didn't know that my aunties and uncles weren't related to me. I didn't know that they were related to me through the Party. I actually thought we were blood relatives for a very, very, very long time. Everybody was called Auntie or

Mama; everybody was called Uncle or Baba, sister, brother, cousin. The elders—who were not really elders because I'm not an elder now, and they were the age I am now—they were in their early thirties, early forties. They were connected by something most people don't understand, this passion for freedom and the willingness to act for it.

I recall as a child going to meetings in Yuri Kochiyama's Harlem apartment, sitting on the floor, under the table, stacks of papers all around.[57] The apartment was dark, I remember that. I remember they were always meeting about something. I didn't know what they were meeting about. I didn't know what they were talking about. But the language about revolution, about police violence, about systemic racism, this is the language I grew up hearing. This wasn't something I was introduced to in college or something like that. I grew up in the context of conversations about colonialism and post-colonialism, Fanon and Marx. My very first gift actually was *The Little Red Book* by Mao Tse Tung. One of my uncles gave it to me when I was born. That's the context that I grew up in.

My First Poem

When I was five, I wrote my first poem at this protest that my mom took us to. My sister was about two, I think. I remember her being in a yellow stroller and my mom had an Afro and large earrings. I remember sitting on my mom's shoulders. We were at an action to protest the treatment of what they called "the Haitian boat people." We were at the edge of the water, I think by the Hudson River, and we were marching. I had a poem in my mind, my first time. So, at this action on my mother's shoulders, I tell my mom, "I have a poem. I need to write a poem!" And she was like, "Right now?" "Yes, right now!" I was getting very agitated. So she put me down and she found someone with a pen. She had an envelope, and she asked someone to lean so she could write on their back. She said, "All right, tell me the poem." So, I dictated my poem, and she wrote it down. When we got home, she put it up on the refrigerator and that was my first poem. My mom taught us to read at Liberation Bookstore, sitting on the floor of Liberation Bookstore reading Paul Laurence Dunbar poems, Nikki Giovanni poems, Langston Hughes poems. She would make us memorize them. We memorized Maya Angelou's poem "Still I Rise," which has many, many stanzas. I loved the way they sounded. I wanted to be a poet.

The Consequences of Activism

I remember going to court quite a bit with my mom and my younger sister. My mother was very involved in the case of Dhoruba bin Wahad, so I would go to court frequently around his case. She seemed to be involved in a lot of cases, was so often at court, and spent a lot of time talking with movement attorneys like Robert Boyle, Joan Gibbs, Elizabeth Fink, and other folks. I just remember a lot of court, a lot of legal battles, a lot of lawyers. That was a big part of my understanding of activism and *the consequences of activism.* From a very young age, I experienced activism as a mandate *and* as a potential threat to your life and livelihood. Years later, my uncle Kamau Sadiki, also known as Fred Hilton, was arrested in 2003 on a bogus charge that was promptly dismissed. The district attorney added a new charge going back to the 1970s—a charge for which there was no new evidence to try him twenty and some odd years later. But with no new evidence, he was tried and convicted. Nothing about the case had changed, what was new was the political and media environment following 9/11. That's what allowed a Georgia court to convict him for a crime he didn't commit: a new context, not new evidence.

I could tell you about my mom and my elders all day. When you ask me about me, I think about them, about her. Everything about my political life as a young person was through my mom and because of my mom. We would walk around and do outreach for Assemblyman Roger Green. My mom was always a poll watcher. We were always at the polls with her, every election, local and state, national—*every election.* So I also understood activism beyond Black activism—the intersections. I did not think that America was something that *just happened.* I thought of America as a place where a set of laws and rules were constructed to result in a racial hierarchy, and that required deconstruction, and that we were—as a family—consistently involved with the construction and deconstruction of the nation at the local level and national level.

Coming Out

I remember when I came out as a lesbian in 1987, and my mom took me to my first women's march in D.C. I remember being on the bus singing, chanting—my mom was right there. A few years later, she was the one who took me on the talk show circuit, on *Sally Jesse Rafael, Montel Williams*, you know, *Best Talk In Town*, all these different shows. She went on *Oprah* to talk about being the parent of a gay teen and didn't even take me! Specifically, because all of those shows were exploring the topic of gay teens—gay youth was a hot-button topic at the time—but the guests were often all white on the shows. My mom was like, "Well, we need to go on a show, to show everybody that it's not only white kids who are gay. We have to help families of color understand."

I was very upset. I didn't want to go on these shows with a national audience. I was thirteen. I didn't want everybody at my school to know I was gay. Not everybody, you know? I came out, but to my family and friends, not to the entire city and country who watched the *Oprah Winfrey Show*, or whatever. But my mom said, "You know, it's not all about you. You have to put your fear aside. It's not about you. One day, some Black parent is going to look at that show and realize that they are not alone and that they don't have to cast that child out because we did this show." That's how she always was. That's how it always was with us in our household.

I never thought that I *wouldn't* be in the movement. It never occurred to me. I really started to come into my own when I came out as queer, when I was about thirteen, because it created other spaces for me. I was engaged in choices more independently around my own freedom and seeing myself. It was a space in which I had to choose to be an activist as opposed to within my family—where it was a responsibility and a birthright. It was something that you, you know, "You was doing that."

When I came out as queer, going to the Hetrick-Martin Institute, a few things happened. It was through that vehicle that I became a spoken word artist and a poet. I had always been writing, ever since I was little. My mother took me to the Black Writers Conference at Medgar Evers. There was a Black women writers' panel. On the panel was Barbara Smith, along with others. During the

Q&A portion, my mother dragged me to the mic. I didn't want to go, and she whispered very, very, very loudly, "Tell them you're a lesbian and you want to be a writer." And I'm like, "Well, you already told them." But she said, "No, you say it."

So I said it. I can't remember if I was fourteen or fifteen. I don't remember the exact details of what happened next, but I met Barbara Smith, and was thrilled. Through Barbara Smith, I met Audre Lorde. Through that relationship, my chapbook was published through Kitchen Table Press, my first and only. I don't even know where that is. I was around fifteen, I believe. Audre Lorde also got me and my friend Nicole Breedlove into a residency at the Brooklyn Academy of Music, a writer's residency. From there, we performed at Audre's "I Am Your Sister" conference. I think I was about seventeen by that point, maybe I was sixteen. Later, when Audre died, I performed at her funeral at the Cathedral of St. John the Divine. Audre Lorde was pivotal in my development as a writer, a lesbian, a feminist, and as a media and Black activist. Not just because she was this amazing poet, but because she was also "difficult." My mom was "difficult." I was "difficult." I learned how to be in a world that seemed to hate me.

Part of coming into my activism was as a writer, just to be honest. My poetry was a reflection of what I saw and what I felt. As a teenager I performed at the Nuyorican Poets Café, at the Knitting Factory with my queer-ass poetry collective the Dark Star Crew, then later with Nia Kuumba. I got to spit poems next to Willie Perdomo, one of my favorite poets. Going to college was another inflection point for me. My activism as a queer person through Hedrick Martin, my activism as a writer and as a poet, being part of the queer arts scene, and my ongoing activism within Black liberation movements all gave me a great sense of purpose.

Building Organizing Skills at College

When I attended Sarah Lawrence College, I was one of very few people of color there. It was my first taste of leading actions, organizing coalitions. I became the head of the Black Student Union and the head of the Students of Color Committee. My girlfriend at the time was the head of the Latino Student Union. I think I started organizing that school the day I enrolled. I was part of that effort along with other students. Of course, student activism at the university level can often be naïve. It can also be very dramatic and precious, because you're organizing for stuff that matters to an elite and rather small group of people, but the stakes are actually kind of high. Organizing for people's tenure, that's important, but certainly not the same as organizing against mass incarceration. We were organizing for ethnic studies and for curriculum changes, for staffing changes. Basically, our organizing focused on the role of the school and what was happening *at the school*. It felt good to be expanding opportunities for students that would come after me and was a great practice ground for me. It was an incredible opportunity to build my public speaking skills, my skills of agitation, and my organizing skills in terms of being able to build coalitions and build organizations.

Because of my mother—again—I worked with my friend and partner at the time to start a program that placed students of color at Sarah Lawrence in a mentoring relationship with at-risk youth between the ages of five and thirteen at the Schlobohm housing projects in Yonkers. Being able to work directly with the people was always part of my commitment and something that I was always interested in. It's where I felt most comfortable. That's partially because my mom always said repeatedly, "If you're not working directly with the people then you're not doing what you think you are." I think that was her rendition of this Cabral quote, "We're not fighting for the things in people's heads, we're fighting for material changes. So, if you're not in the street making material changes, then you really need to reconsider what you're doing."[58] I didn't know yet how to organize in the street, but I *did* know how to deliver a service. I tried to model my program after Serve the People programs in the Black Panther Party. We delivered food. We helped parents. We brought the young people to the college to give them a sense that what they had wasn't all there was. We just did whatever we could think of. I went to college when I was seventeen. I did what I could think of as a seventeen-year-old.

Early Organizing Lessons
The importance of a shared sense of self-interest was one of the first big things I learned. I remember the Coalition of Students of Color.

The Latino students, Asian students, Black students and then anyone who didn't have an organization—Indigenous students, some of the Arab and Muslim students, other students who maybe didn't have an organized force at the school—we had a sense of shared interests. Then I learned that shared self-interest wasn't enough. We also had to have some kind of shared long-term vision and some level of analysis. We did a bunch of political education work to try and build that. We knew that having small differences in analysis— which are fine—could be the difference between whether to choose a campaign that would mobilize school resources to shift the economic base of the poor Black community just adjacent to it or choosing a campaign that would focus on the tenure of a single teacher. We needed to have some understanding of how power worked in order to make correct assessments and to be aligned on what we wanted, what we thought was possible, and what needed to be done. I would say those were some of my biggest early lessons.

There were also the lessons of failure, that it was okay. I took failure very hard when I was in college. I took everything—especially breakdowns in coalition building—very hard. I was very sensitive. I cared a lot, maybe too much. I had been raised in the Black Left, and also alongside so much trauma, so I didn't understand why people wouldn't give every drop, every minute, to the movement. I didn't understand *why*. For example, somebody at the school suggested we should do a hunger strike. I was like, "Cool." I was eighteen and didn't know any better. We were working with the white students, and some of the white women wanted to do the hunger strike. I was like, "All right!" This just makes sense. I mean, of course it *didn't*. You know, you save—you reserve—the hunger strike for life and death conditions that you're trying to change. But I didn't know that. So, I'm like, "Yeah, hunger strike. Let's do it." I got really engaged in the hunger strike. I was HUNGRY. I was furious when I went down into town and saw some of those same white women eating at Denny's, you know?! I was like, "What is going on here?!" It just did not occur to me that we would not do the hunger strike for real, that we would pretend to do the hunger strike.

Another example of how I always do a little bit too much: I was placed on social probation within my first month at Sarah Lawrence

College. There was this tradition of asking incoming freshmen questions like "What do you think of when you hear this word?" And they would publish the answer. Silly, simple, you know? So, one of the words was hygiene. I said, "Something the white girls in my dorm need to do better with." Some white women brought me up to the Committee on Racial Diversity because I used the term "white." They wanted me to write an open letter that they would publish in the next issue that apologized for what I said. I refused to do that, and I was placed on social probation. Social probation meant that I was not allowed to participate in student activities, so I was not allowed to hold office.

I immediately ignored that and became the head of the Black Student Union, violating my social probation. That violation led to losing my student housing the following year. I was lucky, there were a lot of women on campus kind enough to let me stay with them. I made it work; you know? I got my housing back, eventually. At some point financially, I think I lost my meal plan.

Even my introduction into the college was a contest for power. I saw everything about my education—the academics, the classes I took, the books I read, every extracurricular thing I did—as a contest for political, social, cultural, or economic power. I saw it not as something I was doing personally, but I saw myself as engaging in something bigger. I saw it as practice grounds for myself. I thought of it that way. I would say that poetry, queerness, and then college were the three places where I began to come into my own as an activist.

Moving to Oakland

After college I moved to California to be with my girlfriend. When she finished at Sarah Lawrence College, she said, "I'm going to California. You ain't got to come with me, but I'm going." I was like, "Oh, no, she's trying to break up with me. I got to go to California, you know, make this right!" So I was like, "Mom, I'm going to California. I'm moving to Oakland, moving to whatever, the Bay Area." And my mom, being my mom, was like, "Well, I'ma go with you."

My mom came out to the Bay Area with me. There's so many things I can tell you. She came out with me, got me situated, helped me find the gay people. As a matter of fact, we were driving in the

Castro and my mom saw a Black butch walking. She leaned out the car—or she told me to lean out the car—just as she yelled, "Hey! Hey!" She was like, "Hey, ask them where the gay people are at." I'm like, "The gay people are all over." "No, no, the *Black* gay people, where are the Black gay people at? Go, ask 'em."

She made me get out the car in the middle of the street. Go, holler at this person I did not know, and ask them, "Where are the Black gay people? I'm from Brooklyn. Just trying to find Black gay people." They directed me to a place in Oakland, a club called the Bench and Bar. My mom took me to the club, *took me*, but we didn't go at night, we went in the middle of the day. We didn't know it was a club, exactly. We found these gay newspapers, the *Bay Area Reporter*, she was studying them, trying to figure out what's going on.

Even before I came out to the Bay Area, I had a few jobs. One job was with NYC Commission on Human Rights—I must have been fifteen or sixteen. I also worked for Project Reach as a youth organizer, and I was a page at the library. Each one of those jobs was at an intersection of art, communications, and organizing. I've always lived at that intersection. But it wasn't until I was in the Bay Area that I became a media activist.

When I came out here, first I started working at the Applied Research Center, which later became Race Forward. I was grateful when Gary Delgado, the founding executive director, hired me. He was from Brooklyn and our families were both Jamaican. I felt comfortable. But I was a terrible employee. I wasn't on time. I was a millennial. I was arrogant. I had a big old head on me, but I really did see Gary as a mentor. I saw Gary as somebody who was an elder and who could teach me. I learned a great deal from him.

I learned about the racial justice framework from that job. Before that, I was about Black Liberation, Third World Liberation, Internationalism, what my mother raised me in. With Gary and Applied Research Center, I learned about racial justice and structural racism. At Applied Research Center I worked with research, and I worked with their magazine called *Race Files*. Once again, I was working on issues of race, working on issues of justice, but also communications and writing. By the time I got my next job at Building

Opportunities for Self-Sufficiency (BOSS), organizing young homeless people and their families, I was someone who had been engaged with writing at a high level, research, and press work.

Media, Communications, Race, and Racial Justice

Even though the Community Organizing Team of BOSS didn't have a communications arm, or any communications staff, like most organizing shops at that time, when we did our campaigns and it came time to write op-eds or do any kind of press work, I just kind of took it on. I didn't have any formal training in journalism or PR or anything like that. The executive director, Dawn Phillips, was another person whose rigor and thoughtfulness allowed me to learn on the job by doing and by messing up. That job is definitely why my analysis around media and communications became so tied to my analysis around race and racial justice, and was so embedded within organizing and an understanding of power. It was never separate for me. That's how those trajectories and intersections in my life and work came to be. I would say, honestly, it's a birthright. It was given to me. My mom edited the Black Panther newspaper. She was an organizer, an activist, an educator, and a writer, so it just flowed that way. My sister is an educator. My sister Sala ran a school for Black children called Little Maroons for twenty years in my mom's house.

There was no one moment for me when I came into my own as an organizer. It was much more iterative than that. But I will say this. It was a million moments. Throughout that whole time that my analysis was developing, that my understanding of the world was changing and that my role was getting sharpened, I was *also* an extremely sensitive kid. I was getting into all kinds of trouble. I was getting arrested. I got arrested more in the Bay Area actually, than I did in New York. My friends were on the Christopher Street Pier.[59] Many of them were homeless. I'd known intimate loss from a young age. My girlfriend Jackie was raped and thrown off a building in the Bronx and killed. Politics and work wasn't my whole life. Being gay was very hard at that time. I went to Edward R. Murrow High School, and I was the only out person in the entire school. There was a lot of violence. There was a context of violence, you know? I think that also informs, and informed, my politics and my work. Collective action became a way to heal my experiences of collective trauma, and the media had everything to do with both.

Confronting Racist Media Stereotypes

I saw the consequences of the media, the media depictions of young people of color in the 1980s in Brooklyn. I was there then, and in the early nineties. Media coverage of Black teens as "super predators"—everything about the Central Park Five and "wilding"[60] and all of that—was about *me*. These narratives about "crack babies" and "welfare mothers" and all of that. It wasn't some distant thing. It was about me, my community and family, you know? So my work around transforming the media comes from a very personal place. A place where I feel I have experienced the consequences of media racism very directly and very explicitly.

After I worked at BOSS, I was hired by We Interrupt This Message. They wanted to try combining media activism and communications strategy by launching a project focused on building the communications capacity of youth organizing groups in California and engaging those groups in media activism, directly. I was excited by that. I was like, "This feels like the exact right combination of my skills and my interests." But I told them, "I've never run a project before, and also, I'm not a trained communications strategist or a media activist." And they were like, "Don't worry about that. We'll teach you all that." So I went to work there in 2001. I actually worked with Rinku Sen on developing the design for the project, which we called the Youth Media Council. Then, somewhere in 2001, the directors of We Interrupt This Message announced that, due to personal losses, they were leaving. We had gotten funding for the Youth Media Council already. I had started doing the work. I had hired a couple of people. I was excited. This felt like a dream job to me. I was also getting paid more than I had ever been paid before, which was probably like $30,000. It was very little, but it was exciting to me. Then 2002 came, and We Interrupt This Message was closing, basically. I decided not to close the Youth Media Council, and instead, to build it out.

Caregiving

In that same year, things with my mom changed drastically. My mom had come to visit me, my sister and young niece were already in town; but when she got off the plane I couldn't find her. I searched for her, and I searched for her, and I couldn't find her. I was getting very agitated and upset. When I finally found her a couple of hours later, she was just standing in a hallway in the airport and I was like, "What's happening?" you know? And she was just like, "Oh, you know, I was looking for you." So, me being a selfish, ignorant, adult child, I was like, "Why are you playing games, how are you looking for me? I've been looking for you all this time." I was irritated.

We went back to my house, and we were going on a family trip to the mountains—me, my partner, my sister, and my niece—who was very young at the time, maybe she was three or four or something like that. Anyway, we went to the mountains and along the way my mom got increasingly despondent. It seemed like she couldn't, or wouldn't, speak, but every time I tried to say, "Let's go to the hospital," she adamantly refused. At some point she lost control of her bowels. My sister and I finally decided the next day, "We got to go to the hospital."

We took her to the hospital, and that's when we discovered that she was moving into end-stage sickle cell. They were telling us that sickle cell over all these years had done some damage to her organs. She basically wasn't getting enough oxygen. Her hemoglobin was very, very low. Over the next two and a half years, our mom went into a pretty massive decline. She was not offered home care or hospice for a long time, because they said sickle cell—how'd they put it?—"It's not an immediately fatal disease." So it's kind of like you have terminal cancer but you're not eligible for hospice, *yet*. However, unlike cancer, sickle cell can be fatal in a single moment. You can have a crisis and it can kill you then. Furthermore, it was debilitating—she couldn't work. We had to battle for quite some time for her to get her disability. She had been working with sickle cell for many years. So getting it certified that she was eligible for early retirement was a whole battle. Being a Black activist is never just about fighting for some nameless, faceless masses. I was always fighting for my mom, my sister, my nieces, and myself. Caring for my mom was an epic battle.

I just began to come back home once every five weeks, for one week, to help my sister. My sister moved back home. My sister had a young daughter, and we shared the load. I often wonder if I should have moved back home. It's a question that will live in my heart. I'm not sure what the right answer is. But my mom became very ill, and after about three years of decline, she died at the age of fifty-nine at home, in the bed beside me, in the middle of one of New York's biggest snowstorms. She was very young, and she always knew that sickle cell would kill her. She prided herself on being "one of the oldest people with sickle cell that she knew." But it took her life in 2005.

Balancing Leadership and Caregiving Learning Leadership

The beginning of my career as a media activist, the first three years of running the Youth Media Council, which would eventually become the Center for Media Justice, and now is called just "Media Justice," was all about taking care of my mother, commuting back and forth from New York to California. It definitely affected my leadership deeply. Not to mention that I had never run an organization before. It's not like someone hired me and was like, "Yes, you should run this organization." I just happened to become the director because the parent organization closed. I was thrust into a position of leadership because I have certain skills and personality, but my experience was lacking. I was thrust into very public leadership. Well, I wasn't ready. Not with the organizational forms social movements are forced into in this country, not in an isolating and demanding executive leadership role that requires more than many have to give. I wasn't ready to do that, and I was under tremendous personal stress. I have a lot of regrets about how that shaped my leadership moving forward.

The matter of leaving my job and going home wasn't even a question. My mom used to help me financially when I was much, much, much younger. When she became ill, I tried to help financially. I had to continue to work. Also, my sister was receiving welfare at the time, and had a young daughter. My mom had a pension, so it wasn't that we had no money, but my family was very cash-strapped for a while. Especially at the beginning, because initially she wasn't able to receive her pension or disability. So that's number one. I believed, at least, that I had to work, you know? I had to work, and I could not leave my job.

Also, I was getting recognition for my ideas. I was making a difference, or so I thought. I was working with groups all over California and all over the country. The campaign I was organizing, "Unplug Clear Channel," was getting national recognition. I was being quoted in all these books. I was writing book chapters. I was proud of what I was doing, and I was excited by it. So some part of it was a selfish thing. It was like my first opportunity, and I didn't want to stop.

Besides, I truly believed that something very real was at stake. I truly believed that justice was at stake. That media and technology could impact the tide of the domestic movement for civil and human rights. That my work was important and that the work of those who I was supporting was important. My mom loved my work. She was very interested in it. So I was invested. My life and my work had never really been separate. In fact, I think that was part of my problem. I would go to New York on work trips. I would go stay with my mom, work from home, and take care of her.

Boundaries

My life was really different from a lot of people's lives. For many people, they go to work, and their home life is separate. That's *never* been true for me. I mean, when my mom worked at LaGuardia Community College, she hired all Black Panthers. She hired her friends. It was never a situation where "work was here, and life was here." I felt like it was all *one thing*.

I didn't have very good boundaries around any of it, which meant that everything suffered. My attention to my mom suffered and my attention to the work suffered, because I didn't know how to separate them. I do think that the activity of all of it—both taking care of my mom and working—distracted me from other issues that I needed to attend to. The fact that I'm a survivor of child sexual abuse is something that I didn't know how to deal with and didn't want to deal with. So I didn't deal with it. I think that had consequences for me and for my leadership as well.

The fact that I had suffered frequent losses, even by then, was also something that I put aside. Mind you, my mom had sickle cell anemia, which is a genetic disease that she's had her whole life, which means she's had it my whole life, this wasn't the first time. We *grew up* with her having sickle cell crises. It's a chronic condition that could be fatal at any point. So I grew up with anticipatory grief. I was always worried that my mother was going to die. I was very anxious. I always worried about *when* she was going to die. I didn't know if she was going to die when I was six, when I was thirteen, when I was seventeen, twenty-one. Would I be ready? Would I have to go live with somebody? All of these thoughts, you know? As the eldest I also felt some measure of responsibility. So my stress level in life was already quite high. So I would say, if anything, if I was using work to distract me from anything, it was from these stresses. I was using all the activity—all of it—to basically, honestly, to keep me going. I felt like if I stopped to deal with any one of these things, I would just stop. I wouldn't be able to keep going.

Unmanaged and Unmetabolized Grief

When Mother died, it threw me into a seven-year tailspin. I worked harder than ever after my mom died. I built my organization from a very small $200,000-a-year project to a multimillion-dollar organization with a staff of thirteen. We moved from a local and state organization to a national organization. That's what I did with my time. I had complicated relationships. I'm very lucky that most of my exes are people that I continue to love and cherish, and who continue to love and cherish me. They're some of my best friends. But I did have a couple of difficult relationships, both intimate and professional, in that time period. I think that, again, these conflicts were morbid symptoms of my unmanaged and unmetabolized grief.

I don't think that in that time I learned to balance anything. I don't think it's quite so simple. I think that I was just trying to stay alive, to maintain some dignity—oddly by doing everything I could to stay busy and full of intrigue until I became quite ill in 2010. I developed heart disease. I gained a lot of weight. I became diabetic. I really struggled. At some point I became so ill that I had to take a break. I took a sabbatical and moved to Seattle with someone that I was dating and who is one of my best friends now. I then began to recognize that there was some calm available to me. That my work did not have to be at the pace that it had been at.

There wasn't just one direction of the chaos—it wasn't just inward out. There were a lot of external pressures from the philanthropic community and from the conditions themselves. These pressures demanded from me as a leader—and, I think, from others—a certain kind of leadership, a certain breakneck speed, an unreasonable pace of working. If you want to build your organization, if you want to get press, funds, and victories, you can't stop. That was the message I felt I was getting loud and clear, even from people whose words said the opposite. Their actions spoke very loudly. . . . It wasn't until I got ill and moved to Seattle that I began to reject those external demands on me and say, "Well, it don't matter what you want, because I can't do it. I just can't do it."

It felt bad to acknowledge that. It felt like I was weak. It felt like I was going to lose respect if I couldn't keep up. It felt like no one was going to appreciate, and that no one did appreciate, these external pressures. But I went away, I took a sabbatical. It was only three months, but I got a little healthier. I got a little calmer. I was in therapy, which I'd been in for years but not in this focused way. I was just doing better, and some time passed.

And because I was doing better—a lot better—I was ready when I met the woman who would become the love of my life. I shouldn't say we "met." She actually went to Sarah Lawrence College with me in the 1990s. I just hadn't seen her in many years, and we got reconnected through a mutual friend. The point is that I began to find balance. And that balance, let's be clear, it's not some lightweight "work-life balance." It's an extreme boundary, a deep "NO" to the demands that would be placed on me, coupled with a profound "YES" to what I wanted in my life, what kind of life I wanted. Those things are really not compatible with one another, you know what I mean? It was still very hard.

The Love of My Life
Alana Devich—later Alana Devich Cyril—and I fell in love. I was happier than I had ever been in my life. I mean, I've gone through so

191

many things. I had already lost dozens of people, suffered physical harms, and been through a bunch of stuff. I had been arrested, attacked, abused. Until then, life had felt like this difficult experience emotionally and materially. The woman who would become my wife, she just loved me anyway. She loved me so much and she loved me so honestly, and it was just a great feeling. It was the best feeling I've ever had. She taught me to be joyful, and lighthearted, and boundaried, and careful. And my work changed. I found myself becoming less critical, less of a perfectionist, and taking more care with how I spoke to people. I found myself working more slowly. A lot of it was because my wife demanded attention. She was like, "You're not going to be paying all your attention to your job! That's crazy!" It was great. I loved it. I loved that she basically demanded me to focus on *my life*. Not really just on her, but on me.

She was very active physically, so she always had me outside, doing this, doing that. I just was happy. I'm in love with her. I will always be in love with her. We got married in 2015. It was the best day ever. She always would say that, "the best day ever." In terms of the question of work-life balance, it wasn't like I learned to balance, it was that I got called by a different part of my life to show up. It just became more balanced because of that. It wasn't simply some inner choice I made, though my determination toward joy had something to do with it. But conditions matter, and my conditions changed.

The Best Day Ever

Alana was very quirky, very funny. A stand-up comedian. An editor. She called herself a word maven. I've always been a heavier person in terms of my spirit. I'm an organizer, I'm a poet. I'm into those heavy emotions, like, "Let's fight the system." I have experienced all this death and all these different things. She was a light spirit. Alana was like a ray of sunshine. She had her melancholy, but she was funny, always. Everything was funny, and she helped me to see life a different way, through the lens of humor, to not take myself so seriously. Where everything, even the worst things, could be funny. The fact that we went to Sarah Lawrence together, it was just so perfect. We just had been walking a parallel trajectory for so many years. You never know who's walking alongside you, 'til you know.

She had had a crush on me at Sarah Lawrence. I didn't even know that. She told me, "I remember three things about you from college. One is your hands, because they looked like mitts. Nobody has hands like that." So, that became my nickname, "Mitts." Her parents call her Muffy as a joke. That's how we became known as Mitts and Muffy. She said, "The second thing was that you never stop talking." She was a very quiet person, internal. Not me, I talk! The third thing was she said, "You were the smartest person I'd ever met." Now, I don't think that's true, but it's what she said. She had a crush on me back then, but she said she didn't think I would like somebody like her. She was political, but she wasn't an organizer. She wasn't an activist or anything like that. She was biracial. Her dad was white, and she was like, "I'm not like a Black nationalist." Her mom was Black. She was like, "I worried you would think I was frivolous." What's so funny is probably back then I might have thought that, though nothing could be further from the truth. Alana wasn't even remotely frivolous. She was fun. She loved art. She loved live music. She would be one of those people who would go to a museum and stare at a painting and take out her notebook. I'd be staring at the painting and looking back at her like, "What is going on? What do you see?" I love art, but I'm not like that. She loved to travel. She loved life. She was a bon vivant for real. Her parents are a big reason why. They are awesome.

As somebody who had suffered so much, it was almost like I was looking at a miracle. Like, how could a person be like that? Could I be like that? Could I be someone so free? Could I be someone who everyone liked? Everyone liked her. That wasn't true for me. People loved me or hated me. People had strong feelings about me. I wanted to be like her, someone who didn't have this burden, who had not been shaped by harm in childhood. I wanted a different life, a different outcome for myself, and I saw her as not just the incredible woman she was, but also the chance for me to have a kind of happiness that I had not had in the past. So I asked her to marry me, and she said yes. I felt like I had won at life.

Then in mid-2015, she began to feel ill. Not quite ill, but she was having a lot of fatigue. She just felt off. She started exercising a lot. We went to her doctor, but they really couldn't find anything. Then, around September, we went to Maui to celebrate our first wedding anniversary. She was really not feeling well. Something was going on. We came back, and she got diagnosed with H. pylori. They gave courses of antibiotics, but she didn't improve. She finally got an endoscopy, and they found cancer in her esophagus. Then we went and got a CT scan, and they saw cancer in her liver, her lungs, her bones. She had metastatic stage four cancer, gastro-esophageal cancer. They told us that with treatment, she would have likely twenty-four months to live and without treatment, twelve to eighteen months to live.

It was a devastating blow to her. It was a devastating blow to me. She wanted to live, she said, to be with me. Basically, she said, if she wasn't with me, she would not be seeking treatment and would allow herself to die. But she did do chemo. It was very hard on her. It was very hard, period. We suffered many emergencies. It was a terrifying journey for both of us, but caring for Alana was also the most meaningful thing I've ever done in my life. In 2018, on October 27, she died at our home with me and her mom by her side.

Grief, Grievance and Governance

From 2016 when my wife was diagnosed, to 2018 when she died, I lost many other people. Then, from 2018 to now, I've lost many more. Alana died in October 2018. It is not just that various people died. It's that I've been involved with each of these deaths. My friend Art died in August. He was found in his apartment. I organized everyone to clean out his apartment. I organized his funeral. He had really very little family, so his body was turned over to me. My friend Yulanda "Chef" Hendrix died a year after Alana was diagnosed. I emceed her funeral. My god-sister Kafi died in December after Alana died, and again, my sister and I were organizing her care, and we organized her funeral along with some of her friends. My friend Sia moved into end-stage breast cancer a year after Alana died. I became one of her health proxies and helped her daughter coordinate her care until she died in 2019. A father figure, Tony Ishisaka, died. My friend Rahwa died. My friend Lana died. My friend Darshan died. My Aunt Sandy died. So, on and on and on, all during Alana's illness or in the three years since her death. Alana's death and my mom's death have organized and shaped my life, but there have been a lot of losses that shape me and my work. That's why I left my job in December 2019. I've decided to work on the role that grief plays in social movements, and how it shapes our activism and how we need to shape a new public narrative on grief in order to leverage more powerful grievances and demand the governance we deserve.

I'm still formulating it, but my essential thesis is that colonialism, structural racism, patriarchy, are all forces that move death out of balance with life. These are death-producing systems, and they are simultaneously *grief-neglecting systems*. They produce death and they ignore grief. They not only ignore grief, they subjugate grief. They disenfranchise grief. They suppress grief, and under these conditions, under these systems of oppression, grief actually becomes a terrain for struggle. Grief that's unmetabolized, I believe, becomes reactionary and moves into what we've seen as "white resentment." The politics of resentment are really the politics of unmetabolized grief. People who cannot manage loss, rather than grieve, become enraged, and their politics reflect that. When grief is unmetabolized the grief becomes reactionary, the grievances become reactionary, and the governance becomes reactionary.

I believe there's a relationship between grief, grievance, and governance. I believe that we can actually build a more radical grief. I'm inspired, for example, by the mother of Emmett Till, who—after this system of structural racism and white supremacy murdered her son in such a brutal way—metabolized her grief *in community* and made a decision to have an open casket. That decision was intended to inspire activism among Black people for freedom. Her radical grief created the space for radical grievance in a community setting, which, translated into action, becomes the inspiration for radical governance, transformative governance—new rules, new rights, new ways of being.

It began with grief. They define grief as any reaction to loss. But if you think about it, life is loss. What if men could stand to lose? What if white people could stand to lose—could withstand, and comprehend, and deal with loss? This is not just about the uneven losses that people of color and women, queer, and trans people deal with, or the extraordinary, racialized burden of grief that we have to hold. It's also about one of the privileges and benefits of whiteness, of patriarchy—it protects you from having to grieve in the way that it's necessary for freedom to take place.

Our movements have to have the infrastructure for grief. Part of why the civil rights movement was as effective at engaging so many people was because it was through the church. Not because of the religion part of that, but because it was through an institution that was as much about belonging and about emotion as it was about the material change. We need institutions that allow for that level and type of belonging, that allow people to facilitate grief.

We need our organizations to be able to facilitate grief. If we could do that more effectively, I believe that we'll end up with more powerful forms of grievance and it will lead to the kind of transformative governance that we deserve. That's my vision. What does that mean in concrete terms? What does an institution that can facilitate grief look like? What are the practices and ways of being? What does grief-inspired radical leadership look like? What does a grief-inspired movement look like?

Every movement in the history of the world has been facilitated by three things: grief, grievance, and a vision for governance. Every single one. There is a loss, there is sorrow and harm as a result of that loss. There is a grievance that is being petitioned for and there is a vision for new ways of being that involve new leadership, new sources of power, a new economic base. For example, the fight against police violence has been facilitated by the grief of the loss, the grievance at the injustice, and a vision for how that can change. So I'm really trying to forge a new way of thinking about social change that places grief at the center.

The funny thing is, it's not any different from what I was doing before. That's what I've realized. These are all narrative and cultural strategies. At the heart of it is understanding why people do what they do, why people take action, and why people make the choices they make individually and collectively. Then figuring out how to mobilize that "why" towards peace and freedom and justice for everybody. *This is the same thing.*

Organizing around grief is still a cultural battle. It's still a contest for cultural power. It's just a different way of thinking about it. I think the right is very effective at this. I think that the right is effective at manipulating the grief of white people, in particular. The grief around symbolic loss, and convincing them that they should not have to grieve, they should not have to lose, instead of helping them *to let it go*. Let the monuments go, let the institutional inequalities go. Let the privilege go. Let the benefits go. They say, "No, fight for it! Hold on to it! You shouldn't have to grieve the loss of any of that." I think we need to grieve the loss of whiteness. Let it go. It doesn't help anybody, not even white people.

A Spiritual Battle

This is not just a personal battle for me. This is really about a larger spiritual battle. I mean, it's funny. I've never been a spiritual person, but now I am in a way. I mean, I knew it before, because working on narrative is different than working on the material. But I know it now more than ever. There is a spiritual battle. The spiritual battle is not necessarily about God or about religion or about any of that, but it is about emotion, and it is about being connected to something greater. It's about nature. It's about something that sees the individual life as profound, but something that's way more profound than the individual life. That's actually going to connect us to the freedom movements of the past and the freedom movements of the future.

I'm gaining my inspiration from the idea that there's a lineage here. There's something more than the material conditions. If I can establish a way of thinking about that, then maybe I can make a difference informing justice movements to come, and when it's my time to die, this will be something I leave behind that will matter. So that's what I care about right now.

The work around grief is a narrative battle, and I've always been committed to narrative struggle. Both the structural aspects of it and the content aspects of it and the reason for that. At every stage of human development, the way we communicate shapes the economic base of the society, shapes the political structures of the society. Whether you're talking about the birth of the printing press or whatever it is. In this country, the infrastructure of narrative and the infrastructure of the press have always been used in the service of white supremacy. The fact that newspapers were initially used to capture escaped enslaved people. The fact that as we began to build our presses during Reconstruction that the Black presses were burned by the infrastructure of white racism.

Narrative and the Struggle to Change Material Conditions

There is a long relationship between this narrative struggle and the struggle to change material conditions. There is a very clear relationship between those things. Culture organizes the way we think, and infrastructure organizes culture. It doesn't just come out of nowhere, it is built. I started off focused on the narrative. The front end, which you can read, watch, and listen to, because I understood what I just described. But slowly, I peeled it back. Well, who owns these stations? It don't matter how great our narrative strategies are, because at the end of the day, if the infrastructure doesn't allow our content to pass, then we can't move anything. Over time, I kept peeling it back to where I finally started working on media policy. I started working on corporatization of the media.

It must have been the late eighties when we got our first computer. We were the first people on the block to get a computer. This digital transition that we've been undergoing basically since the mid-eighties has profoundly shifted even the nature of narrative structure. This is the thing that's so wild. Now that everything is digitized, it means that every element of racial capitalism is digitized. The separation that used to exist between the economy and media, or between education and media, or between anything and media is gone. It's gone. So, now that data is bought and sold at this high level, everything, basically every part of the economy is digitized. It's no longer like you can deal with media policy over here and deal with the economy over there.

Now, the infrastructure of media *is* the infrastructure of the economy. At the point where it was all print, and at the point where it moved to broadcast, each one of these things had an *impact* on the economy, but it wasn't the economy. Now the internet *is the economy*. It undergirds every aspect of the economy. So, when you have the technology and media being one thing and it becomes an economic base for the nation, you actually have a pretty big problem here, right? It becomes much harder to make cultural shifts in that context.

198

If we think about white supremacy as a material—as a system of relations of power and production—we can see that its function is to intensify the extraction of labor and ensure the accumulation of power. Technology just increases the speed, scale, and secrecy with which one can do that. I don't think people even understand what that means and how much harder it makes change for us, for everyday people. If we're talking about the economic crisis, the climate crisis, the health crisis—these are all high-tech crises which make the racialized economic divide worse. Technology aids voter suppression and denial of basic democratic rights. It intensifies police profiling and punishment, and other kinds of state-sanctioned violence. It generates electronic waste and resource extraction, and it intensifies displacement and dispossession.

This is no longer about media policy. This is about something totally different. This is a digitization of racial capitalism that is profoundly altering the ways we communicate. One obvious example is these data mining companies. We call them "social media" companies. But the real point of calling them social is that there's a "many-to-many" relationship between the audiences, it blurs the lines between audience and producer, and that's not a bad thing, except there are no rules to protect anyone in that environment. It is a Wild West type of situation where surveillance is happening at a high level, where these data mining companies are becoming the purveyors of misinformation and disinformation.

When we talk about an unregulated internet, think about the kind of voter suppression tactics that were used through Facebook in the 2016 election, proven through the Cambridge Analytica scandals. Through all these revelations we know that this is happening. We've seen the intensification of hate speech and how that has directly contributed to intensified hate violence in the streets, and the domestic terrorism of these white supremacist, anti-government extremists, right? This is not an ideological exercise. This is no longer about ideology. This is a material battle in the street every day for life. This idea that you can somehow disappear from that system and divest from dealing with the internet in any way, it's just not real, number one. Number two, that's like an abolitionist saying, "Well, I'm simply not going to participate in slavery." Meanwhile, your clothes were made by the manufacturing that is mobilized by slavery. So you can't say that. It's just not real.

The Center for Media Justice

We started the Center for Media Justice, now Media Justice, to make it clear from the gate that we knew then that this system was going to undergird everything. It was obvious that that's the direction it was moving. What we tried to do was—at every step, every stage—engage impacted communities, marginalized communities, in the decision-making process. We tried to fight for protections that were going to protect rights and life and liberties. We've tried to fight to keep it in the commons as much as we could and as best as we could. We tried to do that because we understood that it was about *education*. It was about *criminal justice*. It was about *immigration*. Look at the digitized border. Look at the high-tech border and the way we're using technology and the internet to keep people out and to *monitor* migration and *criminalize*. Look at electronic monitoring. It undergirds the entire criminal justice system! Even these high-tech cities, what they call "smart cities." Everything about the way we live, the internet is flowing through everything, now.

When we first were in the net neutrality[61] battle, people thought to themselves, "This is about to upend the monopolies." They saw Twitter in the Arab Spring, like, "Yeah, the internet is about to lift up these unheard voices and it's going to smash through the gate-keepers. And now we're all going to be producers of our own content and the stories are in our hands." But what we knew then—and we see now—is that the dynamic of power always wants to maintain the status quo. Simply, we're taught under capitalism—the system that undergirds this kind of neoliberal democracy—that the internet will never achieve those types of goals. So we can't just change the internet. We actually have to change how the internet is funding the economic base on which this nation is perpetuated, and also the political economy in which both the media and the internet exist. It's not just the internet. The same is true for journalism. The reason that the internet could become so powerful is because journalism was so defunded and put on the open market.

Structures and narratives are related to one another. At the end of the day, wherever a structural or material battle exists, a narrative battle should, too. All of these are our battles for belonging. All of these are battles for safety. All of these are battles for dignity. You feel me? All organizing is both a cultural struggle and a material struggle all at once. That's why I work to transform narratives, because I know narratives are also structures and conditions, and at their heart, are people. And that's what I care about: people. I am my mother's child.

EIGHT

Priscilla Gonzalez

✳

It was important to disrupt this notion
that wins are the victories of a sole leader,
to lift up the fact that such wins are actually
the victory of many people
who worked really hard
to make change happen.
That was incredibly validating,
to see that what we had built with intention
was recognized at all levels of society.

Priscilla Gonzalez is an organizer and certified professional coach who has been instrumental in achieving groundbreaking campaign victories and developing movement-building infrastructure in New York City, in New York State, and nationally. The daughter of an Ecuadorian immigrant woman, Priscilla was impacted by the visible economic disparity in the Upper Manhattan of her childhood, and her mother's struggles as a domestic worker. In her oral history, she relates the process of her political awakening and the work of feminists of color, who first gave her the words to understand her own family's place in a broader context. She has organized around issues of domestic work, immigration, public education, gentrification, race, reproductive justice, language justice, and ending police brutality. In 2021, Priscilla founded Catalejo, a consulting and coaching practice that seeks to build meaningful long-term relationships with organizations working toward liberation from oppression. In addition to leading Catalejo, Priscilla serves as Program Director at the Center for Empowered Politics Education Fund, a practitioner-led movement-capacity organization that trains and develops new leaders of color to grow their power-building and co-governing infrastructure.

Priscilla emphasizes the importance of centering relationships and storytelling as an organizing strategy to build community, shift narratives, and educate. The importance of lineages, and where we and the movements we work within fit into those lineages, is also explored. Finally, she reflects on the value of learning how to sustain ourselves in movement work, including the importance of creativity and fun.

Priscilla currently lives in West Texas.

I AM FROM NEW YORK, BORN AND RAISED IN UPTOWN Manhattan. I was born into the New York of the late 1970s, a very rough time. It's still rough, but kind of polished over in many ways. Back then it was *raw* and rough. I was born to a single mom, Marcia Gonzalez. My mom is an Ecuadorian immigrant woman from a working-class background. It was always just me and my mom. She actually stopped working full time and went on public assistance to be able to take care of me, especially because the neighborhood where we lived was hard.

When I was growing up in the 1980s, our neighborhood was sort of known as "crack central." My neighborhood was filled was dilapidated buildings and rubble, a big police presence, and a lot of poverty and daily hardship. My mom did everything in her power to shield me from that. Just a couple of blocks away from where we lived there were tree-lined streets with million-dollar brownstones and buildings that had million-dollar apartments. It was hard *not* to perceive the gross difference between my neighborhood and where the people who had more than us lived. Being born in New York, to my mother in particular, at that time and given that reality, clearly shaped the way that I understood the world and the way that I wanted to change it.

Witness to Disparity

I grew up on 106th Street between Columbus and Amsterdam. Every day I would visit my grandmother, who lived on 96th Street, between Broadway and Amsterdam. Broadway was a major dividing line at that time. On that walk, I saw a very big difference between the surrounding neighborhoods. We were just a block off from West End Avenue and Riverside Drive, and I spent much of my childhood in the playgrounds of Riverside Park. We would rarely go to Central Park. My mom is a devout Catholic, and when I was four she enrolled me in a Catholic school in Chelsea. So, since the age of four, I traveled on the subway every single day to go to school in a whole different neighborhood. My school was on the same block as Barneys, a luxury store. Right across the street from my grammar school was a condominium. So those stark differences were really hard for me to miss. I didn't understand what all of that meant as a kid, but I just knew that there was something there that didn't seem right or fair. I'm not sure how my mom made ends meet. I think while I was in school or on the weekends, she would try to pick up a couple of odd jobs.

My grandmother, Leticia Eugenia Toledo Gonzalez, lived in one of those railroad apartments.[62] I distinctly remember running up and down her long apartment that stretched from the back of the building to the front of the building. My grandmother had sixteen children before she migrated to the United States. Half of those births ended in deaths because of the extreme poverty that my grandparents lived in. Of the remaining half, there's a big difference in all of their ages. At different moments, there were a lot of people who would gather at my grandparents' apartment. It was a place that I have really fond memories of, because we were so close. My grandmother was the nucleus, the glue that held everything together. I still miss her, because she was that grounding force for all of us.

Migration and Trauma

Migration was really traumatic for my family and has resulted in a lot of division and a lot of separation over values, worldviews, and even an understanding of family and community. But before that happened, there was a time when we gathered every single weekend at my grandmother's to share food, a lot of laughter, and joy. My grandmother was married to my grandfather for forty or fifty years before they split up. She had this quiet strength. She had endured a lot of suffering in her life, and her family was first and foremost. I always think of her like a stream of water. Water is so powerful, and it's also quiet and unassuming. I learned a lot just observing how, in her quietness, she was really the backbone of our family. My grandmother had all the strength to hold us together, and for a time, to remind us all about the significance of family. I miss that very much.

My mom was the oldest and the first of the children to migrate to the United States. As such, she took on the enormous responsibility of paving the way for the rest of the family to come. That meant an inordinate amount of sacrifice—the type of sacrifice that I couldn't imagine—regarding what she was able to give to me through a lot of love and hard work. At some point she worked at three different factories, traveling to and from New Jersey while living in Manhattan.

In all of her fifty-plus years living in the United States, she's always lived in Manhattan.

Mom talks often about the harsh winters, harsher than she'd ever known. To this day, she continues to talk about the harshness of the weather, the harshness of the culture, the harshness of this new environment in this foreign country. This is the reality that she lives on a daily basis. When she reflects back on the last fifty years, she recalls the sacrifices that she had to make and often talks about, or laments, choices not made. She laments the fragmenting of her family, whom she worked so hard to bring to the United States to access more opportunities than they had in Ecuador at the time. When I think about the trauma of migration, I am often reminded of my conversations with my mom, because it is a daily hardship for her, and it is part of the collective trauma among many immigrants that has gone largely unaddressed and unacknowledged.

When we talk about migration to this country, it's always about the American dream. It's always about "the better life." It's always rooted in a story that glosses over or invisibilizes what it means to be forced to leave your homeland because of economic reasons, political reasons, environmental reasons. It ignores what that does to your spirit, what it does to your sense of self-worth, and denies the impact it can have on family structures and on communities. It's hard, because when people are finally here in the United States, if they're lucky enough to bring their family, they then have to face the daily struggles of being immigrants, of being people of color, often not speaking the dominant language. These conditions don't create the space for people to address the traumas, sadness, and pain of having been forced to migrate. It also doesn't create the space to be able to bridge the differences between the older generations that migrated here and the newer generations that are growing up or coming of age in this country with a different set of values and perspectives. I don't know if that paints the picture, but that's been my experience of my mother's migration story, and certainly one that I don't see talked about much, but which resonates in different ways with a lot of people.

For a long time, I carried her sacrifice and the hopes and dreams that she had for me. I carried that sacrifice and really saw my work as a way to honor my mother's—and my grandmother's—sacrifices every single day. I made peace with their sacrifice through having that sense of responsibility. A few years ago, when I got to spend some time in Cuba, a friend of mine reflected back to me, "If you weren't doing social justice work, if you didn't feel like you needed to honor your family in this way, every day, what would you be doing?" And I had no idea! I was completely stumped by the question. *I didn't know.* His challenge to me was, "You only have one life, and it's important that you find joy that's beyond the struggle and beyond carrying this responsibility." I'm still working through that, but I am striving to find the balance between honoring my family each and every day and living my purpose.

Gaining a Sense of Purpose

I went to an all-girls Catholic high school. There were two young white teachers there, and they somehow convinced the administration to let them introduce a women's studies class and an African American studies class. My school was largely working-class Black and Latinx girls. As an honor student, I was automatically enrolled in both of those classes. They really changed my life because, thankfully, these teachers had the wherewithal to introduce us to really important histories and perspectives.

I remember having my mind completely blown open by meeting Audre Lorde for the first time in those classes. What she wrote resonated so powerfully with me because the injustice that I had witnessed or experienced through my mother's eyes up until that point finally made sense. I finally had language and an analysis that was beyond my direct experience. That was when I began to understand that there was a whole system in place that designed inequality, racism, sexism, and all of these forms of oppression. I became really energized by this feeling of validation, honestly. Everything that I had been feeling was right. There were things in the world that were designed to keep us poor and struggling no matter how hard my family worked, in particular my mom.

My mom always emphasized education. She encouraged me and pushed me to apply to college. I was lucky to get into Barnard College, which was just half a mile away from our apartment, and my education continued there. I was drawn to sociology and literature. Putting those studies together with my lived reality, and that of my mom and my family, really made me want to do work in the world that could improve conditions and change people's lives for the better. That could actually bring justice. That's how, at that time, I was understanding my sense of purpose. A big part of that was doing good work in the world to honor the values that I was raised with and to honor my mom's and my grandmother's sacrifices. I owe my awakening to Audre Lorde, and Black and women of color feminists, for setting me on the right path to living out my purpose in this life.

Recognizing My Privilege

I would come home and talk with my mom about these things, and it was very overwhelming for her. So at some point I stopped doing that. I was very excited to share with her all of these things that I was learning, because I perceived a sense of shame and guilt and *not-enough-ness* on her part that I didn't think she should feel. I wanted to let her know, "Hey! I learned about all of these things that you're *not* responsible for, and that our neighbors are not responsible for, that our community is not responsible for. There are things that are happening beyond our control that have created these harsh conditions for us and that are making it really hard for us to thrive." My mom found that very overwhelming and just listened quietly, and at some point articulated feeling a greater distance with me.

I was still a teenager when I was in college and as I was accessing this whole new world. One thing that I understood very early on was to be mindful and intentional about how to have conversations about injustice and oppression in our lives. I understood that I needed to be mindful of my privilege and the privilege that having access to higher education gave me. I have taken that with me into everything else I do, thanks to those conversations with my mom and watching her reactions and receiving her feedback.

I was still living at home, and I saw three pathways. One was just staying where we were and not doing anything about it and keeping the status quo. The other pathway, which I think my mom would have also preferred, was a career that would have taken me out, and never having to look back. The third pathway was to stay rooted in that reality and try to do my part to bring about the change that I thought my family and community, and families and communities like ours, really needed. Coming out of college, that third path was the path that I went on. It was an exploration of trying to figure out where I could best contribute, and where it made the most sense for me to be, given my values and what I wanted to do.

A Meandering Path to Organizing

I had an internship with a feminist organization working on reproductive health. It was maybe the early to mid-1990s, and we were going to rallies to fight for mifepristone to be approved.[63] That was my first foray into activism and organizing. I never particularly thought about the specific issues that I wanted to work on. It was just the experience of wanting to fight for something that I thought a community like mine really needed.

For a little while, I entertained international work abroad. I really wanted to get out of New York, and I really wanted a break from the daily responsibilities of being an only child. I quickly realized how that work was very much driven by a savior complex, which I didn't want to contribute to. I never saw myself as being in a position to *help* anybody, because when I looked at my mother, I saw somebody who was strong enough to advocate for herself and who didn't need anybody's help. She just needed opportunity. So I didn't think international work was the path for me. I needed to be somewhere that could engage someone like my mom as a powerful person capable of driving change in their own right. I didn't have the language for that. I didn't know what that looked like. I didn't know what model I was looking for. I just knew that I was looking for a place that had that as a shared principle and that practiced that in some way, shape, or form. Again, I didn't know what that looked like. I was very much guided by instinct and feeling. I knew that when I saw it, I would just know it. The internship that I had done for a feminist organization in Washington, D.C., was so very Beltway focused, and at that time it wasn't the arena where I wanted to be fighting. I started searching for local community organizations, because that's where I thought I needed to be. That was my meandering path to landing at organizing.

Finding a Political Home

I found the Center for Immigrant Families (CIF), which was literally three blocks from my house and organizing in the very neighborhood where I grew up. The organization was rooted in popular education and methodologies and approaches that really engaged community members as agents of change. While I didn't have that language, how they talked about the work and how they practiced the work was exactly what I was looking for.

The Center for Immigrant Families at the time was beginning to launch a campaign to address inequality in public education and the public school system in my neighborhood school district. There again, I didn't particularly have an issue in mind, and I wasn't particularly looking to get involved in public education, but I was very, very compelled by and inspired by the science and the art of organizing. A model that was rooted in popular education, in particular, was especially moving to me. It was about tapping into community wisdom, which I always valued, having watched my mom and women like her navigate housing, fights with the landlord, the welfare system, and doing everything they needed to do to advocate for themselves and their families. I wanted to be able to work shoulder to shoulder with women and community members who were doing the same thing in the public schools in our neighborhoods—advocating for themselves as parents and for their children to have access to quality education. That was what I really consider to be the launch of my participation in organizing spaces.

There was a great deal of intention given to relationship building and care at the Center for Immigrant Families, in terms of how you're treated and how you see others treat people. This was not something I had experienced in any other place that I had worked in or been a part of and made all the difference to me as someone who is an empath. There was, as part of the ethos of this organization, a commitment, and a general daily practice of being kind and caring for one another. The world was harsh enough, we didn't need to bring that into the space. That's not to say that we didn't struggle, but the *way* we struggled mattered. We respected and held each other's dignity. Prioritizing relationship building was a core organizing principle. Paying attention and showing care and being mindful about one another were a central part of our organizing practice. That vibe was important to me and made a big difference in how I wanted to show up in movement spaces.

Centering People's Wisdom, Elevating People's Analysis

The methodology around popular education also taught me a great deal about facilitating community processes to elevate people's wisdom. It was a way to elevate people's analysis of the conditions that they were confronting. We developed curriculum and educational materials to complement people's direct experience and facilitate the making of connections between their immediate reality to the broader patterns in society. That experience to me was very foundational and really helped shape me. It is a through line for me in my organizing work that I carry with me to this day.

We would do workshops at the public elementary schools on the Upper West Side. The context was that gentrification was hitting the poorer neighborhoods in that area really hard. The public schools that presumably are for the public were really catering to the families that were moving in, who were white and had higher incomes. The Black and Brown communities that had historically been there—Black and Latinx communities specifically—were being marginalized.

Storytelling as an Organizing Strategy

We were organizing families who had already been fighting but had been fighting on their own. I began to see firsthand the organizing methodology and principles in practice through the workshops that we were leading. We ran workshops in the schools where mostly Black and Latinx mothers would come and share their stories about what they were experiencing in the classroom and with the administration. They shared how they were being treated as parents, how they were being x-ed out from their own children's education, and how that dynamic was also impacting their children's ability to thrive. Hearing people's stories, and seeing the transformative power of people sharing their stories in that safe environment, taught me the power of storytelling, not just for the sake of storytelling, but actually as part of *strategy* in organizing. It was that kind of storytelling that supported everyone who came through these

212

workshops to build connections with one another and to see that they were not alone in their fight. That they didn't need to stay alone in trying to advocate for themselves and their children. That there was actually a community within the school of other parents who were facing the same thing and that there were also people external to the school who were willing to serve as allies because it was likely that what we were seeing in one school was happening in other schools.

Building a Campaign for Educational Equity, School by School

Starting really small from organizing groups of parents in individual schools eventually helped us grow the campaign to bring more parents together from several different schools. We would meet at the Center for Immigrant Families or other venues to strategize and think about how to make the schools more equitable. We thought through how to bring more parents into this work and how we could engage *our children* in this fight. It eventually became a campaign to implement a lottery in District Three that would take away from administrators the power to pick and choose what families they wanted in the schools. That campaign taught me a lot of foundational lessons about what made for powerful and transformative organizing. I saw how individual people were transformed in the process, how relationships evolved, and how storytelling could be a very, very powerful anchor in the process of bringing about change.

Finding My Second Political Home

I was in my early twenties, still working at CIF. My mom had been working as a nanny and a housekeeper for many years. She was employed at that time by a couple that was in the middle of a divorce. It was a very nasty divorce, and my mom was bearing the brunt of their frustration. In the process, she was being abused and exploited. I had always played a supporting role in my mom's various jobs to help translate, interpret, or negotiate, and I was at my wit's end with these particular employers. I didn't know what else I could do to support my mom, because they were very powerful. I was looking for support online, and I talked to my comrades at CIF. All arrows pointed to a group that had been around for a couple of years called

Domestic Workers United. I contacted them and I was invited to come to a meeting. It was funny because the first meeting I went to was of the steering committee of the organization. I had gone there with the intention of getting concrete support for my mom. I walked out having found a political home, my second political home. I also found some incredibly powerful women, Caribbean migrants, strategizing about how to build power to transform the entire domestic work industry in New York. I remember sitting in that meeting, and swimming in my mind were the words of Audre Lorde and all of these other powerful, brilliant feminists that I had been reading up until that time. It felt like everything had come together in that moment. I still get emotional about it because it really was like striking gold. I don't even have the words for it—it was just an incredible feeling. That I was immediately invited into a strategy meeting was even a bigger bonus. That's where I would be for the next decade, cutting my teeth on trying to win what is arguably one of the most important campaigns in my generation of organizers, and it's been an incredible honor to have been part of that.[64]

Building a Campaign, an Organization, and a Movement

I quickly got involved and was part of base-building efforts and leadership development. I also helped to kick off the campaign for the Domestic Workers' Bill of Rights in New York. At the same time, I was helping to build an organization that would be driven and led by domestic workers. I was focusing as well on expanding the base of the organization to engage Latinx domestic workers. This is when I began to formulate a commitment to and practice around language justice to ensure that the campaign and all the work we were building would be truly multiracial and multilingual. Those were easily seventy-, eighty-hour workweeks. I don't know if it was just because of my youth or because I was so inspired, but I didn't even think twice about how much all of us were dedicating to really building an organization, a campaign, and also a movement. We were engaging not only domestic workers, but employers, students, clergy, labor unions, grassroots organizations like Picture the Homeless, and so many others who really threw down in selfless and visionary ways. Those years

214

in the domestic workers' movement were a really, really, really, really significant part of my life.

I joined the staff of Domestic Workers United as the organizing coordinator. It was a little bit of everything, as is the case with small organizations that have big dreams. That was the thing. We had such big dreams and very little resources in terms of money and material things. But we more than made up for it in people power in terms of our leadership, base, allies, and comrades. It's kind of all a blur, to be honest, at this point. I just remember working all of the time, on all of the things. I joined shortly before we launched the campaign for the Bill of Rights. When we launched the campaign, it was all-hands-on-deck. It was our primary focus, even as we were building the organization, and all the things that go along with infrastructure building. The primary focus was really getting the campaign off the ground and winning in every single legislative cycle. Our goal was to win the passage of the Domestic Workers Bill of Rights in the New York State Legislature, and that was the focus for the next seven years. Once we launched that campaign, it got bigger and bigger every year, and the stakes got higher and higher.

The stories of domestic workers were a significant anchor in the campaign. Their stories encouraged domestic workers to bring into the light the harsh working conditions that had been invisible for so long. We often referred to it as *coming out of the shadows*. It was powerful for the Black and Brown women who were working behind closed doors, away from the public eye, to build a platform where they were exposing the injustices in this industry, and where they were also reclaiming the *value* of this work.

The slogan of the organization was "We make all other work possible." And truer words have not been spoken. In the stories that domestic workers shared, publicly and privately, you could see that if they didn't show up to work, their employers couldn't go out and do their work, so the stories were critical. The stories were also important for building that connection among the workers themselves, to know that they weren't alone and that there were other people who were experiencing similar conditions and who were ready to fight and that there was an organization that had their back.

Innovations in Grassroots Organizing

Another important element was our membership base itself and how we built it. Base-building was such an integral part of our day-to-day work. We went to parks and playgrounds throughout New York City to talk to nannies and caregivers. We engaged the labor union that organized the doormen in those fancy buildings, asking, "Hey, can we post these things in the laundry room?" Or "If there are domestic workers that work here, can you let them know that we exist and that we're here?" It was important having a fixed meeting time, so that if we lost touch with anyone—because that was also a real reality—workers could count on finding us at the same time, same place, every single month for our monthly meetings. Building the base was critical for us to be able to demonstrate our power, to be able to show that workers were in this fight to win, to change this industry. Everyone was engaged in that—from the couple of non-domestic-worker organizers that we had on staff, to the leaders and the members of the organization—everyone going out to essentially *multiply*. That was our daily work.

Solidarity as Shared Interest

I would also say that the power of the coalition we had built was critical. Often coalitions are made up of organizations that have a shared interest in a particular issue. This coalition was so special because the shared interest was one of solidarity. We developed a shared analysis of understanding and valuing the important role of care work in our economy and in our society. So for us to really count on organizations that spanned the gamut of issues from faith communities to labor unions, clergy, and students was powerful. Even employers themselves who under other circumstances would be seen as the opposition or be seen as the enemy were *invited in* to be partners in transforming an industry that would have standards that would be in the best interest of everyone. Building a coalition of all of these different stakeholders and across these many interests that were united behind *one goal* and that honored and respected the leadership of domestic workers, was an incredibly unique and powerful formation. It made all the difference in helping to win this campaign, because our power included our base and extended beyond it.

I don't go around quoting politicians, but it really meant something when Governor Paterson, who signed the Domestic Workers Bill of Rights into law, acknowledged in his speech that domestic workers dreamed, fought, and made this legislation a reality! In the end, it was important to disrupt this notion that wins are the victories of a sole leader, to lift up the fact that such wins are actually the victory of many people who worked really hard to make change happen. That was incredibly validating, to see that what we had built with intention was recognized at all levels of society.

Nurturing Relationships

Even though we had many hiccups along the way, I learned important lessons about the organization-building process. Intentionally building an organization where the leadership of domestic workers was valued and respected in significant ways was a core part of our work also. The leadership of domestic workers was visible and real, and what it took to build that was monumental. It meant a lot of hours devoted to process and collective decision-making. It also involved exploring collective leadership and the contradictions and the hardships that come along with that. One main takeaway that I have—and that I hope doesn't sound trite or cliché—is that we really can't cut corners when it comes to bringing along our people. To me, a big part of that is honoring, respecting, and taking care of individual relationships and not to take them for granted. In this moment where we're challenged to grow our organizations and get to a larger scale, we need to bring in as many people as possible, because the dangers in our world have become that much greater. The stakes are that much higher. Change is hard for people, and in the context of building an organization and growing it, there is a lot of change. A lot of things can go wrong, and a lot does go wrong. One thing that I learned is that all the time that you put into all the things that are seen as important—fundraising and strategy meetings—that same energy has to go into maintaining and caring for the relationships inside of the organization and outside, because that's

217

where the breakdowns happen when we don't take the time to do that.

Seeding the Movement Broadly

Seeing so many of the women that we worked with at Domestic Workers United still in movement—not just in the domestic workers' movement, but showing up in all kinds of other movements, racial justice movements, movements against police brutality—is beyond the best you could hope for! So often, and understandably, we want to keep our best. It's always hard when people make decisions to transition to other spaces, other issues, and organizations. But when you see that someone transitions out of an organization or out of a particular sector of the movement and they go off to play critical roles in other efforts for change, I think that is *exactly* what I want to see and what I hope for.

We can take the lessons we've learned and sharpen them in other contexts and grow them. At the end of the day, what we're all trying to do together in changing the world is made that much stronger when we are sharing knowledge in significant ways by actually grounding ourselves in new contexts, realities, and issues. So I love to see it, and I feel incredibly lucky to have worked with such brilliant people. It's an experience we all share that no one will take away from us, and I'm really happy that many of us are off doing different things. I know that the lessons we learned in that special time, we are continuing to apply today and making them that much better. It's a way to honor and keep alive lineages. There are so many different lineages in organizing. I am proud that the lineage of domestic worker organizing exists and has roots in so many other issue areas and sectors in our movement.

Flexing Different Muscles

For a long time, and maybe even still to this day, I have operated on the principle that when I'm called to serve, I need to go and serve. When I was approached to consider making the move to Communities United for Police Reform (CPR), I applied and was happy to have been accepted. I made the move because I genuinely did want to apply the lessons that I had learned in the domestic worker context elsewhere, because I believed—and still believe—in those strategies. I also wanted an opportunity to build with different organizations and to be in a different fight and sharpen, or maybe flex, different muscles. Deciding to apply to CPR was a mix of all of those things.

I am also somebody who makes decisions based on instinct. When I made the move to CPR, it was really wonderful to learn a little more deeply about the shared lineage between organizing around police accountability and domestic worker organizing, because of Richie Pérez having mentored so many of the organizers that were part of both movements. His lessons and some of his advice were very much alive in both models. You know, from considering "any and all tactics," as I've heard he would say, to using individual cases as organizing opportunities that you could build campaigns around to push forward broader demands for justice, to just getting a deeper orientation to his teachings, all of that was very present within the work at CPR. I felt really validated in having made the move, because I was also still very much connected to my roots. I had been so inspired by the coalition that we had built for the Domestic Worker Bill of Rights campaign, and I was really excited to work directly in a coalitional space like CPR. The campaign and the coalition were unprecedented, and I knew there would be challenges. I didn't know what kinds of challenges, I just thought that they were going to be different. I looked forward to pulling on some of the things that I had learned over my work in different sectors to organizing at CPR.

Building a Movement Against Police Brutality in New York City

Historically, there had always been organizing against police brutality in New York City, but people and organizations had been working in silos for so long. It was clear that efforts needed to be consolidated and coordinated in order to take on such a mammoth force as the NYPD. So in that way, both the campaign and the coalition were unprecedented. CPR was the largest formation of organizations coming together around a clear set of goals to end discriminatory policing in NYC. We were grounded in several unifying principles, but our commitment to respect and elevate the leadership of grassroots organizations in particular was unprecedented, and is what made CPR a special hybrid vehicle. It was visionary in many ways. CPR had formed right on the cusp of what we now can see is a national and international movement against police brutality and in defense of Black Lives and for a redefinition of public safety and community safety. So, for all of those reasons, there are many ways that CPR played a major role in helping to forge a path that created the organizing conditions that we've seen develop in the last few years.

All of the groups shared the big-picture goal of ending police brutality, but each group had its own lens through which they saw that, and there were intersections. Balancing and elevating leadership while keeping everyone on track was something I was doing all the time. It was literally a daily challenge. Here are the things that were grounding for me: Organizing isn't just what we do externally. It's also what we have to do internally. I shorthand it by saying "bringing people along." Really, what I mean is organizing our own people. That's the mindset that I had to be in, in my role at Communities United for Police Reform. What is the organizing that needs to happen internally so that we stay focused on the goals we've all agreed to? Who needs more attention today and who needs more attention this week? Who needs a space to be heard? Who needs to be reminded of the important role that they're playing, and/or what we said our collective goals are? On an interpersonal level, the relationship building was really, really important in order to maintain trust with everyone.

The facilitation of meetings was really intentional. It wasn't just about somebody's facilitation style, but about *the intention* behind facilitating meetings in a person's particular way. First, let's do some analysis. Let's ground ourselves in the current context, because conditions are shifting all the time. So let's first have a shared analysis of what's happening. Then let's talk about what key decisions we need to make today and get clear on next steps, and who's doing what. It wasn't just a question of format and style. It really was "This is how we're going to stay united and clear all along the way and these things are going to be documented, and we're going to be consistently reminded of decisions we made previously, because we know we all have so much going on."

There were also many different interests. As the staff of CPR, part of the relationship-building and the organizing strategy was understanding what every organization's interests were, including what every individual leader's interests were, and being able to forecast where there might be tensions inevitably and where there might be differences that we would need to try to get ahead of or facilitate. It was very much a dance in many ways, striking that balance. The other piece of it, which was always important for me, and I would dare say for the broader staff as well, was anchoring ourselves in the leadership of the grassroots organizations in the coalition.

What are the conditions that our grassroots organizations are organizing in? What are the realities that their membership bases are confronting right now? What is their analysis of why these things are happening? What are the potential solutions? How do they line up, or not, with what the coalition as a whole has identified as goals? There was a lot of understanding of those on-the-ground realities and a lot of analysis of how they connected with what we had all agreed to move together.

Many times there was an alignment so that the coalition and the campaign could help amplify an individual organization's realities and demands. At other moments they weren't aligned, but we could use our discretion to provide support and strategic advice. There was a lot of power, obviously, in being able to use our own judgment. There was a lot of power that we had as staff. I think the coalition leaders were very wise and intentional about the kind of staff that the coalition needed, a staff that would be low ego, humble, and strategic about understanding the politics inside and outside of the coalition. There were only three to five staff at CPR at any given time. As staff, the leadership within the coalition was an important source of support for us. Continuously engaging with coalition leadership was an important practice to keep us accountable, grounded, and always tapped in to moving goalposts or changing dynamics.

Winning Police Reform

The Community Safety Act (CSA) was a historic win.[65] We were in City Hall until four or five o'clock in the morning, waiting for the vote, and it was packed! There were so many of us up in that gallery that night, and it followed so many days under rain, snow, and intense heat with the sun beating down on us on the steps of City

Hall. There were many big actions, including marches and rallies. It brought me back to the power of community. All of these different members of all our different organizations threw down really hard to get this legislation passed, sharing their stories at press conferences over and over and over again.

The Community Safety Act was an all-out effort to hold the NYPD accountable in some way, shape, or form. There's the power of communications, the power of creative actions, and the power of mobilizing huge numbers of people. It was this coalition and our allies flexing their muscle and leveraging contacts in city government that individual leaders and organizations had cultivated over many years. You know, people really flexing political capital and the coalition and the campaign harnessing that and organizing all those different pieces to move in concert were among the elements that led to the success of the CSA passing.

We countered the narrative of the NYPD and the police unions with the first-person experiences of New Yorkers who had been directly impacted by police profiling, by the fact that the NYPD as an institution had no independent oversight whatsoever. Our narrative was powerful enough to stand up and grounded enough to stand up, to the lies and the misinformation and the spin that we heard from the opposition. We were able to harness the specific skill sets and the individual strengths of the respective organizations that made up CPR. From the political leadership of the grassroots organizations to the legal savvy and the data collection and analysis and research by the legal and advocacy and policy organizations, we all worked in concert to paint a compelling picture that influenced public opinion.

The Fight to End Stop and Frisk

When the stop-and-frisk[66] numbers came out, they were compelling enough and revealed that most of the people who were getting stopped and frisked were Black and Brown New Yorkers. Communities United for Police Reform was able to put faces and stories to those numbers and highlight the dehumanizing impact stop and frisk was having on countless people, especially young people, homeless New Yorkers, women of color, and trans folks. We were able to paint that picture for the broader public, for elected officials.

All of our tactics made for a strategy that led to that victory. It was a real honor to have been part of that and to work with so many committed people. I always considered that every one of our organizations that was part of the coalition was also CPR staff. That's how much I was in touch with everybody, every day.

Transitioning to National Immigrant Rights Work

Working with Mijente came next. It was another one of those moments of being called to serve. I applied, and when they offered, I said yes. I was mostly curious about what it would look like to organize Latinx people in this country and to approach my own people—my own cultural people—as a power bloc. That was my big draw. I was also thinking about work at the national level and what it would take to organize Latinx folks to be on the right side of history and to stay on that side consistently, given that we are a multiracial people and come from very complicated histories with the United States, depending on which countries in Latin America we're from. Not to mention the important history of Mexico that is intertwined with the United States.

I was excited about that challenge, and about Mijente, in particular, being a maverick organization, as I like to call it. Mijente is an organization that has really proven itself to be fearless in leaning into fights that other, national Latinx organizations might not have considered or outright avoided. I joined the organization in the midst of the Mijente for Abrams campaign, the electoral campaign to organize Latinx folks in Georgia to elect Stacey Abrams as governor in 2018. I saw that as an incredibly savvy and strategic move on the part of a national Latinx organization in terms of geography, but also in terms of outrightly practicing the principle of being a Latinx organization that is pro-Black, given the pervasive anti-Blackness in Latinx communities.

I stepped into the role of directing the campaigns team. I had the opportunity to design what the approach of a national organization like Mijente's issue-based campaigns would be. It's an organization that has an individual membership base across the United States and Puerto Rico and up until that point had not yet launched an issue-based campaign. They had done electoral campaigns and had been doing a lot of building in the first few years of its founding. It was at a moment where they were ready to launch issue-based campaigns, and there was a desire to be intentional about it to ensure that the campaigns would be aligned as well with Mijente's values and its flavor—or *el sazón,* as we call it in Mijente. I was really excited to sink my teeth into that and play. For the first time in my organizing life, I had embraced the idea of play and experimentation, and I was there for two and a half years. I'm still a member of Mijente, and although I have transitioned off of staff, I'm still very much engaged.

Experimentation and Throwing Things at the Wall

I was part of the team that helped to shape the No Tech for ICE campaign. It came to our attention from organizers on the ground who had been noticing a pattern of ICE knowing exactly where to pinpoint migrants' locations despite the fact that they lived and worked under the radar. Our team homed in on the fact that technology and tech companies were more involved in immigration enforcement and surveillance than anybody had been previously aware.[67] Our assessment was that in the absence of a petitionable government, which at the time we're talking about Trump, we needed to get creative with our targets. Silicon Valley was both a viable and a perfect target for defending our people in that moment. Delving into that space, which was new to all of us, there was an opportunity to do a lot of learning about how tech colludes with the federal government against migrants. Looking at the obscure processes and funding that happens that no one is privy to in the general public allowed us to access different partnerships. There have been organizations that have been paying attention and doing advocacy and organizing against surveillance that were already closely watching Silicon Valley from different vantage points. But no one had really launched a fight that connected immigrant rights with Silicon Valley greed. So that was an opportunity to do a lot of experimentation and a lot throwing things at the wall to see what could stick, and it was an example of thinking about the methodology of campaigns that made sense for an organization like ours.

We thought about the role that Mijente had historically played in organizing, so we designed a methodology that was in line with the roles that we felt comfortable playing. For example, responding when we're called to come in and help on the ground, playing a role of the first responder or scout who can see—or predict—fires on the horizon. An example of Mijente playing these roles can be seen in its No Tech for ICE campaign when we said, "Hey, we're seeing this thing in the field. We think this could be a way bigger problem. Nobody's paying attention to it from this vantage point. Let's start drawing some attention in this direction and let's start building some momentum around it."

Over the last couple of years, Mijente has grown into the role of sustaining campaigns that can serve as vehicles for people to jump into fights and get activated. One example of that is how college students have been activated in the No Tech for ICE campaign. Students have organized to get some Silicon Valley companies kicked out of career fairs and recruiting on their campuses because of their complicity with ICE.

FueraTrump

The year 2020 was a big one in terms of the global pandemic and being a critical election year. The organization's attention veered exclusively toward getting Trump out of office. Mijente launched the FueraTrump campaign, which organized Latinx folks in key states to turn out and to vote him out of office. During the Democratic primaries, I got the chance to be part of a membership process that did a presidential endorsement for the first time. It was a real exercise in democracy with a lowercase "d." Democracy is so *fraught*, but it was a real practice in engaging our membership in debates to consider the different candidates, really consider the issues, and then to run a process where members could make their voices heard and decide who we were going to endorse. Ultimately, we decided to endorse Bernie Sanders. I've never been a fan of elected officials or candidates running for office, but it was a moment to be crystal clear about the narrative. Our narrative was that we're not endorsing a candidate, *we were endorsing the opportunity to organize*. We were fighting for the conditions that would allow us to organize in ways that we could really leverage for power and drive some change. That was a really important part of that experience too.

Transitioning to Texas

I moved to Texas from New York City right before the pandemic. It's been challenging to get in deep with communities in my part of the state, but living here has certainly opened my eyes to a number of things. I live in West Texas, which is the seat of oil and gas and a Republican stronghold. There are also a lot of folks who don't vote. I haven't quite figured out if those folks were mobilized to go and vote, which way they would vote, but I think there's opportunity here for sure. It's compelling because of oil and gas, which is an incredibly powerful target, so I'm paying attention to what could be possible here.

I'm not yet doing work on the ground in Texas. I am still working at the national level. But one of the things that has become clear to me in visceral ways is how much of a bubble the Left is in. I think we've broken through to the mainstream in many ways, at least I would say rhetorically and in popular culture. But in terms of organizing and winning back ceded ground, we have a lot of work to do. Living here in West Texas and having had some interactions, albeit limited because of the pandemic, with native Texans, and in particular folks who are native to this part of the state, there is a lot of opportunity to learn about people's perspectives. This includes learning what has gone into shaping these folks' worldviews, understanding the dynamics in Washington, and understanding the messages and images that they're seeing in popular culture through the media.

I think we need to do a better job of communicating beyond the choir on the Left, and really figure out ways to get back to organizing basics. How do we have curious conversations with everyday people, the way that many of us *used to do* when we were first starting to organize? How do we tap into what's most important to people who live in places like West Texas? They're not the majority, but they certainly have a big influence in national politics when they're turning out to vote for Republican senators who then go off to Washington and do bad things. I have a newfound appreciation, and have been challenged in many ways to think outside of the East Coast mindset, the West Coast mindset, all the liberal strongholds. That's what I've been paying a lot of attention to and really thinking about.

The other thing that I've been thinking about in this phase of my life in organizing is how we also have to move beyond intellectualizing everything. As I get into my mid-forties and I am experiencing changes in my body, I'm really paying more attention to that. I'm accessing insights about any number of things that I don't think I would have thought my way into. Practicing meditation and doing regular physical movement are giving me the kind of spaciousness that I need to be creative and think of new ideas and come up with new questions as I move into a new phase of my work.

My Ongoing Compass

I wrote four very simple but grounding words on my whiteboard to help serve as an ongoing compass for me. They are love, fun, rigor, and impact. I had always focused on the love, rigor, and impact part. I'm especially excited about the fun part, because I think we need that to sustain us in this work. It's really hard and I've experienced burnout. I know a lot of people have experienced burnout and there's high turnover in our organizations and in our movement. I want to invite us all to think about how we make organizing and social justice work fun and enticing and sustainable for all of us. There's so much to experiment with. When I think about how much intellectualizing we do, I think about how we need to build in much more time to experiment with new models and new ways of being, new forms of governance or new organizational forms. I think that could be a lot of fun and be really inspiring for people so that we're not always only deconstructing things, but we're also nurturing people's imaginations and actually creating alternatives.

NINE

Hilary Moore

⁂

This life is short,
and if you want to use your life
toward creating a world
that we all actually need to live in
and have dignity
and have our needs met—
if you want to make that a priority in your life—
I think committing yourself
to organization
and committing yourself to movement
are really important compass points
or touchstones
to keep coming back to.

Hilary Moore is an organizer, author, and educator raised working-poor in an area of rural Northern California steeped in the politics of white supremacy and the far right. Among her first experiences of the possibilities of resistance was witnessing anti-fascist battles with neo-Nazis during a punk rock concert as a pre-teen. Moving to the Bay Area, she was drawn to housing and anti-gentrification struggles that resonated with her own experiences of housing precarity and displacement, exposing her to racial justice work. Organizing as a member of Rising Tide and of Mobilization for Climate Justice West taught her the necessity of leadership by people of color, as well as the power and beauty of direct action. She is the author of several books on race, resistance, and climate change.

Hilary works within an anti-racist framework that links movements to abolish the police and the military with environmental justice, racial justice, and anti-imperialist struggles in the US and internationally. She draws connections between eco-fascism, white supremacy, policing, and the military. Her training at the Anne Braden Anti-Racist Organizer Training Program within the Catalyst Project focused on mobilizing low-income white people. It also supported understanding her own class identity and the importance of organizing poor white folks through an anti-racist lens. In the following oral history, she reflects on the process of her own political development and explores the meaning of belonging, creating community, and connection. She describes the importance of mentorship and the role of storytelling as a way to build connection, leadership, and movement.

Hillary currently resides in Louisville, Kentucky.

I WAS BORN IN 1985 IN SACRAMENTO AND LIVED IN THAT area most of my life. My family moved around a ton. I think before I was thirty, I had moved over forty times. My parents had split up, so there was lots of staying in one place for a year and then having to move for all kinds of reasons. The relationships in my family are pretty fractured. They are kind of shredded. That's how I feel about it. My parents' divorce was a huge part of my youth. It was pretty aggressive between my parents, and Child Protective Services was involved, so we had to go to court dates and go through a whole bunch of legal shit.

Growing Up with White Supremacy

I say that I'm from Placerville, California, which is in the foothills, maybe an hour and a half or so drive east and a little bit north of Sacramento. My grandparents had a house there all my life, so it was a bit of a home base that was consistent. My dad, aunts and uncles and cousins also live in Placerville. That's where I go back to when I do visit. I would say that the area where I grew up is conservative. Where my dad lives especially is politically far right. There is a lot of State of Jefferson[68] stuff, people wanting to secede from California. That's the vibe, and the family I grew up in, for sure. My grandpa was pretty influenced by the John Birch Society and conspiracy theory shit. That was his milieu. This is a side note, but after he died, I had a really intense moment of, "Wow, we never had a lot of money, but what money they had they put towards this worldview." All of that to say, I got out.

Everybody thinks California is all surfing and progressive politics, and I'm like, "Y'all don't know." There are little pockets of really cool shit, of course, but most of the state, at least in my experience, is conservative, if not more deeply entrenched in domination politics. I think that's a huge reason why I am who I am. Some people ask, "If your whole family was this way, what makes you different?" I have no fucking clue. I just took the whole "what is fair in life" thing more seriously, perhaps, or took it to heart in a certain way. My safety strategy was to get out as soon as possible.

My dad's side is more heavily influenced by far-right-wing stuff. My grandfather lied and told the Sacramento newspaper that he was a photographer, and in the 1960s and '70s he was taking pictures of the fucking Black Panthers and AIM, going to this rally and that rally. He was a right-wing guy taking pictures of liberation movements! I have some of his negatives.

Something that's very meaningful to me is *how to come back*. Because you don't want to throw all of it away. A couple of years before my grandfather died, I went up to the house in Placerville and sat with him and talked to him about the different stories and stuff like that. That was how I could come back and spend time with him.

I'm not close with my mom, and I haven't had a close relationship with her family. I did live with her father when I was in high school, because things were so hard between me and my mom. I didn't know my mom's mom for most of my life, because my mom and her mom didn't have a close relationship. There's grief there, for sure. I did get to interview her before she died and talked to her about growing up in the Depression in Chicago, in a little German neighborhood and how she made meaning of life. My mom's dad was in the Air Force. He's very militaristic in a "my way or get the fuck out" kind of way. I lived with him in high school for a couple of years. When I left, I had to put up a big wall on that side too. So yeah, it's been picking and choosing which walls to take down and how to have particular relationships with the people I can. I would say that's important, and it comes back to the work we did around "White Trash Up for Grabs" stuff.[69]

Rednecks, White Trash, and Hillbillies

I would say my dad's side is more redneck. I mean, there's so many ways to describe it. My mom's side is more white trash. On my dad's side, some people would say, "Hell, yeah, we're fucking rednecks!" Other people would be like, "No, we're not." The same thing on my mom's side. My aunt just died a couple of weeks ago at fifty-five years old. I think it had everything to do with class as to why she died at fifty-five years old.

I asked my paternal grandma, Gum, what the difference is between redneck and white trash. It's fucking fascinating and complex. Both names indicate an economic status, so that's real. But then there are really different cultural feelings or connotations in the different ways someone may identify. Redneck, how I experience it, is a term of pride, like, "We get shit done." I asked her, "Tell me, why do you all call yourselves rednecks?" And she was like, "I'll tell you."

We had this fox on our property and it was killing the chickens, and we were trying to get rid of it. When there was a dead deer that got hit down on the road, Papa brought it back up to the house and set up a trap to get the fox. He tied a rope around the deer, and then somehow put a string to it and connected it to the doorbell. When the fox attempted to pull the dead deer, the doorbell would ring and then he'd go get his shotgun and then go out and kill the fox. Gum was like, "That's what I mean." I was like, "Understood."

I think "redneck" has within it a bit of a "fuck you, we get shit done and we take care of our own." Even if that's not true, there's the idea that we look out for each other. How is white trash different? I don't know how to answer that. I know it's different than hillbilly. Gum, and that whole side, is like, "We are not hillbillies." That's very clear. They would talk about it in terms of intelligence, like, "We are smart." I'm like, "You're up in the hills." So it's not about geography. It's complex. There's a judgment about white trash. You're disposable, you are *literally trash*. It's what they think, it's what I experience, it's what society says. It's so loaded. Everybody has a different connotation and meaning when they use those words.

If I had to, I guess I would identify as a redneck, even though I don't actively live it. In certain contexts, of course, I will claim it, to make a point or whatever. Even now, I live in Louisville, Kentucky, and the neighborhood I live in is super working-class. You know, cars without wheels up on blocks in the middle of the street, five cars on the street that haven't moved in ages, all that. I'm like, "Oh, this is familiar to me." I'm in Kentucky, but this might as well be Placerville, California!

I have an older sister. Her name is Heather. I'm thirty-six, she's forty. Since we were young, we've never been close. My mom ended up moving to Reno for a while, and I think now she's in Oregon. We haven't talked in like twelve years. I think my sister is in Roseville, which is a suburb outside of Sacramento. She's been in that area for a long time. What's wild is that I kind of got started on this track through my sister. You look up to your older sister in some ways. She was an atheist in high school, and I was like, "Oh, let's get in on that." Then, some of her friends were listening to punk, and that's a little bit of how I got into punk. But then she really flipped, and now she's a Christian therapist. We have really different experiences or stories about our childhood, different understandings of what happened.

We moved between poor and working-class. I sometimes call it working-poor. There are not a lot of *strong* relationships in my family, so I got real good, real fast, at making family with other people. I spent all my time with other people and their families and friends pretty early on. I'm starting to realize just how important gender queer people were in my life at that time. Even though I'm mostly straight, I needed to be around people who saw the world differently. The words weren't there in the 1990s, but a lot of my friends were gender nonconforming or trans. Those were the folks that I tended to hang out with.

Punk Rock Saved My Life

I was maybe ten or twelve when I went to my first punk rock show. That show was kind of scary because I came from the hills, and this was in the big city of Sacramento. At my first show there were Nazis, or, you know, kids that identified with Nazis, or some bullshit. At that show, they got kicked out and beat up, and that was my first encounter with anti-fascism.[70] It was messy. It was all kinds of things. It was probably couched in some aggressive patriarchal shit, but that was my first "Oh, we have a thing to protect or to defend in some kind of way." That left a big impression on me.

Soon after, I started to get tattoos and joined punk bands. In my early twenties I toured in bands around the US multiple times. I was becoming more political, but what I was doing socially was music. I wanted my music community to be more political and more active and to have more impact. Not everybody in punk rock wants to organize. There were also some pretty intense stories of abuse that was happening, like sexual abuse, and I was really galvanized by that. One of my friends was abused and assaulted by another friend, and people wouldn't respond. My young self was like, "This is so not OK." That was a moment that I took a huge step back from prioritizing putting my time and investment in the music world. Music was still a huge part of my life, but I started to turn towards mobilizing, organizing, and trying to spend time with people who took social change a lot more seriously and were trying to not just say, "Fuck you," but who are actually trying to bring that world into being.

Awakening to Climate Change

I was pretty young when I first became aware of the threat to our natural environment. I think what changes is the *meaning* we make out of it. When I was really little, it would snow around Papa and Gum's house in Placerville. We were above the snow line, in the mountains, and snow was a part of winter. We would have snowball fights and all that kind of stuff. In the 1990s that started to change. It started off much more personal, like, "Why isn't the snow coming down at Papa and Gum's house?" Now it rarely snows there, and if it does, it doesn't stick. If you keep going up the mountain, you get to Tahoe, where all the ski resorts are. Within a five-year span, all the ski resorts were making snow with machines. Because it doesn't snow naturally anymore, they're trying to keep their business up by making it with machines.

You can't *not know* that shit's fucked when you're living in California. There has been a drought there for the past twenty or thirty years. *The ground literally dropped.* There are these big measuring sticks. The ground used to be here and now the ground is nine feet lower than where it was. I'm sure it's changed even more since I left. Drought—how devastating it is to agriculture and the people who work in the fields—is very well known in California. Even if you are a suburban kid who doesn't give a fuck about anything else about yourself, *you know.* In Central California all the farmland area used to be a gigantic lake. Of course, things change, but you can see that the water table, the water underground, has also gone away.

Then the fires! There was a *fire season* when I was growing up. Now, it's just year-round, with whole towns going up in flames. Everyone's leaving. I think that's the other way I knew—because people were being displaced by fires and drought. Then Big Tech came in and it's a class issue of who gets to stay and who has to leave. I don't know where people are going. I think to Nevada, that's why my mom went to Nevada.

Where I grew up, fires were happening, but now you have to have your head in the fucking sand if you don't understand that our natural systems are out of balance and see who is most vulnerable. Or the prison system?! Throw that in there! California has so many fucking prisons, and we have so many fires and we make—or we "employ" prisoners to fight our fires. It is one of the most dangerous, necessary jobs in California. People who are incarcerated get paid a dollar a day, and then, if and when they get out, they can't become actual firefighters.[71] Clearly, it's environment, class, and race all mixed in. I think that you could probably have that same kind of realization in any state. In my experience, the awareness of these climate changes started around drought and fires.

Leaving Was My Survival Strategy

I left my family because I couldn't tolerate the contradictions I was in. *I cut out.* I went to college and took out as many loans as I could so that I could get out of the Sacramento area. I didn't go far, but it felt far. I went to Sonoma State. That's an hour and a half north of San Francisco. That was where I first learned words for some of the experiences I was having as a younger person. I remember I had one professor in a Women's and Gender Studies class that blew my whole world open. Going to college was culture shock, *times a million*, and one that I was looking for. It was extremely exciting. I took out all the loans I could, and that meant I got to live in a really nice dorm. I was living by-myself-ish, but with roommates. I was living on my own for the first time in a really, really nice dorm away from Sacramento and Placerville. I was both petrified and overwhelmed, but I would never admit that. I was mostly just like, FREEDOM!

I used school to get out, but school wasn't easy for me. I double majored in women's and gender studies and human development, with a minor in anthropology. Then I did a master's at Prescott College, a liberal arts college in northern Arizona. I never actually lived there, but I would do online stuff and you got school credit for fucking organizing. So I have a master's in social ecology. I met the Institute for Social Ecology through Prescott. That shit was $40,000, and looking back, I am like, "Oh God, Hillary!" So I'll be paying that off for the rest of my life, I'm sure. But I wouldn't change it, either.

I have a relationship to debt, and I think it's a class thing, for sure. Debt is just a reality. I want to make sure that I'm doing the work that I want to be doing, because money comes and goes. Sometimes you have more of it, sometimes you have less. I have other friends who grew up working-class, and everything they've done since they got out of college has been to pay off their student loans. I haven't paid that loan since I graduated! To qualify for not paying it back I've worked as a nanny, not made enough money, or lived outside of the country. At thirty-six years old, I now have a job where they can find me, so now I will start paying my student loans. When I think of school, I think of student loans, but school was also a really important time where I just let my heart lead the whole fucking way. Who makes money after getting a degree in women's and gender studies? Nobody! Or a social ecology degree? No one.

Being Welcomed into Community

As soon as I could drive, I spent all my time in the Bay, trying to find something that felt more aligned with the world that I wanted to be a part of. I lived in Oakland for close to fifteen years. I've lived in Germany, and now in Kentucky. An important part of what shaped me is being from a really right-wing area. People don't call it that, it's just the norm. In the Bay Area, I was influenced by movements for self-determination, but it was housing struggles and things around gentrification that I so identified with, because people were losing their homes. That's what got me into racial justice work. I wanted to be a part of collective projects that keep people in their homes. Then I began doing more climate work and saw some of the environmental connections about people being able to choose if they stay, leave, and how—all that kind of stuff.

I can look back now and say that most of the people that shaped my life when I changed tracks from music to organizing, were Indigenous mothers in the Bay Area who were really fucking politicized. They were really clear about how we need to be together, what we need to build, and what matters. There was a handful of people that totally changed where I was going. That's really important for me to always bring back in. I was able to change tracks because of powerful

Indigenous women that I had the honor to be in the same organizations or the same projects with. That was huge.

Anti-Racist, Environmental Justice Work

The first group that I got involved with was Rising Tide. It's a national direct action network in the States, oriented around root causes and stopping extractive industry. I and a couple of people started a Rising Tide chapter in the Bay. It took a while. There were already—and this is the really important part—really brilliant, powerful organizations led by people of color led trying to stop Chevron. I started to do public activities at first with Rising Tide and other parts of my life. "Oh, flyer here, or flyer at this education event." That kind of stuff.

Rising Tide is where I first started engaging in direct action. Being public was a huge step. We don't do that generally where I grew up. Then I started to come to the *art of direct action*, and then its function and purpose within a campaign. "We'd been doing x y z for two years. The shareholders meeting is happening *here*. This is the intervention we're going to make, and these are the demands. Then depending on what happens there, these are the actions we're going to take." I came to understand how direct action can be used as a tool.

The Chevron refinery in Richmond is over a hundred years old. The communities there, and other communities connected to the fights in Richmond, were disrupting the shareholders' meetings, doing direct actions, having big gatherings trying to shift awareness and push policy on the ground to prevent the expansion of that refinery, because they were going to get Canadian tar sands. The Richmond refinery is super old, fucked up, and has been destroying the local community for a long time. They were trying to expand it and connect to Canada. So everybody was like, "No."[72]

Rising Tide was a majority white group, and there were a couple of other organized white groups who were part of the Coalition. It was a concrete way to participate in anti-racist work and movement. This is where I came into contact with Carla Perez and Sharon Longo, two of the Indigenous women who were leading really important work around direct action and community defense. I was in Rising Tide when we joined the groups that were moving things on the ground. I just happened to be in the right room at the right time. I was in the room of the people that founded the Mobilization for Climate Justice West, which became a coalition of forty-some organizations that were putting up a lot of political pressure locally and nationally and getting ready for the 2009 Climate Change Summit in Copenhagen.

Collective Risk Taking

During that time, people involved were taking different risks in different ways. Some did it through messaging or putting their stories out. We took a legal risk. I really saw ourselves as the white group that could do the lockbox thing. We could do civil disobedience, get arrested, and take those kinds of risks that don't make sense for other people in that context or this moment. It felt so deeply satisfying to be used well. It was also scary. I had never taken those kinds of risks before. The risks that I was used to were not choices, whether it was domestic violence or other kinds of shit that happened in my life. None of those were choices, but this was a choice, and for a positive thing, a collective thing. So it was huge, it was powerful.

Communities for a Better Environment and the Richmond Progressive Alliance and the Asian Pacific Environmental Network were three core community-based organizations that had shared campaigns around shutting down the refinery, or at least preventing the expansion of the refinery in Richmond. Those were our core organizations. Then there was a whole smorgasbord of organizations that were down to support what their demands were. Rising Tide was one of those organizations. That's what became the Coalition for Mobilization for Climate Justice West. It was the lead-up to Copenhagen. Almost every month for ten months we chose to stage direct actions leading up to the climate summit, which was amazing, and holy moly, a lot of work! Almost every month, we had a kind of direct action, *or something*. Some of the actions were in Richmond, and then there were also political education tours. We went around the whole Bay and did talks, with puppets and art, painting the street, and all kinds of things. David Solnit was a mentor of mine, so it was also "How can direct action be beautiful? How can the direct action have a particular message that shapes the whole thing in the positive future?" It was exciting.

Chevron was expanding and already had refineries all around the world. This was before Copenhagen, and we were trying to connect to the resistance in other countries. One of the actions was staged against Chevron shareholders. We turned the gates of Chevron into a community stage, and we had speakers or video of speakers. The community-based organizations, the media, the videos, the children, the food, everything got to fill up the road where we had created that space, and it was beautiful. We had practiced and coordinated our ability to lock to each other using lock-box tubes. Our team locked down early intending to prevent the shareholders from getting into the building to meet and make decisions related to the expansion. It was also cold. I remember being real cold. We were out there for hours. What the cops decided to do was just let us sit there. We didn't really have a way to end. We expected a little bit more confrontation. It didn't go exactly how we wanted, and we had to escalate to get arrested. Some of my mentors, like Gopal Dayaneni and folks in Movement Generation, were like, "Okay, what do you all want to do? Do you want to unlock and then get up?" And a bunch of white kids were like, "No! We want to have more confrontation!"

The plan shifted to going further into the property. We unlocked ourselves and then tried to get in, and that's when they arrested us. It was kind of anticlimactic, but we got to tell a story of "This many people were arrested, and here are the main stories of what that space created." We were trying to build up momentum to Copenhagen, and drama is important, depending on the narrative of what the people are doing.

I learned a lot. You need to have an exit plan when you are doing direct action. I mean, we did, but we had to make choices. I remember it being complicated. It was different than what we had imagined. Some people in the coalition were like, "That wasn't how we wanted to end the action." Some people were like, "Yeah, it was." I remember being at a debrief meeting shortly after that action. It was complex, and I was grateful for being a part of that. I had some decision-making power, but really there was a whole crew of folks who were making the core decisions, especially from those three organizations I mentioned earlier. It was a whole lesson on thinking through what actions we take, and the importance of considering what impact they might have on the most vulnerable folks, or the folks who are leading the way. I am so grateful that I had all those conditions that set the foundation for the rest of my political life.

I was with the Mobilization for Climate Justice West for a few years and then that changed. The three core organizations started to shift priority in their campaigns and the Mobilization for Climate Justice West kind of petered out. I had to think about where I was going and what I was going to do next. When I was in high school, I organized a walkout in protest of the AP English test that cost a hundred dollars. I couldn't afford it, so I got people pissed off about that and we walked out. That was just reactionary activism. During 2008 and 2009, I got more involved with people mobilizing and organizing for reasons that are not only about their own material interests but are really about societal transformation.

The Importance of Mentorship

There was a very distinct ethic about mentorship being a priority in those organizations. I wouldn't say it was talked about consciously, I remember it being just a thing of common sense. I remember coming in and being welcomed. I didn't know anything, if I look back at it. Who is this little white girl from the hills? But they welcomed me like I had a purpose.

Mentorship and intergenerational work was tended to and shared collectively. Development and bringing people along was also a really important ethic. That was also true of the Center for Third World Organizing. In the Bay, there's a culture of political expectation. This is what I wrote about for my master's. There are generations of political people. For me, it comes back to my family history stuff. When I feel my place within history, it's easier to feel like I belong. It's very important for how I understand who I am right now and where we are going.

That is probably why I stuck like glue to those Indigenous women. That was a big part of how they oriented to the work. Who do we come from? Who are our ancestors? Who are we right now? What are we leaving behind? That was always part of the conversation as we were locking down at Chevron. That was the stuff that just meant a ton to me, and it still does. It's still part of how I do political work. That, I would say, is the milieu that I got brought up in, politically.

Looking back now, Sharon and Carla and those folks, I don't know what they saw in me, but they made a lot of room for me, this random white girl. They brought me in and called me family. I'm pretty sure I said a bunch of terrible shit at some point. I have this Día de los Muertos tattoo on my arm. I got that in my punk days. I remember Carla asking me on BART, "Tell me what that means to you?" She just listened. I'm pretty sure I told her, "Oh yeah, in my family, you know, we're part Cherokee." Shit like that, and she was like, "Oh, well, let's talk about why it is that you are white." She met my ignorance and still kept me in. I never felt shamed by her or anything. I was the youngest person in that space, and I liked that. I like learning from powerful people.

Confronting Whiteness

Richmond is a majority Black city, with lots of Brown and Asian folks. I went door knocking with the Richmond Progressive Alliance. They had a local electoral campaign. I didn't really do much. Sometimes white folks get politicized around anti-racism because they are around people of color and that's what politicizes them. I grew up in a majority white area. There was some shared economic status, but poor and working-class Black neighborhoods have a whole different *weight* to them. I grew up poor and working-class. But I remember feeling like, "I don't know shit." That's good, but I also remember that it destabilized me in a way, "Who am I? What the fuck am I doing? How do I do anything that's worthwhile?" I wasn't clear on who I was or what I had to contribute. But I felt that if this is where the people I deeply respect and want to be in movement with are making interventions and doing good work, I need so much more help in understanding how I can be a part of this, because it was so shocking.

Understanding Race and Class

I was fumbling all over, especially around white shit. That's when I looked for the Catalyst Project and found the Anne Braden program, an intensive, anti-racist organizer training program. I missed the application deadline, and I wrote a letter to Catalyst, and Carla wrote a letter to Catalyst, saying something like, "Hey. Get her in." They made special room for me to get in that program. Not everybody has access to movement leaders that have that much clout, and having that was a huge privilege. When I started to do the Anne Braden program, some of what I did was family history research. It's been family history work that has helped me to put my family into context.

Catalyst was life changing. When you get a bunch of white people together, it gets messy. I think that they held us well. I started as just a participant in the program and a few years later became a collective member. We were a very difficult cohort. We tried to make it hell for the collective members. The first part of the program, all of us were like, "Everything that's wrong with white supremacy is wrong with Catalyst Project." The trainers made an intervention in the middle like, "Hey, what is happening? Is this how you want to spend your time?" Then it totally shifted into a different experience.

Going through that arc was so important, because I think anytime you get a group of white people together around racism, the last thing they usually want to do is talk about racism. They want to just tear each other down. I had started off in multiracial spaces. That was magical because people looked out for me, but when I left that magical space, I was fucked. Being in the Anne Braden program with the Catalyst Project gave me tools to stay in and gave me tools to understand.

This was the first time I understood class. Before I was in the Anne Braden program, I really couldn't articulate what class was. I think because of the right-wing shit that I came from, I knew that race was really important. I think that's why I got in on some of the projects that I did. It wasn't until I was in the Anne Braden program that I understood why I identified with the housing struggles, with people being able to stay. I understood my own stake in it. For the first time, I realized I was working-class. Before, I had zero concept of that at all.

One of the other things that comes to mind from Catalyst is they name mentorship very intentionally. They pair participants up with folks that have related experience, both to process what the program is for folks while they're in it, but also to make movement connections. It's a chance for people to ask questions about how other people make sense of what they do in the world.

A really important piece involves shifting from a framing centered on white privilege and education into *how do we organize working-class communities for collective power?* Those are really different strategies. Those are really different end goals. I think the Anne Braden program and Catalyst were a huge reason why I even shifted in that way. It helped me to find context for the systemic function of white supremacy and imperialism. The piece around internationalism often gets dropped off. All over the world movements have been doing this shit for a really long time. The US has a lot to catch up on and we have a particular role. Context and strategy got filled in for me, a millionfold. A lot of the leaders in Showing Up for Racial Justice (SURJ) are alumni of the Anne Braden program. There is something very important about collective study. There is something very important about seeing everybody on the path of their long-term leadership, and what it means to invest in each other.

The Catalyst Project was my intervention for a lot of years. There was a mostly white environmental movement and a mostly people of color, Indigenous, and Black–led *climate justice movement*, with a big gap in between in terms of resources, culture, and impacts. When I was at Catalyst, I pursued 350.org. I pursued Sierra Club. I pursued Rainforest Action Network. I was trying to use that role to move the bigger greens, in terms of shifting their internal understandings and resources to movement organizations led by people of color. That was my intervention for some time, and it's still something I really care about. That work really deepened my understanding of the importance of organizing white people around racism, particularly poor and working-class white people. It could be with any issue or movement sector. That's my lifelong intervention now.

That whole experience really lit a fire under my ass around the ways that the climate movement at that time understood racism so little. I moved more into anti-racism work. That's also when I was dabbling in the PhD program in human geography at Berkeley. I did that for a year because I wanted to study. I wanted the fucking resources that a university could give you. I wanted time away from movements to think differently about race and climate. Then I had a cancer scare, plus class and culture shock at Berkeley, and realized that I couldn't do a PhD program because that wasn't how I wanted to use my life. After the Mobilization for Climate Justice West, I was like, "Oh, I'll do a PhD." Then I was like, "Nope, back up."

The John Brown Anti-Klan Committee and Lessons for Today's Mvements

I was working on the book *No Fascist USA! The John Brown Anti-Klan Committee and Lessons for Today's Movements* with James Tracy. Richmond, the Richmond Police Department, and a faction of the Richmond Police Department known as the Cowboys were a big part of that history. Learning about them was like a punch in the stomach. I think people learn in spirals and life happens in spirals. You come to things the first time, then other things in life happen, and then you come to similar things, but in a deeper way, perhaps. That's the hope. In writing about the John Brown Anti-Klan Committee, it totally time-traveled me back to Richmond and painted a whole other historical context for the work that we were doing in 2008, 2009, and 2010.

We were writing about the 1980s. I was born in the fucking eighties! Working on that book put my life into perspective, in a lot of ways. Some of the places that we talk about in the book are some of the places where I was part of door-knocking campaigns at nineteen and twenty years old. Even if I had read the book that I would later write, I wasn't in a place to receive the depth and the breadth of all of that.

The Cowboys, a Klan-like organization within the Richmond Police Department, were picking up young Black men, especially, and driving them out to the suburbs and leaving them there or just committing the regular police murders that were always happening. I wouldn't have been able to comprehend or understand when I was nineteen years old how that is related to the fact that there is a global corporation doing whatever the fuck it wants in Richmond, and taking up both the illegal practices it was doing and the way it was legalizing more horrible practices on this community. What is the ideology, what is the common sense, what's in the water that we're all swimming in, where both the Richmond police can do whatever the fuck they want in this place and Chevron can do whatever the fuck they want in this place? What does that mean about Black and Brown folks in Richmond? What does that mean about Indigenous folks who are resisting the tar sands? I was connecting those resistance points. I have chills right now. I had a whole experience writing that chapter. I know even more deeply the ways that we're all connected, the ways that all of our movements need each other and how systemic this shit is. Writing that whole book really deepened my politics and understanding and commitment, particularly for movements fighting for self-determination. That was a trip.

Organizer/Author/Educator

The term organizer was always this contested term from back when I started doing work in the Bay Area in 2008. Everybody wants to call themselves an organizer. Maybe it's only the people that do the door knocking and do the one-on-one stuff, and all those things. But recently, Steve Williams visited with folks at Showing Up for Racial Justice and talked about people who are organizers. He said, "You're part of an organization and you're trying to build an organization. There are many ways that you can do that." I am committed to collective projects, and when I say projects, I mean organizations. This life is short, and if you want to use your life toward creating a world that we all actually need to live in and have dignity and have our needs met—if you want to make that a priority in your life—I think committing yourself to organization and committing yourself to movement are really important compass points or touchstones to keep coming back to.

An Organizer in the Broad Sense

It was really hard for me to move to Germany and switch movement roles. I became a writer full time, and literally had a visa as an author. The principle of building organization is so central to how I understand being a political person. But I am an author. I am a writer, dammit. I've gotten used to being rigorous and studying and writing and doing research. It's still not easy for me. I write books, but I hate writing, honestly. I love editing.

I love making things that are relevant and that come out of movement. That's what I love. My writing is coming out of organization and it's coming out of movement. What I've been trying to do is put some life into our reflection, because we're moving so fast all the damn time. We don't integrate the wins that we have, or if we do, it's for just a hot minute. We don't have much space to grapple and pause with the lessons, distilling the lessons of what we're up to and how we have changed it. So I am a writer. I hate writing, but I am a writer because we have a lot to build on.

Let us not re-create wheels. A lot of shit *hasn't* worked. Let us let go of the things that haven't, and let us really refine what does work and create some new shit based on that. That's what I care about. So I would say that I'm an organizer, but in the broad sense. I'm going to knock on some doors in Louisville, but I'm not the person leading that campaign about ending cash bail. But I am committed to organization and committed to movement, so I do different things within that.

Germany, Connecting Family History, and Political Movements
I initially went to Germany because I was trying to reconnect with family. I had cut out so early on that I didn't really have anything to reconnect about, but I knew that my dad's parents really cared about family history. It was something to come back to, and I interviewed and recorded them a bunch. That was also from the Anne Braden program. I knew that we were German. That mattered to me, even as a young person. I took German in high school. Nobody takes German in high school. It was just me and the Goth kids because they wanted to understand what the Rammstein lyrics were.

I was a kind of a punk in high school, but I was also a jock and I hung out with the Goths. I took German classes because I knew that I was going to go at some point. My dad's side is from Austria. I was connecting with my grandpa, with Papa. His name was Robert. It was my way of coming back into the family somehow. I would go up specifically to talk to him and Gum, about who we came from and why we got to where we are. We had really lovely conversations, and I still re-listen to him even though he has passed away. That is really hard because I feel like I have missed a lot too. After he passed away, I told myself that I had to go. I just had to go to Germany. I just had to go to Austria.

At the time, one of my friends who is German was living in Oakland. I had a couple of pieces of information from the conversations

247

with Papa about what village we came from in Austria. My friend
helped me write an email to the church in that region. Every village
has a little Catholic church. I sent emails asking, "Do you know anything about these people who left in 1900?" I thought that maybe
something might come out of it. The day before I got on the plane, I
got an email from a man named Johann Limburger, Hans. He wrote,
"I'm your relative and I am retired, but have spent the last ten years
researching our family history. I can show you ten generations of
your family from this one village. So come and meet me on this day
at this time, and I'll show you all of this."

Belonging

This was one of the most life-changing experiences I've ever had.
Riding this tiny little Austrian train into the Alps, which are stunning
and gorgeous, and having this visceral experience of coming home
and returning in some way. My family never was able to come back.
They had plans to come back to Austria, but my great-great-grandfa-
ther died, and my great-great-grandmother was stuck with six kids
in the States. But I met Hans, and he brought his family, and everything changed. Whatever is in me that deeply wants to belong to
place was just like, "Don't let this go." I visited every year or so. I
would meet him at his house, and he would drive me around: "OK,
your ancestors lived here before they left. One hundred years before
that, they built this house down the valley. A hundred years before
that, they built *this* house down the valley." So, I know for the last
eight hundred years where my family has lived.

Having that historical context for how you became who you are
means everything to me. Both the family that stayed and became
Nazis, or the family that came to the States and were so fucking poor
but who worked for the railroad and saved money and said, "Fuck
you" to all the other immigrants. All the different ways that empire
and class and whiteness combine. The short story is that I went because Papa died and I needed to go, and we had always said that we
would go together. When I finally went, all these doors started to
open up, in terms of family history, and in terms of the powerful climate justice movement in Germany. Folks there had translated my
book *Organizing Cools the Planet*. I had worked with them on the

German translation, and so there were all these really rich lessons across nations also happening at the same time.

I had also fallen in love with the Germans, so it was the whole heart-opening, mind-opening thing. Mostly it was family stuff, but of course it was also political. I was really impressed by, and wanted to learn from, anti-imperialist, anti-racist movements in Europe. I am not comparing myself to James Baldwin or Angela Davis by any means, but there is something about being outside of the States and knowing who you are from a different perspective that is so fucking valuable. Being in Germany these last three or four years has actually been really hard, kind of brutal, but I would not change a damn thing because of how meaningful and rich it is to literally switch to a global perspective. Granted, Europe is also Western, but I was in Berlin. That city is so internationalist. I was around Turkish people. I was around Kurdish people and folks that are seeking asylum from West Africa and Cameroon.

This is that thing that we talk about in *No Fascist USA!* "Can the white working class in the US be revolutionary, given imperialism?" That's an old, old, old debate and fight. I want it to be a yes. It took me being outside of the States to get the depth of what the difference is between Third World countries and being in the belly of the beast. I feel like my experience in Richmond was my first time in the Third World within the US, and my experience in Berlin was being around more of the Third World, but also outside the US, especially folks that are organizing from the Middle East. My commitment to Palestine and Free Palestine got so strong in Germany. Yeah, so family history, politics, but also race, class, nation, all that stuff.

Eco-fascism, Policing, Imperialism, and Race

Doing work connecting eco-fascism, policing, the military and surveillance systems felt like the obvious progression of racial justice work. Writing the *No Fascist USA!* book was a reframing of a bunch of things. Now, it feels like I'm going to be working around abolition of prisons and policing for the next twenty years. I wrote another small book, *Beyond Policing: Community-led Solutions to the Violence of Policing in Western Europe*, which is similar to *Burning Earth, Changing Europe*. It's about the demand to defund the police, the global uprisings of 2020, and what those movements look like in Europe. Europe loves to say that the US is so racist, and the US police are so terrible. "Good thing we have nice police over here." Guess what? There's a whole bunch of communities, people of color, Black communities, African communities in Europe that are like, "Fuck y'all. There's a reason why there were mass uprisings in Europe." Ten countries in Western Europe had the biggest anti-racist uprisings in their history in 2020. It wasn't because it was *just* solidarity with the US. It was because that shit is real in Europe too, and a global crisis.

Coordinating with Critical Resistance, I translated their Defund the Police Toolkit into a European context, and used case studies of where people are doing Defund the Police work, but not calling it that. Like *No Fascist USA!*, it has a section of lessons and reflections. In dominant white society, police are perceived as a given, and like the definition of what makes something safe. It's a really strong, strong, strong impulse in German society. Almost as strong and getting stronger is the very real fact that the far right in the German police and military do whatever the fuck they want. People are making these connections in new ways, hopefully. Those are the pieces that I was trying to pull together. How can you be anti-fascist? How can you be socialized as a German and be so anti-fascist, and say that Nazis are terrible, but because of your commitment to policing you can't make the fucking connection? Why is it that there was not a really thorough de-Nazification process? Nazis still kept their jobs and became police and became military. Germany sees itself as "We did a real good job. The Holocaust was fucked up, and we have a lot of memorials." There's a whole industry around the politics of memory, but the focus on memory also allows for a turning away from the current state. It's really oriented towards the 1940s and not looking at what's happening *right now*. So, given who I am in the world, I was like, "Oh, I can do this while I'm here."

I thought I was going to live in Germany for the rest of my life. I even got married so that I could live there for the rest of my life. But it was the uprisings, and it was COVID, and a whole bunch of things within that, that shifted my gravitational pull back to the States. I had always stayed on the board of SURJ, and was always invested. But I got galvanized in a new way around Defund and around

Critical Resistance's leadership. Rachel Herzing is another really important mentor and friend of mine. I know that I'm more useful when I'm in an organization and in my context, even though I hate the US in so many ways and I can do cool shit in Germany, but ultimately, if I'm not a fluent speaker and I don't know the intricacies, I'm not as relevant. So much got shifted and changed around the uprisings and Defund and abolition. When SURJ committed to abolition in a huge way, I was just like, "I have to go back."

Standing Up for Racial Justice

I was in Germany for four years, mostly Berlin. When the pandemic came down, I was living in a collective house with forty people. Even leftist Germans don't have great threat assessments. So I left to live in the countryside with a different group of friends. Then I moved to Louisville, Kentucky. I had started to feel like I needed to go back to the states over the winter. I've been on the board for SURJ for the last five years. I was going to come back, and I knew that we needed a whole bunch of new roles, given all the state work and state strategy that we're moving forward. One of those roles was making sure that we strengthened our internal systems and our internal processes, including how we are with each other. We went from a baby organization to a massive organization. We're still catching up to being able to hold that much weight on our bones. I got invited to the position of director of people and culture. We have a very clear external strategy about who we're organizing and why. We need internal systems and structures to reflect that politics. It's political education, it's communication systems, it's conflict resolution. I'm on the human resources team to make sure that our internal policies actually take care of our folks.

We're organizing poor working-class white folks. Our organizers are of those communities. Well, guess what? If you bring in folks who have had a shit ton of trauma and this is their first movement job, then the middle-class shaping of the previous versions of the organization don't hold up. They don't take care of our folks. So we're creating new policies and we are updating out-of-date ones. I'm taking care of the insides, the innards, and making sure that we can do what we need to do on the outside.

I'm six weeks into the job at SURJ. It's a lot of shaping culture. One, if we're moving from a position of whiteness around racial capitalism, *we're already late.* The intervention should have happened a long-ass time ago. There's already a context of urgency, especially with the trauma and the impact of everyday life. So what do you do with that context? How do you find ease? How do you find ground? It's a constant dance, for sure. Our organization struggles with urgency, absolutely. We're trying to start all of our meetings with purpose, whether that is the mission statement or something else about "Why the fuck are we doing this work?" So starting with purpose and ending with beauty. We're trying to do a lot more story sharing and storytelling, because we are a cross-class organization with mixed abilities. We're also a mostly female socialized organization with a lot of gender-nonconforming folks and trans folks. It's a whole complex beast, for sure, but these are the folks that we need to do the work, and there are contradictions and challenges within that.

What we're finding is that when we make enough space and time regularly for people to talk about what they love and why it matters to them, that shifts a lot. Having a lot of room for celebrations at the ends of things, whether it's the end of the year, or end of a campaign, really helps to integrate those lessons. That helps also with urgency, not to just fall into the next thing, but to be like, "Oh, we can have this. We can let this in."

I'm also trying to build up the practice of *culture sharing.* What is anti-racist culture? What is anti-capitalist culture? *Let's build that together.* Whether it's your grandma's recipe and your grandma was an anti-fascist, and that's why it matters to you, or just your favorite song, or a ritual or practice that you are in. We have to lead with the things that are compelling. Externally, those are the conversations we're aiming for, including during door knocking. That's the thing that I'm trying to pump up the muscle for internally as well, to get more practice in. We need to do that with each other as staff. Because there are a bunch of differences between us on the inside, we have to get real clear about the things that *do* connect us.

SURJ is a multiracial organization, but it is majority white. That's an important part of it. It has taken a lot of time and struggle to center class in an anti-racist way. I know this by being on the board for years. We're not perfect, it took a lot of struggles to get to that place, but I would say that we are there. We need a culture that's fucking *inviting*, and that people want to join from the communities that we want to join. So that is a priority. It's a constant dynamic tension in the organization. When you get mostly white people together where class matters but the overall context of why the fuck we're organizing is building multiracial anti-racist movements, it takes skill and nuance and development and time. It is different for all individuals, and also for different projects. Historically, there's been a lot of left organizations in the States that were trying to deal with class with white folks and then totally lost the race piece. So we feel *very aware* of that legacy that we teeter around.

What has been so exciting is Southern Crossroads' work around Rednecks for Black Lives, and their intervention to really identify with the miners at Blair Mountain. They got gunned down alongside their Black coal miner co-workers. Those stories are what lead the work. We try to center those stories and that ethic, and continually adjust along the way. You've got to do both things at the same time. Make room for folks to finally fucking identify with class struggle and how they are personally moved and traumatized by that shit *and* have a space that is big enough and wide enough to *galvanize* that positioning toward the larger project of an anti-racist society, an anti-racist intervention, and movements that are powerful. There are reasons why it's hard, because it hasn't been really done at this scale before.

SURJ is moving thousands and thousands of people, in all kinds of ways. The chapter-based work is mostly middle-class work. There's campaign work and then there are these local projects that are doing deep listening and deep canvassing and building really deep connections in rural, poor, mostly Southern communities. We're doing all kinds of things at the same time. We know that it's important that there is room for all the strategies, and that it's not one strategy over another, but that they work together. There are a lot of contradictions, and it doesn't mean we're all on the same page at the same time, not at all. But there's enough of a political will and an internal compass of "This is the direction we're going, and contradictions are going to be part of it." Considering who our movement partners are and what we're committed to, I think our compass is going in the right direction and we'll just keep getting better and more fine-tuned with it.

I've taught with Generative Somatics since 2014. It's a lot of understanding trauma within movements and an analysis of trauma as to what movements are responding to. I think it's a really important piece, right? I think about it with SURJ and some of the projects that we're taking up. Sometimes you need to make a certain intervention at the city council meeting. But if the story that's running inside you is "I don't belong. Why am I here?" you're not going to have the impact that you want, and you're not going to have the impact that maybe that campaign or the organization *needs*. So what are all the tools and practices for making sure that we can be powerful in our work?

Generative Somatics is embodied leadership. Do our actions, our moods, our worldview, who we are, match up with our values? You can be dedicated to something so beautiful and profound, but if you don't know how to hold a boundary and you perceive everything to be someone attacking you then how are you going to bring that change about? We're shaped in all kinds of ways.

How do we make sure that who and how we are in the world aligns with where we're trying to go? It's healing trauma work, but it's also leadership development work in a body-out kind of way.

Abolition and Environmental Justice

I am really influenced by Ruth Wilson Gilmore around how abolition is an environmental issue, *a justice issue*. Given who I am, given the last thirty-six years in the US context, given the uprisings last year, the work at SURJ just feels like the most ripe and pertinent expression of what I care about around climate justice, what I care about around anti-racism, what I care about around anti-imperialism, and what I care about around abolition. So I feel quite satisfied. I don't do the chapter work; I'm mostly tending to the internal national organization. But I feel well used in a good way, and I feel like there's nowhere else I would rather be. You know, it can be stressful coming into a new job, but this role with this organization at this moment in time, given the lane that we're in, in movement, it feels like a lot of right-on-time-ness.

The thing that feels worth emphasizing is the role of mentorship in my life, and most of those people being Black or Indigenous women, some of whom are gender nonconforming and trans. There is really important mentorship in my life. Carla Wallace, for instance, is a white Southern woman, queer, and a *huge* part of my life. But I feel like I wouldn't even have found Carla if I hadn't had those folks from before, or Rachel now. If anything, I know that I'm clear on the work because of the people I've been around.

I think my superpower is finding really good people all over the world. That has been what saves me and why I have a rich life. I know how to find good people, people that *do* take care of each other in a way that I so wanted members of my family to take care of each other, but that wasn't on the table. That's why I'm in Louisville. I know that there is an awesome core community here where that is the priority. I'm sure we'll go through our ups and downs and all that. Where I'm going to make home as an adult, I want to be with people who know how to do that, or who want to know how to do that, and will *stay in*.

ACKNOWLEDGMENTS

ORAL HISTORY INTERVIEWS ASK A LOT OF THE NARRATORS, before and after the interview itself. I am grateful to each of the women interviewed for this book for taking the time to consider my request, reviewing materials prior to the interview, making time for the interview itself, reading their transcripts afterwards and making changes as needed, and responding to my emails and texts for clarifications.

This is movement history as told by women who've led from the front and from behind, holding down multiple roles. They have created a better world because they saw the need to do so. It isn't that they are fearless, because resistance brings risk. There is beauty in their resilience and commitment to remain in movement in spite of its challenges and all the ways that systems of oppression create obstacles to birthing a more just world in every aspect of our lives. Their brilliance, creativity, generosity, and dedication are a gift to all of us. Organizing isn't only about fighting *against* oppression, it is about supporting the process of building a collective vision of a just world, with love.

I have always dreamt of recording and sharing stories and lessons from organizing, probably because I didn't hear these stories growing up. Histories of resistance matter because contained within them are the lessons and tools we need to change our world. It is essential to document history from the grass roots, where histories of social change is least likely to be recorded and preserved. Not only do we need to understand how change has come about in the past, we need to use that knowledge to shape the future. By being able to see ourselves in others who are engaged in social justice work, we may be able to imagine ourselves as agents of change, even if we don't know where to start. There is always a way forward, even if we don't always see it. I hope these oral histories shed light for the reader about the potential each of us has to help bring forth a better world.

Additionally, the power of these oral histories to contribute to social change lies in the hundreds of historic references in each chapter. Each interview reveals a complex ecosystem of relationships among individuals, organizations, and movements that span continents and generations. There are linkages and lineages across these interviews—some of the narrators have crossed paths and/or share movement roots. The breadth of their experience, knowledge, and impact is beautiful, particularly in the context of the arc of their stories.

Some of the women interviewed for this collection have published their own articles, essays, websites, and zines, written or edited books, developed curricula, taught courses, been interviewed for podcasts, and exhibited their artwork or multi-media pieces. Others have a much smaller media footprint. This in no way diminishes their knowledge or significance to the social justice movement. Deeply respected within their organizations, communities, and beyond, their analysis and impact are reflected in the collective consciousness of community members, co-workers, and comrades who've had the blessing of working with them, who know of them, or who have been impacted by their work without even knowing their names. While the endless flyers, brochures, meeting agendas, campaign plans, letters to allies, funding proposals, murals, action props, et cetera are all expressions of a political analysis and vision, these ephemera dissipate with time, nor is their authorship attributed to one person. Brilliant organizers and their analysis often remain unknown as individuals, their contributions subsumed within organizations. The need to document histories of resistance bears witness to the importance of oral history and social movement archives. It is in that spirit that this book is offered. I hope that readers will be inspired to begin recording the changemakers in their lives.

I want to thank my dear friend and comrade James Tracy for his unflagging support for me as an organizer and (now) oral historian during nearly twenty years of friendship. James is the type of person who understands that if he gets in the door, it's his joyful duty to hold that door open for others. James introduced me to Greg Ruggiero at City Lights Publishing. Although I have never written a book and

There are several women in my life whose light has helped to illuminate my own path. I was blessed to be mothered by my grandmother Violet. She was only thirty-six years old when I was born, yet took on the task of mothering all over again to raise me, with the help of my grandfather John. That many grandparents step in to this role doesn't lessen my love and gratitude to them. I was doubly blessed to have had two of my great-grandmothers in my life until I reached adulthood. I saw my mom work until her hands were raw, cleaning and cooking and creating a beautiful life for her family from little material comfort but an abundance of love. Her kindness was never dimmed by the hardships she faced. I met my birth mother Carol when I was seventeen. Her refusal to conform to social norms frightened my grandmother but inspired me. One of the few photos of her that I saw as a youth was her standing on her fire escape on Longwood Avenue in the South Bronx with an Impeach Nixon banner behind her. Meeting Frances Goldin at age twenty-one changed my life. She was the first woman that I ever met who was actively fighting injustice. She welcomed me and countless others into movement with a raised fist, something to eat, and a list of things for you to do. She was strategic, fearless, glamorous, a warm and welcoming host, loyal friend, excellent cook, and a true believer in revolution.

I returned to school in my late fifties to study oral history after being immersed in organizing for several decades. Oral history felt like the best strategy for inviting folks to share and reflect on their own experiences in movement work and to document that knowledge. Too often, we are so busy doing the work that we neglect making time for reflection and learning from the work. I am thankful for Amy Starecheski, director of the Oral History Master program (OHMA) at Columbia University for supporting me on my oral history journey. Amy is a longtime ally of Picture the Homeless, where I worked for nearly two decades. She not only attended actions supporting homeless folks organizing for the right to housing, she dedicated the royalties of her book *Ours to Lose: When Squatters Became Homeowners in New York City* to Picture the Homeless. When I considered applying to OHMA, Amy welcomed me into that academic space. I had for so long desired to return to school, but was anxious about actually making the transition from community organizing to oral history. I am still working through those old working-class/white-trash impostor syndrome demons. Amy's continued support as I bridge the worlds of oral history and community organizing are a blessing.

No words can express my deep respect and gratitude for all of the women organizers with whom I've shared conversations, strategy sessions, debates, disagreements, and amazing moments of clarity, prop-making session, arrests, tears, not enough victories, and too many disappointments, as well as many a night on the dance floor. Some of these encounters were in cramped meeting rooms, in borrowed offices, in someone's kitchen, riding a subway, at an action, or in the back of a pickup truck. Combining family life with political work is an endless balancing act, and it isn't always pretty or perfect. My children will surely attest to that. For the women who have shared space with me, from New York to California, Florida, Nicaragua, and Venezuela and back, thank you from the bottom of my heart.

My daughter Rocio, James Tracy, and Janet Richmond read and made comments on the Introduction, and Michele Orwin proofread an early draft of the manuscript and helped improve the flow. While I appreciate all the support and encouragement I've received, working on a book is a daunting process, and any and all messiness is my own. I want to do justice to the women interviewed and to our collective struggles, but I am sure this book can be improved upon, just as we as individuals and our collective movements must be if we are to change the systems of oppression described within these pages. I can only hope for the reader's grace and constructive feedback, so that I learn and do and be better with future projects.

ENDNOTES

1. Frances Goldin was founder of the Cooper Square Committee in New York City in 1959. She dedicated her life to radical social change as a community organizer and founder of the Frances Goldin Literary Agency. When I was a single mother living in the Cooper Square community in 1981, it was Frances who knocked on my door to invite me to my first tenant meeting.

2. Angela Y. Davis, *The Meaning of Freedom* (San Francisco: City Lights, Open Media Series, 2012), 198.

3. From a recorded interview with Ella Baker by Gilda Lerner, published as "Developing Community Leadership," in *Black Women in White America: A Documentary History*, ed. Gilda Lerner (New York: Vintage Books, 1973).

4. One resource is *Nēpia Mahuika, Rethinking Oral History and Tradition: An Indigenous Perspective* (New York: Oxford University Press, 2019).

5. Nora Almeida and Jen Hoyer, *The Social Movement Archive* (Sacramento: Litwin Books, 2021).

6. A helpful guide is Cliff Mayotte and Claire Kiefer's *Say It Forward: A Guide to Social Justice Storytelling* (Chicago: Haymarket, 2018). While I don't subscribe to the term "best practices," there are also helpful resources to be found on the Oral History Association's website.

7. One example of a neighborhood oral history project is Black Bottom Archives, "a community-driven media platform dedicated to centering and amplifying the voices, experiences, and perspectives of Black Detroiters through digital storytelling, journalism, art, and community organizing with a focus on preserving local Black history & archiving our present."

8. The Chicana Por Mi Raza Digital Memory Collective is a group of researchers, educators, students, archivists, and technologists dedicated to preserving imperiled Chicanx and Latinx histories of the long Civil Rights Era.

9. "Goin' North: Stories from the First Great Migration to Philadelphia," https://goinnorth.org.

10. Patrisse Cullors, a founder of Black Lives Matter, shared the story of Malkia Devich-Cyril first chanting what has come to be known as the Assata Chant in Oakland, California, after being inspired by a letter written to the Grassroots Movement by Assata Shakur. See: www.youtube.com/watch?v=zmuaWInh8BQ.

11. Howard Zinn, *A Power That Governments Cannot Suppress* (San Francisco: City Lights, 2006), 11.

12. Ibid.

13. Kimberlé Crenshaw, "Demarginalizing the Intersection of Race and Sex: A Black Feminist Critique of Antidiscrimination Doctrine, Feminist Theory and Antiracist Politics," *University of Chicago Legal Forum*: Vol. 1989, Article 8.

14. Angela Davis at an Occupy General Assembly, Washington Square Park, New York City, quoting Audre Lorde, recorded October 30, 2011. See: www.youtube.com/watch?v=HlvfPizooII.

15. Dr. Wendsler Nosie Sr. is an American University of Sovereign Nations professor, a member of the American University of Sovereign Nations Board of Governors, former Chairman, San Carlos Apache Nation, and the founder and leader of Apache Stronghold.

16. Oak Flat, known as *Chí'chil Biłdagoteel*, is a sacred site for the practice of the Apache people's spiritual and religious beliefs. The Battle for Oak Flat challenges a "land swap" authorized by the 2015 National Defense Act permitting a copper mine to swallow their holy ground in a nearly two-mile-wide crater.

17. John R. Welch, "White Eyes' Lies and the Battle for Dził Nchaa Sí'an," *American Indian Quarterly 21*, 1997: 75–109.

18. *Usen* is the Apache word for God, or Creator.

19. Zinaida Carroll, "The Spiritual Connection of Indigenous Women to the Land and Its Crucial Role in the Apache's Battle for Sovereignty," *Restoration Magazine*, June 2021, Volume 18, Issue 2. The article describes the significance of the Sunrise ceremony for Apache teenage girls entering adulthood, practiced at Oak Flat.

20. According to a July 14, 2022, Apache Stronghold Press Release, "The Mount Graham Sacred Run spotlights the ongoing occupation of the mountain for scientific pursuits by research universities and institutes, including the Vatican, the University of Arizona, Ohio State University, Notre Dame, Germany's Max Planck Institute, and Italy's Arcetri Astrophysical observatory."

21. The mining company Resolution Copper (owned by BHP/Rio Tinto, an Australian/British company), owns land throughout the state of Arizona but covets Oak Flat, hence the misnomer "land swap" for what is really a land grab. The proposed "swap" will trade 5,300 acres of private parcels owned by the company to the Forest Service in exchange for 2,400 acres, including Oak Flat.

22. The midnight rider authorizing the "land swap" was attached to The National Defense Authorization Act of FY15 by Senators John McCain and Jeff Flake.

23. On June 24, 2022, the Ninth Circuit Court of Appeals, in a 2–1 decision, ruled that the request for a preliminary injunction to halt the land exchange of Oak Flat be denied. Apache Stronghold, which is represented by the Becket Fund for Religious Liberty, has vowed to appeal to the US Supreme Court immediately. The preliminary injunction would have stopped Resolution Copper, a foreign-owned mining company, from gaining control over Oak Flat through a

land exchange until the court case *Apache Stronghold vs. the US* was decided. The court ruled that Apache Stronghold's case against the United States had no likelihood of winning.

24. Judge Marsha Berson called the decision "absurd," "illogical," "disingenuous," and "incoheren[t]." The court ruled that the government's decision to transfer Oak Flat to Resolution Copper "does not substantially burden" Apache's religious practices—even though the mine will swallow the sacred site in a massive crater, ending those practices forever.

25. Rep. Raúl Grijalva (D-AZ) introduced the H.R. 1884 Save Oak Flat Act (SOFA) to permanently protect the Oak Flat area of Tonto National Forest from destructive mining proposals in March 2021. It is now included in the House's $3.5 trillion budget reconciliation bill. H.R. 1884 will repeal the Section 3003 land exchange of the 2015 National Defense Authorization Act. Sen. Bernie Sanders (I-VT) introduced an identical bill (S. 915) in the Senate. The Save Oak Flat Act (SOFA) would protect a 2,422-acre site known as *Chí'chil Biłdagoteel* (Oak Flat).

26. A report by the Greensboro Truth and Reconciliation Commission was completed in May 2006 after a two-year process, and is available on its website.

27. On August 12, 2017, when white supremacists descended on Charlottesville, Virginia, in a Unite the Right rally, James Allen Fields drove his car into the people protesting the rally, killing one protester and injuring 35 others.

28. Given the rise in white supremacist violence as of this writing, it is important to note that members of both the Klan and the American Nazi Party participated in the Greensboro Massacre.

29. Claire Butler, was a member of the Communist Workers Party.

30. See Catherine Fosl's interview with Anne Braden, June 17, 1999, Anne Braden Oral History Project, Louie B. Nunn Center for Oral History, University of Kentucky Libraries.

31. This interview was conducted just after the historic leak of US Supreme Court Justice Alito's opinion regarding *Roe v. Wade* in spring 2022.

32. The Personal Responsibility and Work Opportunity Act of 1996 denied cash benefits or childcare assistance to families receiving welfare if they were attending a four-year college or university.

33. After the murder of Amadou Diallo by the New York City Police Department's infamous Street Crimes Unit, the Coalition Against Police Brutality (CAPB) organized several demonstrations across NYC, and was also instrumental in litigating *Daniels, et al. v. the City of New York*. The National Congress of Puerto Rican Rights, led by Richie Pérez, was in the leadership of CAPB. The combination of street protests and the Daniels litigation brought by the Center for Constitutional Rights resulted in the disbanding of the Street Crimes Unit and a settlement agreement around Stop and Frisk.

34. Organizing efforts by Mothers on the Move contributed to stopping American Marine Rail (AMR) from establishing a waste transfer station in Hunts Point.

35. Open Society Institute, now known as Open Society Foundation.

36. An infamous juvenile detention facility formerly located in the South Bronx.

37. Camaradas was a neighborhood venue for music and spoken word in East Harlem, particularly for Puerto Rican culture. Bomba is a genre of Puerto Rican traditional music and dance. At one time, Thursday nights at Camaradas featured live Bomba music.

38. Kathleen Cleaver, now an attorney, was the communications secretary for the Black Panther Party.

39. Ai Jen Poo is executive director of the National Domestic Workers Alliance.

40. 256G falls under the 1996 Federal Illegal Immigration Reform and Immigrant Responsibility Act, and allows state and local agencies to act as immigration enforcement agents.

41. Alina Das, *No Justice in the Shadows: How America Criminalizes Immigrants* (New York: Bold Type Books, 2020), 46.

42. Betty, her sister, and her mother are profiled in Miriam Ching Yoon Louie's book, *Sweatshop Warriors: Immigrant Women Workers Take on the Global Factory* (Cambridge: South End Press, 2001), 179.

43. Manhattan Neighborhood Network (MNN) is Manhattan's public access television station, which for several years provided grassroots organizations with equipment, instruction, and airtime. Many of the groups that Betty taught created their own programming and had monthly television shows.

44. The Manhattan Detention Center is known as "the tombs."

45. Uniform Land Use Review Procedure (ULURP) is required by the New York City Charter for certain development projects and involves multiple levels of government review prior to approval.

46. Artwashing is a term that describes the relationship between gentrification and support for art and gallery spaces in low-income communities, often of color, as a strategy to attract residents of higher incomes, who are often white.

47. The COVID shutdown in NYC took place in mid-March 2020, before most of the US adopted similar measures.

48. *Spatial Deconcentration* by Yulanda Ward is a seminal analysis of the housing crisis, and was first published in 1981 for a national housing activists' conference held in Washington, D.C. It has been reprinted and is available online.

49. Evelyn Queen later became a judge in the D.C. Circuit court.

50. The Dalkon Shield was a contraception device that went on the market in 1971 and was promoted by the manufacturer as safer than birth control pills. Within only a few years it was found to cause severe injury and even death, leading to numerous lawsuits, in which juries awarded millions of dollars in compensatory and punitive damages.

51. Loretta Ross, "Measuring the Empowerment of Women of Color at Mainstream Organizations" (unpublished).

52. Dr. Lynn Roberts is an assistant professor at the City College of New York's School of Public Health and Associate Dean for Student Affairs and Alumni Relations. She is also co-editor of the anthology *Radical Reproductive Justice*.

53. See Ngọc Loan Trân, "Calling IN: A Less Disposable Way of Holding Each Other Accountable," bgdblog.org.

54. Unschooling and homeschooling both occur outside of institutional school structures, but differ in that unschooling is based on a philosophy of respecting a child's self-determination, unlike homeschooling, which may be based on standard curricula but offered in the home.

55. Denver's Right To Rest Act, HB19-1096, would establish basic rights of persons without housing, including but not limited to the right to rest in public spaces and to shelter themselves from the elements.

56. Sweeps refers to the practice by government agencies, including police departments and departments of sanitation, of destroying the belongings of homeless folks who are sleeping and living outdoors, often in public space but sometimes in areas, such as along highways or under overpasses, that are State-owned property. The destruction of homeless folks' property has been challenged in court and determined to be unconstitutional.

57. Yuri Kochiyama was a political activist who survived a Japanese internment camp during World War II as a child and later became active in Harlem in the early 1960s, befriending and collaborating with Malcolm X. She participated in Asian American, Black, and Third World movements for civil and human rights throughout her life until her passing in 2014.

58. Amilcar Cabral, *Return to the Source: Selected Speeches of Amilcar Cabral* (New York: Monthly Review Press, 1974).

59. The Christopher Street Pier is a gathering place for queer youth in New York City's Greenwich Village.

60. Wilding was a term often used to stigmatize youth of color in New York City, amplifying racist stereotypes of criminality, popularized in mainstream media after the brutal rape of a white female jogger and the unlawful arrest of five youths, who came to be known as the Central Park Five, now known as the Exonerated Five.

61. Net neutrality is defined by the Electronic Frontier Foundation as "the idea that Internet service providers (ISPs) should treat all data that travels over their networks fairly, without improper discrimination in favor of particular apps, sites, or services."

62. A railroad apartment is the apartment version of a shotgun shack. One room leads into the other, like a series of train cars; they are found in older housing stock built originally for working class people.

63. Mifepristone is an oral medication that can induce an abortion during the early stages of a pregnancy.

64. In 2009, New York became the first state in the US to pass a Domestic Worker's Bill of Rights, led by Domestic Workers United.

65. The Community Safety Act was two bills passed by the New York City Council in 2013 that established the office of the Inspector General of the NYPD and an anti-profiling bill. It was an historic win and prefigured much of the Defund the Police and police accountability organizing that continue as of this writing.

66. Stop and Frisk was a discriminatory policing tactic used by the NYPD. The New York Civil Liberties Union successfully sued and obtained the data proving that the NYPD were primarily using this tactic against Black and Latinx New Yorkers, eventually leading to a class action lawsuit resulting in Judge Shira A. Scheindlin, ordering a federal monitor to oversee reforms. Communities United for Police Reform was recognized by the courts as a stakeholder in the joint remediation process.

67. The #NoTechforICE campaign was widely covered in the media largely due to organizing by Mijente and other immigrant rights organizations, and Mijente, the National Immigration Project, and the Immigrant Defense Project commissioned the report "Who's Behind ICE?: The Tech and Data Companies Fueling Deportations."

68. The State of Jefferson is a secessionist movement in Northern California and Southern Oregon that dates back to the mid-1800s and has flared up again in ways that mirror the political polarization in the rest of the US. It has been recently animated with right-wing, white supremacist, and anti-COVID measures.

69. "White Trash Up for Grabs" was the name of a panel organized for the Left Forum in New York City.

70. Stuart Schrader, "Rank-and-File Antiracism: Historicizing Punk and Rock Against Racism," *Radical History Review* 1 October; 2020 (138): 131–143.

71. The increase in the frequency and intensity of fires throughout the U.S. West has prompted media coverage of the use of incarcerated folks as firefighters although once released from prison they are ineligible to be hired as firefighters.

72. As of this writing, Chevron's Richmond oil refinery has been in operation for approximately one hundred years and continues to be the subject of protests by community members.

ABOUT LYNN LEWIS

LYNN LEWIS IS A COMMUNITY ORGANIZER, ORAL HISTORIAN, and educator. She is the former executive director and past civil rights organizer at Picture the Homeless. Lewis is the recipient of a 2022/2023 National Endowment for the Humanities Oral History Fellowship, and is currently working on an oral history of Picture the Homeless. She lives in New York City and is a mom and a grandma.

Rising Up
The Power of Narrative in
Pursuing Racial Justice
By Sonali Kolhatkar, Foreword
by Rinku Sen

Twenty Dollars and
Change
Harriet Tubman and the Ongoing
Fight for Racial Justice and
Democracy
By Clarence Lusane, Foreword
by Kali Holloway

Build Bridges, Not Walls
A Journey to a World Without
Borders
By Todd Miller

The Path to a Livable
Future
A New Politics to Fight Climate
Change, Racism, and the Next
Pandemic
By Stan Cox, Foreword by
Zenobia Jeffries Warfield

No Fascist USA!
The John Brown Anti-Klan
Committee and Lessons for
Today's Movements
By Hilary Moore and James
Tracy, Foreword by Robin
D. G. Kelley

Loaded
A Disarming History of the
Second Amendment
By Roxanne Dunbar-Ortiz

Have Black Lives Ever
Mattered?
By Mumia Abu-Jamal

United States of Distraction
Media Manipulation in Post-
Truth America (And What We
Can Do About It)
By Mickey Huff and Nolan
Higdon, Foreword by
Ralph Nader

Narrative of the Life of
Frederick Douglass, an
American Slave, Written by
Himself
A New Critical Edition
By Angela Y. Davis

CITY LIGHTS BOOKS | OPEN MEDIA SERIES
Arm Yourself with Information